Martial

Arts

Talk

Martial Arts Talk

Conversations with Leading Authorities on the Martial Arts

MARK V. WILEY

TUTTLE PUBLISHING
Boston • Rutland, VT • Tokyo

First published in 2000 by Tuttle Publishing, an imprint of Periplus Editions (HK) Ltd, with editorial offices at 153 Milk Street, Boston, Massachusetts 02109.

Library of Congress Cataloging-in-Publication Data

Wiley, Mark V.
  Martial arts today : an oral history / Mark V. Wiley.—
    1st ed. p. cm.
  ISBN: 0-8048-3182-3(pbk.)
  1. Martial Arts—History. I. Title
GV1101.W546 2000   99-27411
796.8'09—dc21   CIP

Distributed by

USA   JAPAN
Tuttle Publishing   Tuttle Shuppan
Distribution Center   RK Building, 2nd Floor
Airport Industrial Park   2-13-10 Shimo-Meguro, Meguro-Ku
364 Innovation Drive   Tokyo 153 0064
North Clarendon, VT 05759-9436 Tel: (03) 5437-0171
Tel: (802) 773-8930   Fax: (03) 5437-0755
Tel: (800) 526-2778

CANADA   SOUTHEAST ASIA
Raincoast Books   Berkeley Books Pte Ltd
8680 Cambie Street   5 Little Road #08-01
Vancouver, British Columbia   Singapore 536983
V6P 6M9   Tel: (65) 280-1330
Tel: (604) 323-7100   Fax: (65) 280-6290
Fax: (604) 323-2600

First edition
06 05 04 03 02 01 00   10 9 8 7 6 5 4 3 2 1

Design by Joyce C. Weston

Printed in United States of America

CONTENTS

Introduction   vii

PART ONE
THE MARTIAL ARTS OF A COUNTRY

Patrick McCarthy
The History and Evolution Okinawan Martial Arts   3

Alexander Co
The History of Kung-Fu in the Philippines   31

J. Christoph Amberger
The Evolution of European Sword Arts   48

PART TWO
ON INDIVIDUAL SYSTEMS AND STYLES

Cheong Cheng Leong
Chuka Shaolin: Art of the Phoenix-Eye Fist   69

Hawkins Cheung
Fighting Theories and Principles of Wing Chun Kuen   81

John Little
The Art and Philosophy of Jeet Kune Do   102

PART THREE
MARTIAL ARTS AS SPORT

Hayward Nishioka
The History and Evolution of Judo   135

Bill Wallace
The History of Martial Sports in America   150

PART FOUR
MARTIAL ARTS AND ENTERTAINMENT

Andre Morgan
The Martial Arts Film Genre   175

Mark Dacascos
A Career in Martial Art Films and Television   199

James Lew
Martial Arts Stunts and Action Choreography   211

PART FIVE
MARTIAL ARTS RESEARCH AND PUBLISHING

Hunter B. Armstrong
Hoplology and Combative Culture   221

Curtis F. Wong
Martial Arts Book and Magazine Publishing   246

PART SIX
MARTIAL ARTS AND LIFE

Christopher D. Hess
Toward a Total Quality Martial Art   263

Afterword   283
About the Author   285

INTRODUCTION

Martial arts are traditions.
Specifically, they are oral traditions based on myth, legend, oral testimony, and individual perspectives, recited and recorded over time and across space. As Jan Vancina so astutely defined it in his seminal work, *Oral Tradition as History* (Wisconsin 1985, p. 3), "The term 'oral tradition' applies both to a process and to its products. The products are oral messages based on previous oral messages.... The process is the transmission of such messages by word of mouth over time.... Hence, any given oral tradition is but a rendering at one moment...."

Storytellers, then, are essential to the historical process in general, and to the perpetuation of martial arts in particular. Martial arts are, after all, orally transmitted physical, mental, and spiritual disciplines. What would a martial arts class be like without the teacher explaining the minutiae of a given technique or concept? What drives a student to aspire to greater physical heights than stories of how the masters of yesteryear were able to effortlessly kill a bull with a single punch, jump up to a second story window with a single leap, or single-handedly defeat a dozen foes in seconds? It is the oral traditions that connect us to the past, offer us obstacles to be overcome, and endlessly motivate us to the pursuit of perfection.

Storytellers and their stories, then, offer us unusual keyholes through which we can view the martial arts and come to better understand and appreciate them, the cultures that foster them, and the people that embrace and perpetuate them.

Rather than haphazardly gathering a collection of interviews in this volume, I aspired to document the history of specific aspects of the martial arts through conversations with a leading authority in each given area. As such, *Martial Arts Talk* offers fourteen such keyholes through which, in individual chapters, the reader can discover the history and development of Japanese, Okinawan, Chinese, Filipino, and European martial arts, Bruce Lee's training methods and the forging of his art and philosophy of jeet kune do, reminiscences of field research in Southeast Asia with the late Donn F. Draeger, the evolution of the martial arts film genre, how to balance physical, interpersonal, and spiritual dimensions of life through the martial arts, and the shaping of the publishing business through which the arts have been documented over the decades.

To offer the reader a more well-rounded and accessible discussion on the history and development of the martial arts, this book is divided into six parts, each focusing on a specific dimension of the arts, and containing between one and three perspectives.

Part One: The Martial Arts of a Country presents a history and development of various martial arts within three specific areas. Patrick McCarthy's interview focuses on the history and development of Okinawan karatedo, tracing its roots in China to its modern Japanese conception and sport form. Alexander Co's interview focuses on the history and spread of Chinese martial arts in the Philippines. And J. Christoph Amberger's interview discusses and analyzes the history, development, and role of sword arts in Europe, both in their dueling and sport forms.

Part Two: On Individual Systems and Styles presents in-depth descriptions and analysis of three specific martial art systems. Cheong Cheng Leong discusses the history, art, and healing dimension of the Chuka Shaolin system, also known as phoenix-eye fist kung-fu. Hawkins Cheung's interview focuses on the fighting concepts, principles, and training methods of wing chun kuen. And John Little speaks about the evolution of Bruce Lee's jeet kune do, its various contemporary interpretations, and how it can—and perhaps should—be looked to as more a philosophy of life and less a fighting art.

Part Three: Martial Arts as Sport outlines the history, development, and trends of many of the world's most popular martial sports. Hayward Nishioka speaks on the evolution of judo from jujutsu, its spread around the world, and contrasts the Japanese and European models of practice. Bill Wallace, on the other hand, discusses the entire spectrum of martial sports as they unfolded and evolved in the United States, from light- and no-contact karate to full-contact kickboxing, muay Thai, and savate, from bare-knuckle karate to the no-holds-barred martial arts events popular today.

Part Four: Martial Arts and Entertainment presents the spectrum of martial arts film and television from the production line to stunt fighting to acting. Andre Morgan discusses in detail the history of martial arts movies and the creation of an entire martial arts film genre. Mark Dacascos shares with us his personal triumphs and tribulations as an actor in numerous martial art films and in his dynamic new television series. James Lew's interview offers behind-the-scenes glimpses into the stunts and action choreography that make the viewing of martial arts films and television so exciting.

Part Five: Martial Arts Research and Publishing rounds off this collection of conversations by focusing on the ever-important research and publishing industry. Hunter B. Armstrong offers insight into the history and development of hoplology, the study of human combative performance and behavior, its resurgence in the twentieth century by the late Donn F. Draeger, and how it is applied in today's world. But what use is research to the masses without a venue through which to spread one's findings? Curtis F. Wong's interview, then, focuses on the business of martial arts book and magazine publishing and how it has evolved and grown over the past quarter century.

Part Six: Martial Arts and Life is the anchor interview in this collection, as Christopher D. Hess discusses the philosophical and practical underpinnings of the martial arts and how they can teach us to balance our physical, interpersonal, and spiritual lives.

As the subtitle indicates, this is a collection of conversations with the masters, competitors, researchers, and pioneers of the martial arts. In essence, it is an oral history of a period in world martial arts history as told by a cross-section of people who helped to uncover, define, and in some cases redefine what the martial arts are and how we have come to know and understand them. And even though trying to capture an oral tradition in writing is, as the saying goes, like "trying to capture the sea with a fishing net," there is always the hope that these interviews show the kinds of things a martial artist has to deal with on a day-to-day basis, the things they like to talk about, the things that construct their very sense of being. These interviews, then, can be read on many levels.

Actually, these aren't interviews as much as they are directed conversations. *Martial Arts Talk* is constructed of open dialogues through which ideas are explored, common misconceptions questioned, and the happenings of a time and place documented. Although the individuals included herein are contemporary martial arts figures, what they have to say is at once historical and timeless and sets a verbatim record of things happening today and that have transpired in the years that these men have been involved in the arts. As such, these accounts offer future generations of practitioners and researchers a more vivid account of how the martial arts were practiced, developed, and perceived during the twentieth century, as well as offering a more clear picture of what these arts were, are, and have become in an ever-shrinking and multicultural world.

I owe the martial artists whose conversations appear herein much thanks for their candid insights and willingness to participate in this project. In addition, I extend my deepest gratitude and respect to Robert Chu, Karunakaran A/L R. Chindan, Oscar Ratti, and George Donahue for their very generous, though perhaps not overt, contributions to this project, and, of course, to Tuttle Publishing for their willingness to publish it.

Mark V. Wiley
Philadelphia, 1998

PART ONE

THE MARTIAL ARTS
OF A COUNTRY

PATRICK McCARTHY
The History and Evolution of Okinawan Martial Arts

Patrick McCarthy is well known as an authority on the history of the fighting traditions of Okinawa. A student of karate for over thirty years, McCarthy has been awarded a 7th dan, kyoshi, teaching license from the Dai Nippon Butokukai. He has also studied t'ai chi ch'uan and White Crane, Hung Gar, Monk Fist, and Five Ancestor Fist kung fu. As a result of the influence of his mentor, Richard Kim, McCarthy undertook the study of karate's history and philosophy that engages him to this day. His research has taken him to Japan, China, Taiwan, and Hong Kong to interview and train with the world's most famous masters of karate and kung fu. Among McCarthy's credits as an author and translator are The Bible of Karate: Bubishi *and the two-volume* Ancient Okinawan Martial Arts: Koryu Uchinadi. *A native Canadian who lived and trained in Japan for a decade, Patrick McCarthy now makes his home in Australia, where he administers a college-level degree program in martial arts when not traveling the world to teach and continue his research.*

3

**Why don't we begin this discussion with your assessment of the histori-
cal roots of Okinawan karatedo?**

Well, I'm sure that an entire dissertation might better illuminate
that specific issue, but I would like to say this. It has always been
the human body, its unique function, and common anatomical
weaknesses that have ultimately dictated how to seize and what personal tools of impact and methods of transferring low intensity and
higher velocity kinetic force best impedes motor performance.
Based on this hypothesis and man's fight for survival, defensive traditions were born and profoundly influenced by the anthropologi-
cal forces of those individual cultures in which they evolved.

In the case of Okinawa, a symbiotic liaison with the Middle
Kingdom, dating back to 1392, provided the window of opportunity through which that culture embraced tributary status. This
explains how members of the *uchinanchu* class learned the ways of
their more sophisticated Chinese mentors.

I think that Okinawa, like any other culture, has always instinctively possessed the motivation and means with which to defend
itself. In 1372, four years after the Ming Dynasty (1368–1644) was
established, China sent envoys to contact its geographical neighbors
and surrounding cultures in an effort to establish commerce and
obedience.

The Ryukyu Kingdom was one such culture. It wasn't, however,
until 1392 that the first Chinese settlement, described as the
Thirty-Six Families, was established in Okinawa. Hence, Chinese
culture (politics, business, commerce, music, literature, and martial
arts, and so on) were funneled into the Ryukyu Kingdom.

**Were there some specific time periods or events in Okinawan history that
forced its people to adopt or develop sophisticated self-defense systems?**

Yes, there are several historical events in Okinawa's culture that
gave rise to why Okinawans might necessarily need to shift their
attention to alternative means of self-defense.

Shoshin's prohibition of weapons after the unification of the
three rival principalities in the late fifteenth century certainly compelled concerned Uchinanchu to consider developing an alternative

means of defending themselves, their lands, and their possessions.

In 1477, after an intense and bloody military effort, King Shoshin unified Okinawa's three rival principalities. In bringing them together, he spent the next generation (his time in office) establishing a centralized administration with which to oversee the growth and development of commerce and culture in his Kingdom.

By 1507, his administration had forged the "Age of Eleven Distinctions" document, in which there appeared a prohibition—aimed at all those who were not part of the central administration—that outlawed the private ownership and stockpiling of weapons under the guise that there wasn't a need for them as the centralized administration would oversee both domestic and national defense. Of course, opposition to the decree believed that it was done purely to prevent wealthy and powerful landowners from rising up against the government at some later date.

King Shoshin called the outside lords from those areas he had militarily subjugated to come and reside in the great castle district of Shuri. He then supported them and sent administrators to oversee their own territories. As you can imagine, that very act itself threatened the grip on their own land and family possessions.

Many historians are of the opinion that this one act in 1507 forced the people of wealth and position—whose belongings and family were threatened by this act—to consider alternative defensive measures. Hence, they turned their attention toward their liaison with the Middle Kingdom and the Chinese in Okinawa. By taking defensive principles and applying them to weapon-usable implements used in everyday industry (e.g., sticks, sickles, bits of chain, boat oars, and so on) they could in fact establish a secret line of defense in times of despair.

The Japanese subjugation of 1609 is also recognized as yet another principal force behind the development of personal self-defense traditions during Okinawa's old Ryukyu Kingdom. However, when this hypothesis is more deeply explored, it becomes evident that "Okinawa's" civil defensive traditions were, for the most part, introduced from China and embraced by *keimochi* and *chikudon pechin* (upper-class and law enforcement officials).

Is there another source from which fighting disciplines may have been introduced to Okinawa, other than the Chinese connection?

Yes, there is. It is commonly referred to as the Minamoto (Tametomo) hypothesis. The legend maintains that toward the end of the twelfth century Minamoto Tametomo, the eighth son of the Minamoto Yoritomo, who had been taken captive during a minor skirmish with the Taira, escaped his bondage in Izu and sailed south to Kyushu, where he resided for several years before heading off to the Ryukyu Kingdom with a garrison of soldiers.

There it is further alleged that Tametomo, arriving with a superior military force, was greeted and embraced as the powerful military leader he was. Tametomo married the daughter of the island's most powerful lord and had a son named Shunten, who became the so-called first king of the Ryukyus.

If this history is true, then it would be safe to further conclude that Tametomo, in addition to the garrison of warriors who accompanied him, would have had to recruit and train local Okinawans in the standard warrior traditions of that day: spear, sword, horsemanship, archery, and battlefield grappling.

It is based upon this theory that I believe *tegumi* grappling concepts (originally introduced to Japan from China by the Kentoshi) form the plebeian foundation upon which ongoing foreign influence forged what is commonly referred to as Okinawan martial arts.

That's interesting. With that as a foundation, what happened in the years after 1507?

Fortunately, the culture of Okinawa, despite the 1609 subjugation, remained a peaceful society and ultimately rose to the apex of cultural prominence. However, its treasury was methodically milked dry by the Japanese over the succeeding centuries. Okinawa's Japanese neighbor to the north, after the battle of Sekigahara (where Tokugawa Ieyasu rose to prominence and ushered in a military government), was plagued by hundreds of peasant uprisings during the nearly three centuries it lasted. Okinawa's old Ryukyu Kingdom experienced no such history.

Speaking of peasants, doesn't island folklore maintain that the premise

upon which karate unfolded was the pre-Meiji peasant-class theory?

That's correct, however, such unchallenged oral traditions remain suspect, and have been plagued by historical inaccuracies and hidden agendas. My research, published in *The Bible of Karate: Bubishi*, was the first that I know of to challenged such myths.

The pre-Meiji peasant-class theory would have us believe that karate and kobudo unfolded in the secrecy of nightfall, unbeknownst to the occupying samurai warrior, who allegedly raped and beat women and cruelly cut peasants down for no reason at all. The theory further maintains that peasants, trained in this clandestine "combative" overcame the unsuspecting samurai warrior in personal confrontation. While I am certain that the occupation was not without incident, nowhere in my extensive research can I find any accounts of such a history. It is simply not true and I do not think that any serious researcher believes that.

That certainly has been the perpetuated and much-quoted myth of how Okinawan, and indeed most, martial arts were developed and practiced. What do you feel actually happened during that time to spur interest and development of the Okinawan fighting traditions?

While we are certain of the Thirty-Six Chinese Family phenomenon, and Shoshin's "Age of Eleven Distinctions" in 1507, my research concludes that although the 1609 Japanese occupation of Okinawa completely disarmed Okinawa's centralized government, it allowed officials to cultivate those basic skills necessary in domestic law enforcement. I believe this single act provided the infrastructure upon which the karate/kobudo phenomena unfolded.

When I studied the history and evolution of this island culture I found that local law enforcement officials came from within the class of people commonly referred to as *pechin*. These were people with position and referred to as *keimochi*, as opposed to *mukei*, people without position. There were several levels of *pechin* that looked something like this: *pechin, satunushi-pechin, chikudun-pechin, satunushi, waka-satunushi, chikudun*, and *chikudun-sashiki*.

Not unlike today, so too did the local law enforcement of that tiny island culture, during feudal times, need to serve and protect its communities. Crowd control, working premise security, private protection, transporting money, courtroom security, jailers, prison guards, transporting criminals, and local law enforcement restraining methods all needed to be addressed. In all cases, the skill of physically restraining people or forcibly rendering a person(s) compliant, as one could easily imagine, was of enormous value and vigorously cultivated by the *pechin* class.

Moreover, in a culture where weapons were prohibited by the occupational forces, local law enforcement policed their streets (long before the Japanese ever did) with little more than an iron truncheon (*sai*) and a wooden cudgel (*bo*). Occupational samurai concluded that such implements were of little real threat to them, the professionally trained warriors with a three-foot razor blade on their hip.

In my humble opinion, this is the real history behind the development of karate and kobudo. In fact, if we closely examine such history nowhere can we find even one instance of peasant intervention, only the emergence of such *pechin* class heroes as Makabe Choken, Sakugawa, Matsu Higa, and Bushi Matsumura. These men were all members of the *pechin* class, and were certainly the most influential of all karate/kobudo pioneers.

One can clearly see a history and development of these arts separate from the common belief that they were transplanted in whole to Okinawa from China. In what ways, though, did Chinese martial arts come into contact with and affect Okinawan martial arts?

Again, it has always been the human body, its unique function and common anatomical weaknesses, that ultimately dictated how to seize and what personal tools of impact, along with the varying ways in which to transfer both low intensity and higher velocity kinetic energy, best impedes motor performance. Based upon these universal realities, the *uchinanchu* (Okinawans) continually pursued a deeper understanding of traditions which promoted related skills. Hence, they cultivated, reinterpreted, improved, and perpetuated *their* teachings in the same way that their Chinese mentors did. In fact, much of what they learned came from Chinese defensive themes and application principles.

Because of Okinawa's geographical proximity and political connection to Fujian province, most of the interaction with China was focused there. Hence, most of the martial arts that made their way back to Okinawa came from Fujian, and most notably included white crane, monk fist, and tiger boxing.

Who was it specifically, though, that traveled to China from Okinawa's old Ryukyu Kingdom, thus introducing these foreign fighting systems to Okinawa?

Cross-comparing Chinese culture with that of Okinawa, during that period of time, we can see that, in addition to official and commercial excursions, the first-born male of each of family of wealth and position was, by virtue of their societal values, entitled not only to inherit everything from the families, but also to a first-class education. A first-class education meant studying in China during those times. That included the five Taoist classics, the five Confucian classics, what we refer to today as traditional Chinese medicine, and of course the martial arts.

This is an expression of what we also see in Western culture, as far as the sons of wealth and position learning fencing and the way of the sword, or what we refer to in Japanese as *bumburyuodo*. In English we say "the pen and the sword." It's not enough to understand physical assertion, it needs to be balanced with scholarly pursuits.

Hence, like scholars, doctors, statesmen, politicians, men of medicine, monks and priests, so too were the first-born sons of high ranking *keimochi* in Okinawa sent to China for such an education. And it's in understanding this that we see that there is yet another avenue of influence into Okinawa's martial arts culture.

Moreover, understanding this rarely addressed evolution, we can more clearly recognize what is commonly referred to as "family styles" or "clan practices," which have never gone outside of a family or, perhaps, a small village or community to be exploited in the same way that modern karate has.

When we are able to cross-compare, evaluate, and analyze the methodology used, what we see is that there is nothing really different other than what we refer to as personalized or signature methods through which to impart the very same principles. Remember what I said earlier about the human body?

When we look around the martial arts community today, we see the same thing happening.

Are you referring here to the way contemporary practitioners of the arts feel a need to develop their own, "new" styles?

Yes. People always find a need to reinterpret things in their own way, for varying reasons. However, I can assure everyone reading this presentation that nothing new is ever created that hasn't existed before with regard to application principles—there are just more improved ways to impart the same thing!

In the words of the late American anthropologist, Joseph Campbell: "Every generation produces leaders who, in an effort to keep the traditions, myths, and ritualized practices of the tribes of man a living experience for the cultures, societies, and people they serve, continually reinterpret the common principles upon which they rest. In doing so, it is not necessarily new traditions forged as much as it is more innovative ways of teaching the same principles."

You have been known to illustrate this point in a very real way during your seminars. Would you care to share with us your method for doing so?

Sure. Sometimes I try to illustrate this point—because in modern times we suffer from the proverbial "best style, best school, best teacher" phenomenon—when teaching open or multistyle seminars.

If I have eight or ten different styles there, I'll take a volunteer from each group and a guinea pig—usually the guy most clouded by narrow vision. I blindfold him and tell him to prepare himself to withstand controlled impacts to the chest, the stomach, and a joint lock. I call one of the volunteers to strike, kick, and joint lock him. So various "styles" execute the said techniques and then sit down. Then I remove the blindfold from the recipient and I ask him the $64,000 question: What style punched you first? What style kicked you second? What style bent your joint third?

Invariably, the answers are always the same: "I can't answer the question because I wasn't visually stimulated, I was only impacted. At the end of the day—regardless of where you are coming from, what uniform you wear, or what language you speak, and so on—a punch is a punch and a kick is a kick. Your joint only bends one way, and pain never discriminates.

With that in mind, I believe that learners are better prepared to recognize the common principles upon which all karate rest. Force equals mass times velocity and travels according to common scientific principles: the anatomy is unique and responds to specific physical stimulation. Hence, the tools of impact and varying ways of employing them (styles) are little more than personal interpretations of these principles.

Your analysis of and commentary on the *koryu uchinadi*, or old-style karate styles, are quite detailed and systematize that which has been obscured in the last century. This is an important element in (re)discovering what karate was and, in fact, has always been. Would you care to discuss your views on the universal nature of defensive themes and application principles?

Well, based upon this universal truth, man has continually pursued different ways through which to learn and improve these infinite principles. Through generations of empirical observation spiritual recluses in the monastic sanctuaries of ancient China were able to identify and catalogue no less than thirty-six different defensive themes. In an effort to address each of these random yet habitual acts of physical violence, that plagued the plebeian society in which they dwelt, individual application principles were meticulously forged which also employed as many as seventy-two different variations. Ultimately, eighteen individual exercises (called *hsing/kata*) came to represent a total of one hundred and eight defensive themes and application principles. Historically, this phenomena represents the foundation upon which karate unfolded.

Kata has customarily served the principal vehicle through which the "secrets" of karate have been handed down over the generations. Profoundly influenced by the culture in which it is embraced, the knowledge of those people who re-impart it and its competitive popularity, modern karate "styles" represent varying interpretations of these common defensive themes and application principles.

During this generation there has surfaced growing and independent movements aimed at rediscovering the original purpose of *kata*. The International Ryukyu Karate Research Society is one such movement dedicated to rediscovering, analyzing, improving, and imparting our discoveries. We strongly believe that it has been the emphasis upon the modern competitive aims and objectives that have given birth to corresponding training methods unlike that which were originally known. It is only natural that rule-bound aims and objectives are supported by corresponding training methods.

It is through this phenomenon that researchers have discovered how and why the original art of karate has become all but obscured. In this research department, the Society stands alone.

What, in your opinion, are the hows and whys of traditional Okinawan karatedo?

The five principal sets of tools used in *koryu uchinadi* include: (1) punches, (2) kicks, (3) blocks, (4) stances, and (5) strikes.

The six kinds of classical exercises which facilitate the development of these tools are: (1) techniques of punching, (2) kicking methods, leg maneuvers, and associated practices, (3) posturing, (4) the use of the empty hand, (5) corresponding tools of impact, and (6) checking, trapping, and blocking.

The twelve fundamental defensive themes intertwined within *koryu kata* include: (1) seizing nerves, (2) attacking blood passages, (3) twisting bones, (4) attacking tendons, (5) joint locks, (6) takedowns, (7) throws, (8) grappling, (9) groundwork, (10) counterattacks, (11) impacting anatomically vulnerable zones, and (12) digging into the cavities of the body unprotected by the skeletal structure.

The four fundamental categories of application principles into which these defensive themes fall include: (1) techniques of restraint, (2) neurological shutdown, (3) attacking the respiratory system, and (4) methods of temporary paralysis.

Indeed, these principles don't appear to be overtly known or understood

by today's martial artists. I think, for the most part, that most martial artists today either focus on perfecting forms, without a proper understanding of their intended applications, or just care about the sport aspect, with little interest in the true fighting techniques and principles of the arts, as preserved in kata.

How was _kata_ originally introduced into Okinawan karate?

How many times have you learned a _kata_ but remained unaware of what the defensive themes intertwined within its technical myriad actually mean? In this regard, _kata_ can be likened to learning a song in a foreign language; Melodic, but unless you understand the language in which the song is sung, its words will forever remain a mystery.

Long ago, before written language, the ancient tribes of man passed their knowledge on through physical emulation. This living phenomenon not only served as an excellent vehicle through which to impart existing knowledge, it also provided the very platform upon which more progressive learners could extrapolate and interpolate more improved methods of studying infinite principles.

It is the Society's official position that karate's ritualized paradigms (called _kata_) date back to this early seed planted by prehistoric man. The fundamental concept of _kata_ is not the commodity of any one specific culture, but rather the product of humanity. As civilizations evolved, languages developed, and the tribes of man began to take on individual characteristics, so too did his rituals reflect such changes. Built upon ancient customs, profound spiritual conviction, and disciplined social ideology, the kata of karatedo are then but a microcosm of the austere cultures from whence they come.

Kata has always served as the principal vehicle through which the art of karate has been transmitted from master to disciple, father to son, mother to daughter. Its defensive themes were not originally forged to be used in a rule-bound arena, against a professional fighter, or a warrior on the battlefield. This does not preclude such application, but suggests that they were developed, and constantly improved upon, for the expressed purpose of being used against someone who had little or no understanding of such application principles. As such, ritualized techniques represent classical responses to the random, yet habitual, acts of physical violence that have plagued civil society across the spectrum of humanity.

Do you think karate can exist without a moral philosophy or with a lack of spiritual introspection?

No. Karatedo cannot exist without a body of moral philosophy to govern the behavior of those who embrace its empowering practice. Learning karatedo without its corresponding philosophy creates a terrible imbalance which is usually reflected in attitude, character, and behavior.

Moreover, one will never go beyond the immediate results of physical training without looking inward. Karatedo teaches that the source of human weakness is internal, not external. Hence, the journey must always be inward, not outward. Discovering that the source of human weakness lies within, reveals the location where our personal battles must first be fought and won before inner harmony can ever be achieved and the living of daily life improved.

I, for one, hold that a system's applications are only as good as their training methods. What are some of the training methods used in Okinawan karate to make the art come alive, so to speak?

Training methods must always reflect one's aims and objectives, or confusion is bound to materialize. Conversely, aims and objectives must be supported by corresponding training methods. In other words, if you're learning martial arts for *ippon shobu* rule-bound competition, but training at a club which emphasizes submission grappling, for example, you're not going to fare well in your form of competition. Alternatively, if you've taken up training for self-defense but are being taught sport or rule-bound karate, isn't it time to look elsewhere?

Lastly, while karatedo can be many different things to many different people, and embraced in many different ways, society holds the position that karatedo can be: (1) an interesting alternative to conventional Western physical fitness; (2) a challenging rule-bound sport; (3) a form of self-defense limited only by one's understanding of its defensive themes and application principles; (4) a way of improving daily life (i.e., a ritualized empowering defensive, holistic/therapeutic tradition punctuated with moral philosophy, and highlighted by introspective practices as a single study); and (5) a respectful, rewarding, and meaningful occupation.

It is interesting that you say karate, as a self-defense system, "is limited only by one's understanding of its defensive themes and application principles." I couldn't agree with you more, although it seems most practitioners don't quite grasp this concept—they would rather just blindly follow an instructor's interpretation of the techniques, or routinely go through movement without a clue as to what they are truly doing.

Indiscriminate learning must be recognized as one reason why there exists such chaos today. I believe that the French mathematician and philosopher Henri Poincare summed it up best when, in 1905, he wrote in his book, *The Hypothesis of Mathematics,* that "science is built upon facts, much in the same way a house is constructed of brick. The mere collection of facts is no more a science than a pile of bricks is a house."

And so, too, when we learn the fighting traditions indiscriminately, we cannot possibly understand the magnitude of what the tradition represents, without moving inward to understand the principles upon which they rest.

I sincerely believe that Okinawans, like every other human race in the world, were able to perceive and understand these common realities. I refer to these as infinite principles. In other words, it's better to learn to comply with the infinite rather than to resist the inevitable.

An ancient proverb reads: "It may be true that there are many paths that lead up a mountain, but there is only one moon to be seen by those who achieve its summit."

It is widely known that the Okinawans acquired and further developed their fighting arts from kuntao (or quanfa, as you prefer) systems of Southern Chinese. In what ways did the Okinawans come into contact with these arts and the masters who were willing to teach them?

For the most part, *uchinanchu* of Okinawa's old Ryukyu kingdom could only travel to places in the south like Fujian and Nanjing, as opposed to the northern capital of Beijing which was restricted. That's where most of their commerce and business was done. Political issues were also handled in Nanjing, despite the last word always coming from Beijing.

The Chinese port of entry for *uchinanchu* was Fuzhou, in Fujian province, one of the principle deep water entry ports for South China. In my personal research, I located the official records of various ships that plied those treacherous waters during the Okinawa's old Ryukyu kingdom and sailed in and out of Makiminato, the deep water port of Maki in old Okinawa. Studying this history I also learned that Ming (1166–1644) and Ching (1644–1911) China usually sent one or two official ships to Okinawa every time a new king came into office. This ritual continued on even after 1609. Tributary ships were sent and Chinese envoys arrived bearing gifts and to oversee the transitional ceremonies. Such delegations, often with hundreds of people, stayed in Okinawa anywhere up to five or six months at a time.

How is it that the Okinawans were able to acquire knowledge of these Chinese fighting arts, since mere contact does not necessarily indicate a sharing of combative knowledge?

Well, understanding that the Ryukyu kingdom was, for the lack of a better description, a Chinese tributary colony, I think that the answer is quite evident.

An interesting historical passage that comes to mind when considering the value placed upon Chinese martial arts training in Okinawa's old Ryukyu kingdom comes down to us by way of a local seventeenth century Nago district statesman named "Te" Junsoku (1663–1734) In 1683. "Te" literally means hands, but actually is an old local expression once used during the Ryukyu kingdom to describe martial arts. "Te" Junsoku wrote: "No matter how you may excel in the art of 'Te,' or in your scholastic endeavors, nothing is more important than your behavior and humanity as observed in daily life." The passage can be read in its full context in Nagamine Shoshin's *Essence of Okinawan Karate-Do*.

A popular saying during that time went something like this: "Young men should go to Fujian; it's 'the place' where an Okinawan can learn the real martial arts." We have reason to believe, therefore, that all interested young men who wanted to model themselves after stalwarts like Bushi Matsumura in Okinawan culture, always dreamed of one day going to Fujian to learn the fighting traditions. Of course, Higashionna Kanryo is one such man.

I believe that is why so many *uchinanchu* who were unable to make the pilgrimage to Fuzhou, cultivated personal relationships with local Chinese residing in Okinawa, or other *uchinanchu* who had learned in Fujian.

Moreover, my English translation of Nagamine Shoshin's Japanese book, *Tales of Uchinadi and Tegumi Meijin* (*Tales of Okinawa's Great Masters,* in English), provides historical testimony from the late nineteenth and early twentieth centuries of local *uchinanchu* who actually did travel to Fujian for the express purpose of learning specific types of Chinese martial arts. In fact, Nagamine's book clearly outlines some very provocative personal testimony which I recommend as mandatory reading.

You had these people traveling back and forth to study Southern Chinese martial arts, and now you have this ancient text in Okinawa called *Bubishi*. This text has become, and indeed is, so important to the development of Okinawan martial arts. What is the origin of the text and why have Okinawan karate masters held it so sacred?

Well, let me explain it like this, in Japanese classical martial arts there is what we refer to as the *makimono* phenomenon; this is where the secrets of the tradition are committed to several scrolls (*makimono*) and usually handed down to the *jikideshi* (personal direct disciple) best suited to carry on that tradition.

Koryu Uchinadi (the "Okinawan" old-school defensive traditions) never had such a phenomenon, but rather used an anthology of Chinese martial arts. The text, called *Wu Beiji* (in Chinese) and outlining Fujian white crane quanfa and Shaolin monk fist boxing, focuses upon defensive themes and application principles, history, martial arts strategy, philosophy, and traditional Chinese medicine.

Reading this important historical work and its supporting research, one will recognize that there are several hypotheses surrounding its arrival in Okinawa and how it was subsequently used by nineteenth and twentieth century *bujin* (Okinawan martial artists).

So how does this relate to the *makimono* point you mentioned earlier?

Well, rather than receiving a *makimono*, the person most suited to carry on the tradition/interpretation of whatever the master had imparted, was required to hand draw the *Bubishi* so that he/she could carry on the core principles and have a written source with which to refer to and later pass on.

It is my opinion, then, that the *Bubishi* had been handed down from master to disciple, and has in fact served in many regards as a *makimono* of Okinawan karate. And in light of a deeper knowledge, we can see why this text was so valued by many of the pioneers of modern karate. Yamaguchi Gogen of the Goju kai referred to it as his most treasured text. Miyagi Chojun, the founder of Goju-ryu, actually selected the name Goju for his interpretation of quanfa from the book and even referred to the text as "the bible of karate." We see that the book served as the foundation upon which Funakoshi Gichin wrote his early books. In fact, on p. 249 of Oshima's English translation of *Karatedo Kyohan,* we can find two sections of the *Bubishi* which remain untranslated (please refer to Chapters 14 and 16 of my translation of the *Bubishi* to locate the English translation of this passage in *Karatedo Kyohan*). Motobu Choki also embraced the *Bubishi,* not only in the writing of his own books but in the way he practiced as well, and certainly with the medicinal concoctions he used to remedy injuries in his practice. Mabuni Kenwa actually published the *Bubishi* in 1934, but to no avail as few could understand its obscurity. Shimabuku Tatsuo of Isshin-ryu also used the *Bubishi* to compose his *dojo kun.*

In a tradition plagued by the issues it seeks to eradicate, and one that seemingly has no single formula for success, the *Bubishi* has to be seen as the single most important source from which to evaluate the legacy and heritage of Okinawan karate.

There are certainly many factors involved in the forging, development, and spread of Okinawan martial arts. You already discussed two theories on the development of karate, is there a third?

Yes, toward the end of Japan's military government, the era we now refer to as the *bakumatsu.* From about the mid-1800s to the demise, we can see in Okinawa that the Japanese had methodically bled the kingdom dry. And from early as 1724, the *keimochi* class, or upper class, were drastically reduced in size. In light of this knowledge we can better understand how and why virtually thousands of people, from the centralized administration, once on a government stipend, were financially cut off and had to move out of the castle capital to fend for themselves.

Because of this phenomenon, we can understand how those *pechin*, who may have also been martial artists, ultimately became merchants, tradesmen, craftsmen, artisans, farmers (and or any other profession which would allow then to keep food on the table), and carried their traditions into the countryside and surrounding districts to where they eventually settled. And it is from this that we sometimes see as family or clan "styles."

This is also the case during and after the King abdicated and the Kingdom was abolished in 1879. The only people who actively pursued martial arts were young men, local law enforcement officials, and a handful of wealthy merchants.

At what point do we start seeing the emergence of some of the existing Okinawan karate styles today and the masters who made them popular?

In 1891, the military draft found its way to Okinawa and medical examinations were carried out for first line conscripts to serve in the Imperial Army. It was from that point in Okinawan history that Japanese military officials recognized the physical conditioning of young *uchinanchu*. Men like Hanashiro Chomo—my teacher Kinjo Hiroshi's teacher—and Yabu Kentsu along with a hoard of other nameless martial art enthusiasts of the time.

The military reasoned that if there was some way in which karate (then referred to as te or toudi) might serve to enhance military effectiveness, then a deeper investigation into its potential battlefield value was sanctioned. It was believed that toudi might be used as a vehicle to funnel physical fitness and character development in the same way that kendo and judo was being used on the mainland.

By reading the word of people like Funakoshi, we also know that Admiral Dewa sailed into Nakagushiku Bay and had a dozen of his officers attend seminars with local teachers of that generation in an effort to better evaluate what karate had to offer. However, in the

end, and according to the Dai Nippon Butokukai—the organization that facilitated the growth and direction of martial arts
throughout the nation—the military decided that they were not
interested in pursuing their study of karate simply because—and we
know this even today to be a factor—what can you learn in six or
eight weeks of doing traditional karate? Nothing but a bunch of
sore muscles and total confusion. One thing that has never changed
in the classical transmission of the fighting arts is that they are lifelong studies.

**But somehow Okinawans were able to establish karate as a cultural arte-
fact that spread widely. How was this eventually accomplished?**

Look, even my own Okinawan teacher, considered one of the
most senior (if, in fact, not the most respected) historian of karate
maintains that *uchinanchu* themselves were virtually astonished that
karate became so popular. No one ever believed that it would ever
become as popular as it did.

Even though the Japanese abandoned their military interest, as it
would serve them little or no military purpose in six or eight weeks
of boot camp, that was not before an independent campaign surfaced under the direction of a single man. Fountainhead by one of
that era's most prominent authorities of karate, Itosu Anko had
been a statesman with the central administration until the king
abdicated and his Kingdom was abolished. Itosu reasoned that if
Okinawa could make some significant contribution to Japan's esca-
lating war efforts, they would really being doing both country and
emperor a great service.

Itosu, and those who supported his movement, believed that if
karate (uchinadi) could be introduced at the school level by the
time students graduated and were entering the military for their
two-year obligation they would be both physically fit and mentally
prepared.

Besides his own personal command over uchinadi/toudijutsu,
Itosu was heavily supported by local sources and ultimately established his own "modern" interpretation of the tradition. Drawing
upon *kata* like *gojushiho (useishi), kushankun, chinto, jion, nai-
fuanchin,* and *passai,* etc., Itosu forged the five *pinan kata.*

His concept ushered in typical Victorian-era physical discipline into Okinawa's school system. By introducing various set patterns, as preset paradigms of physical fitness, that could be embraced by large groups of learners each year for the five years they attended public school, Itosu assured the Ministry of Education and the Department of War that Japan would have a continuous source of healthy and mentally prepared patriots to serve the Imperial nation.

I believe that his 1908 October address to the ministry of education and the department of war pretty much sums up his ideas: "We must not forget what the Duke of Wellington said at the Battle of Waterloo, when he overcame and defeated Napoleon Bonapart, 'Our victory today was gained on the playing fields of Eaton.'"

Didn't this, then, change the face of karate from being an effective fighting art to being a mere physical vehicle for enhancing personal growth and development?

What Itosu did, in fact, by bringing various traditions (*kata*) together and standardizing a teaching method, was to diametrically alter its original practice and purpose. In so doing, Itosu laid a different foundation upon which a new generation of modern "masters" surfaced. The way he envisioned his tradition did not focus upon its brutal defensive themes, application principles, or corresponding practices, but rather, emphasized physical fitness and character development in large groups. Today, many see this phenomenon as having obscured an otherwise omnipotent and brutal tradition and metamorphosized it into a cultural recreation for the purpose of enhancing military effectiveness. However, when we look beyond the obvious we can more clearly recognize that Itosu's innovation was the single stimulus that revived an otherwise dying tradition.

Not unlike the learning curve of today's enthusiasts, regardless from which school or "style" they come, so too did the learners of Itosu's generation (who continued on with their studies in uchinadi) ultimately seek out the deeper teachings, defensive themes, application principles, and corresponding two-man training methods which supported such original practices.

You mentioned the introduction of a formulated karate *kata* into the education system. Prior to this event, was karate or uchinadi basically a Chinese art being practiced by Okinawans?

Well, understanding Okinawa's lengthy tributary Chinese status, it probably comes as no big surprise to readers that much of karate is based upon Chinese quanfa reinterpreted by *uchinanchu* in a culture unlike that from whence it came. However, let me explain further. The concept of perpetuating infinite teachings through a conduit of ritualized physical paradigms is not a monopoly of the Chinese. It is hypothesized that even the earliest tribes of prehistoric man of ancient Africa used ritualized physical emulation to hand down its wisdom. However, the ritualized defensive paradigms (*hsing* in Chinese; *kata* in Japanese) practiced in uchinadi/karate are Chinese in origin—forged over hundreds of generations in monastic sanctuaries by spiritual (Daoist, Buddhist) recluses. More specifically, they are Southern Chinese and can be traced back to a handful of stylized eighteenth and nineteenth century Fujian Shaolin quanfa traditions that haphazardly found their way to Okinawa.

How did the introduction of karate into Japan's university sports clubs in the 1920s affect the growth, spread, and direction of karate?

Well, the social, cultural and political climate of the *uchinanchu* was completely alien to the Japanese; as a matter of interest, the Japanese historically thought little of the *uchinanchu* or their culture. This is paramount for readers who do not understand how the anthropology of a powerful culture profoundly influences the growth and direction of those foreign ritualized practices embraced within their society.

The Japanese saying, *"Deru kugi wah utareru"* (A protruding nail ultimately gets hammered down), aptly describes how people/things which are not "Japanese" conform to cultural guidelines or are ultimately ostracized or excluded. In Japanese society there is a cultural phenomenon referred to as the principle of wa (harmony or peace), which is paramount to understanding their mentality. *Wa* is an attitude that, to varying degrees, is customarily practiced in all aspects of Japanese society. In his best seller, *The*

Enigma of Japanese Power, Karel van Wolferen describes *wa* as the uninterrupted display of a readiness to sacrifice one's personal interests for the sake of communal tranquillity. Together with kokutai (National Polity), shushin (representing diligence, regimentalism, conformism, the commitment to mass productivity, strict adherence to seniority, Emperor worship, and lifetime loyalty to one's organization or business), and Nihonjinron (Japaneseness), uchinadi, in its new sociocultural setting, simply became influenced by forces beyond its control.

The central location in which that metamorphosis took place was in the universities that were busy forging the new minds of an imperial nation. In many ways, uchinadi, like judo and kendo before it, became yet another conduit through which to funnel Japanese imperial ideology during a period of radical military escalation. By virtue of the culture into which they journeyed, *uchinanchu* were forced to conform to the following Japanese *budo* standards: (1) adopt standard training apparel, (2) adopt the *dan/kyu* pedagogy, (3) adopt the belt system, (4) adopt the customary Japanese suffix "*do*" to help identify a domestic tradition, (5) adopt a prefix which might better the depth of its study rather than revealing its foreign (Chinese) origins, and (6) adopt the *ippon-shobu shiai* practice to test the technique and spirit of its participants.

Weren't many of the classical Japanese martial arts come martial ways— like judo and kendo—already a part of these university social club systems at this time?

Yes, that's right. Judo and kendo were compulsory subjects in Japanese normal schools, in addition to being part of the university *bukatsu* (sports club) system.

So what was going on with karate in Japan at this time? Wasn't Funakoshi Gichin spearheading its movement?

Well, I think that it might be more appropriate to also include other leaders like Motobu Choki, Mabuni Kenwa, and Miyagi Chojun (along with others) rather than continuing to perpetuate the myth that Funakoshi did it all by himself. There were several *uchinanchu* on the mainland during that era vigorously campaigning to promote the island discipline.

As to what was going on with karate, I think that much of what I have already mentioned provides a pretty good chronology up to this point. However, an important point I would like to introduce in this interview is the subsequent metamorphosis karate experienced in the university *bukatsu* (sports clubs) during the time after it was introduced to the mainland.

Before I describe the way karate was taught during that era, I believe that it is necessary for the reader to appropriate some fundament knowledge about kendo and judo, as these two modern Japanese *budo* had an enormous impact upon the way karate unfolded.

Based upon the defensive and offensive principles used in several schools of jujutsu, judo was the product of synthesizing and simplifying their most effective techniques into a safer modern competitive format. In judo one learns basic *ukemi* (break falling) in order to protect himself in the event of being thrown; one learns *ashi-sabaki* (footwork) and *tai-sabaki* (body movement) to support the execution of fundamental throwing techniques. Within a few lessons the learner is actively partaking in *randori* (sparring) and on their way to mastering the tradition. In short, judo is a great form of conditioning and a way through which to forge character and fighting spirit.

The study of kendo, an older competitive practice, parallels judo in that it unfolds in much the same way by bringing various schools of swordsmanship together to arrive at four basic offensive patterns: *men* (striking to the head), *kote* (slashing the wrists), *do* (cutting the body), and *tsuki* (thrusting into the throat). Once these are learned and combined with the *ashi-* and *tai-sabaki*, deflecting principles and associated methods of responding or creating and exploiting weaknesses, learners gear up and engage in sparring. Like judo, it's a great workout and helps to develop character and fighting spirit.

Unlike judo and kendo, where specific principles of movement and associated training methods supporting the actual application of its corresponding technique are embraced, the instruction of karate during that pioneering era was void of such teachings. When people like Funakoshi introduced karate into the mainstream of Japanese culture, the focus was upon *kata*, the principal vehicle through which the tradition had been imparted in Okinawa. While what he was doing was admirable, and keeping in mind that the Japanese had never seen the human limbs oscillated in the brutal way that karate employed them, the restless sounds that keep reverberating during that embryonic generation were of young university stalwarts dissatisfied with training methods that did not support application. In other words, there simply were no training methods that linked *kata* to its corresponding defensive themes and application principles.

Moving toward the peak of their athleticism and fueled by testosterone, students anxious to engage their training partners in the same way that fellow *kendoka* and *judoka* did, were growing weary of infinite punching and kicking and repeating *kata* as a solo practice. The common questions being asked by young enthusiasts like Ohtsuka Hironori (1892–1982) and his colleague Konishi Yasuhiro (1893–1983) was, "When are we going to get around to testing our technique, character, and fighting spirit?"

In trying to help beginners or inflexible thinkers better understand this natural evolutionary process, I sometimes like to quote the late American anthropologist, Joseph Campbell, who said: "Every generation produces innovators who, in an effort to keep their ritualized traditions a living experience for the people they serve, reinterpret the common principles upon which they rest. In doing so, it is not so much new traditions that are forged, as much as it is more innovative ways of imparting the same principles."

Against the better judgment of their Okinawan masters, a few Japanese karate students during that first generation eagerly ventured out on their own to reinterpret those common principles and establish a way with which to develop a fighting spirit, like kendo and judo. In the image of kendo and judo, and using the very same *ippon-shobu shiai* principles, Ohtsuka Hironori and his colleague Konishi Yasuhiro vigorously spearheaded a movement that witnessed the development of more innovative ways of using karate as a sport.

A prominent *kendoka* and *jujutsuka*, Ohtsuka met Funakoshi in

September of 1922, and by 1924 received his first *menkyo* from him. Similarly, Konishi was also an expert in jujutsu and kendo and an early student of Funakoshi as well. Together, they took the concept of blocking, punching, and kicking, and used corresponding combative engagement principles used in kendo and judo, and meticulously forged the fundamental paradigms from which came one, two, and three step sparring. Ultimately, and from their brainstorming, *jiu-kumite* unfolded.

Naturally, in an effort to achieve their common competitive outcomes, corresponding training methods needed to be developed. Hence, the various signature training methods (commonly referred to as *ryuha* or "styles") which gradually unfolded reflected individual interpretations of a common rule-bound themes, complete with corresponding assessment criteria for achieving levels of proficiency.

You mentioned earlier about aims and objectives of a system matching its training methods. Since the essence of what karate has become in Japan so vastly differed from what it was on Okinawa, did there also develop new aims and objectives?

Yes, well, I think I have already covered that aspect. However, it might be worth reviewing here that the original defensive objectives, application principles (addressing the random yet habitual acts of physical violence which plague civil society through *kata*), and corresponding training methods which once supported such intent (old-style karate now referred to as koryu uchinadi) seemingly became obscured from Itosu's time. Then there is the subsequent modern generation introducing the practice to mainland Japan where it underwent yet another metamorphosis based largely upon developing it into a sport and cultural recreation.

Somewhere in these historical circumstances I believe that we can more clearly recognize the transition between what the old tradition represented, and what its modern counterparts now represent.

You certainly have provided us with a rather detailed explanation of the origins, spread, and development of karate. In concluding this conversation, is there anything else that you would like to share with us?

Thank you, Mark. Yes, there is. During this generation there has surfaced growing and independent movements aimed at rediscovering the original purpose of *kata*. The International Ryukyu Karate Research Society is, to the best of my knowledge, the only movement dedicated exclusively to rediscovering, analyzing, improving, and imparting the common and infinite truth, rather than focusing upon any one particular style or signature practice. In this research, the IRKRS stands alone, yet beckons like-minded thinkers to join our campaign in an effort to deliver the truth.

Bushi Matsumura (1809–1901) once said: "For those whose progress remains hampered by ego-related distractions have yet to learn the value of humility: the spiritual cornerstone upon which the self-defense traditions rest." Humility serves to remind us all of the importance of placing virtue ahead of vice, values ahead of vanity, and principles ahead of personalities. Styles are nothing more than varying interpretations of those universal principles upon which karatedo rests. Understand the virtues, values, and principles of karatedo and one will discover why vice, vanity, and personality defeat the ultimate aim of karatedo.

Mastery without delusion can only be discovered by sincerely embracing the precepts upon which karatedo rests. This is why foreigners get such a good feeling about training in Japan, the culture is so nonconfrontational, unlike the West. Traditionally speaking, Japanese understand and live in accordance to the principle of "*wa*." This message has made a significant impact upon the pioneers of this ancient fraternity. Like the karate enthusiasts who have walked before us, we too need to establish a symbiosis with karatedo so that our lives are just as much a product of the art as is the art a product of our lives. In understanding these ancient precepts, enthusiasts can come to know and respect the genuine difference between karate and karatedo: the exciting competitive recreation and the "Way" of karate.

This is a concept rarely observed in Western culture, but one that represents a cornerstone of Japanese society. When one cannot get beyond the immediate results of physical training, karatedo remains purely a recreational pursuit. Captured by the essence of introspection karatedo becomes a fascinating vehicle of inner exploration, through which untold personal rewards are made possible.

Those who are familiar with the power of combining rigorous physical discipline with philosophical study, methodical and protracted introspection can readily testify to the self-conquests made possible through karatedo. However, before the light inside each of us can ever be turned on we must balance the physical with the mental, we must master the ritual of introspection, breath, and silence. Introspection is vitally important to the growth and maturity of each and every one who studies the *kata* of karatedo, regardless of how ignorant or skeptical they may at first be.

The research process is equally as important as is the end result and I caution anybody who embarks upon such an adventure to understand this. Get interested in the race and not just the goal; the process, not just the possession. Quite often we are so preoccupied by the ends to which our choices would be a means that we, rarely, if ever, give any attention to the causes for which our choices are effected. What can we ever discover if we are not first willing to explore? Only a fool takes no joy in understanding. Karatedo teaches one that the source of human conflict is internal and not external, hence our journey must be inward, not outward. Change must occur from within before it can be measured without.

The results of one's research usually holds more personal value when interest develops from attraction rather than promotion. In short, it is better to discover on your own how valuable research can be rather than someone else telling you how great it is. With one's attention drawn inward, the prolonged physical discipline of karatedo has a way of influencing the mind. It is in that regard that a student of karatedo begins to recognize the depth of this tradition. However, it usually takes one a long time to understand that there is something beyond the immediate results of physical training. Beyond exhaustion, despite aching muscles, we have all experienced a peacefulness flowing quietly within the brutality of karatedo. And, it is through this inner tranquillity that our pursuit of spiritual fulfillment is realized.

Rather than gaining or acquiring excess baggage in life, karatedo teaches us to remove useless and ego-related distractions. Instead of always striving to acquire more, genuine happiness can come from learning to appreciate less. Rather than only taking from karatedo, we must also consider putting back into that which has given us strength and power. Consider that all power and success has to do with putting knowledge into action through mastering the world within.

To be the very best one can ever be, regardless of whether or not it is fighting, sports, business, or just life in general, an indescribable resolve and inner strength is required. Transcending the barriers of the ordinary, such indomitable fortitude is never made possible without first making enormous personal sacrifices.

Through adhering to the age-old precepts of karatedo one comes face-to-face with one's weaknesses. And it is through these precepts that weaknesses are turned into strengths and strengths into even greater strengths, hence the tradition fulfills its purpose. Indomitable fortitude provides the resilience to withstand the personal failure, which tests each of us along life's path.

A mind tempered in the tradition of karatedo will remain impervious to worldly delusion and illuminate the darkness of selfishness and ignorance. As with the samurai warrior undaunted in the face of fear, preparation, patience, and humility are ninety percent of fighting, winning, living. With greater control over our mind, or the "world within," we can have greater control over our body, lives, and the "world without." It is by putting this power and knowledge to work every day that our lives are enriched and fulfilled in ways we never thought possible.

Through cultivating our spiritual nature, faith, courage, and enthusiasm, brings forth the rewards of accomplishment. Our spiritual nature can only be cultivated by "doing"; "we can only get as much as we give," "only reap that which we sow." In fact, the law of inner-growth depends entirely upon reciprocal action: we receive only as we give. Cultivating our spiritual nature begins with mastering a ritual of introspection, breathing, physical stillness, and humility long before its benefits can be put into practice.

Karatedo is a vehicle through which an even balance of austere conditioning, philosophical assimilation, nutritional intelligence, methodical and protracted introspection, builds a strong and healthy body, wards off illness, destroys ego-related barriers, cures human misery, and draws one's attention inward to where a journey without distance teaches us that spiritual freedom and genuine happiness can be realized, not by having more, but by learning to appreciate less.

When captured by the essence of introspection, the relentless practice of kata draws one's attention so deeply inward that thoughts are focused upon until the mind attracts the conditions necessary for their fulfillment. Concentration must become so intense that one is able to identify with the object of one's inner reflections, so much so that one is conscious of nothing else. Ultimately, thought is transmuted into character (we are what we think), and character is the magnet that creates the environment of the individual.

We need only to recognize the omnipotence of our spiritual nature and the desire to become the recipient of its beneficial effects to begin our journey. However, austerity, self-deprivation, and modesty—the essential elements of self-mastery—must surface from attraction and not promotion.

The passing of time, the changing of the seasons, the erosion of land, and the death of loved ones; the "Way" of karate teaches, to those willing to learn, that everything in the circle of life is seasonal, changing, dying, reborn. A microcosm of life, karatedo is but one path leading up the mountain; it teaches one to understand these changes, accept them, and live in harmony with them. It is the circle of life. Our aging, the way we think, one's urges and sexuality, man's questions about the universe, our necessity to know ourselves, and the need to find a reason for existence, even accepting our own death, will always need meticulous examination and action.

Because these questions will always exist, there will always be the need for a tradition that has the answers. Karatedo is one such tradition: a tradition that can only be brought to life by teaching its participants to look inward to discover the truth and live in harmony with nature.

ALEXANDER CO
The History of Kung-Fu in the Philippines

No name is more synonymous with kung-fu in the Philippines than Alexander Co. He spearheaded the Chin Wu Club in Manila, wrote the first kung-fu book ever published in the Philippines, and also published its first martial arts magazine, simply titled Martial Arts Magazine. *Co has studied a dozen different kung-fu styles, was an "in-door" disciple of ngo cho kun's late grandmaster Tan Ka Hong. In addition, Co studied praying mantis and Hung-gar kung-fu under Shakespeare Chan, Wu style tai chi chuan under John Hu Chuan Hai, and hsin-i liu ha pa fa under David Chan. Co is vice-chairman of the Hsin-I Society of Internal Arts and chairman of the Tsing Hua Ngo Cho Kung-Fu Center. In addition to his dozens of magazine articles, Co has written three books,* Secrets of the Seven Star Praying Mantis, The Way of Ngo Cho Kun, *and* Five Ancestor Fist Kung Fu, *and recently filmed a series of six instructional videotapes on ngo cho kun and seven star praying mantis.*

Although you wouldn't think it to be so, there are a vast number of Chinese martial arts and well-known kung-fu masters in the Philippines. Who were the first Chinese to emigrate to the Philippines?

I think as early as the Ming dynasty Chinese merchants were already coming to the Philippines. Before the Spaniards came over, there are stories about a Chinese pirate name Lima Hong. He came to the Philippines and was disgusted with the place. He just wanted to use it as a home base. In China at the time, life was real hard for the merchants. After the Ming dynasty and the Ching dynasty most of the history books claim that the government was corrupt and life was hard. So, most of the Chinese, especially those from Fukien, Canton area, started going overseas to look for greener pastures. A lot of the Chinese came to Manila.

Which of these new settlers brought kung-fu with them?

Among the businessmen, some knew some kung-fu. But basically, because it was a big community, they relied more on Chinese medicine and all those things. So, some of the Chinese bone setters and doctors came here to make a living serving the Chinese community. A lot of them knew kung-fu. This was during the early 1900s.

Did these men begin teaching the people within the Chinese community by opening clubs? If so, what did they call their arts during that time?

In the early 1900s, they used to call the kung-fu styles from Fukien province kun-tao. Usually the term kun-tao is used by those who Chinese are illiterate. As a term, it is generally used only by those who live in Fukien province. So only after the establishment of the Central Kou Shu Institute, did Chinese martial arts begin to be called kuk sut in both China and the Philippines.

What does kuk sut mean, and why did they use this term as opposed to another?

Kuk sut comes from the term meaning *chung Hwa busut,* meaning Chinese martial arts. So they shortened it to kuk sut. Actually, kuk sut is the Fukien pronunciation of kuo shu, or national art.

So how did those within Binondo, Manila's Chinatown, find an instructor and learn these fighting skills?

At that time, some of the Filipinos were still hostile toward the Chinese. The Filipinos look to the Chinese as people who are taking part of their livelihood. And the police thing is not so good. So at lot of Chinese rely on their kung-fu for their own protection. A lot of them knew that someone knew some kung-fu. So, they usually tried to hire them as private teachers or to study under them in small groups. Those who were rich could hire a kung-fu master for protection as a bodyguard. But the ordinary people couldn't afford this, so they grouped together and shared a small class.

What were some of the first kung-fu styles that were taught into the Philippines' Chinese communities?

Ever since the beginning it has always been ngo cho kun because it is the art of the Fukien people. Earlier, they say there was a master of kau kun—but nobody had seen anything of him. From my research, I have found almost everyone to do ngo cho kun because Manila's Chinese community is made up of eighty percent Fukien people.

So what happened to the other Fukien styles, like white crane and wing chun, for example?

The wing chun white crane, there was maybe a few people studying it. The masters here never came out with their arts openly, even within the Chinese community. It has always been the ngo cho kun clubs that really prosper.

That art was being taught by whom?

At that time it was being taught by Tan Kiong Beng, who originally came to the Philippines to work as a bone setter. Tan was the father of my *sifu*, Tan Ka Hong. But people heard of Tan's fame as one of the ten tigers of ngo cho. They soon began to practice with him. If I am not mistaken, the Chee Kong Tong, which is a Chinese mason, hired him to be their kung-fu instructor. But most of the Chinese at that time only looked at the Philippines as a place to make some money, and would rather just stay here for six months or so and then return to China. Then, after spending their money, they would return to the Philippines again. So, Tan Kiong Beng was here, and after teaching for a while he didn't feel like staying in Manila and went back to China, leaving his students to continue their practice on their own.

Under whom did Tan Kiong Beng study ngo cho kun?

Tan Kiong Beng was quite wealthy in China. As a result, he was able to acquire the services of the founder of ngo cho, Chua Giok Beng, as a private instructor at his house. Since Tan wanted to learn the art so badly, he spent almost his entire family fortune to pay for his lessons. That's why he had to go overseas to start earning some money again. He didn't want to work in China because of his family pride.

Is Beng Kiam the oldest kung-fu club in the Philippines?

During the early days there were a number of private training groups, but they didn't go by any special name. In the early 1930s, Chang Tzi Jiang, a government official who was active in kung-fu, organized the Central Kuo Shu Institute. That is from where most of the old Taiwanese kung-fu masters came. Chang organized a group of kung-fu masters and went on tour throughout Asia to promote the art. He went to Malaysia, Singapore, the Philippines and other places. When he came to Manila—I think Tan Kiong Beng was here at that time—the community asked some of the students to participate in the exhibition. This started the craze in kung-fu, and everyone began looking for kung-fu.

So the group of Tan Kiong Beng's students decided they were going to open a formal kung-fu school. By the time they made the final decision to do so, Tan had already gone back to China. The group sent Tan a letter asking him to come back to Manila since they were prepared at this time to open a school. But Tan Kiong Beng didn't feel like returning to Manila again because he wanted to enjoy his old age in China. So, in his stead, he sent Tan Ka Hong. That was in 1935.

So the oldest kung-fu school in the Philippines is the Beng Kiam Athletic

Association. How did it get started?

Tan Ka Hong came over with a few of his father's disciples based in Manila. They grouped together the rich businessmen at that time to finance or sponsor the club. At that time, the kung-fu clubs served as a kind of protection agency for their sponsors, doing the police work for the local Chinese in Manila. When Beng Kiam was established it was a really big thing because everyone knew the powers of Tan Ka Hong. They relied on him and his students since they saw their exhibitions and were amazed by the strength of their kung-fu. Ngo cho is a very strong style, so they were able to get a lot of supporters for the club. Beng Kiam started out real big, with a lot of students. It kept changing sites until the club had enough money in the 1950s to buy their own lot and put up their own building.

So members of the local Chinese community would hire Beng Kiam students for protection?

Well, actually, not hire them for protection. The prominent people in the community who came to study in Beng Kiam, whenever there is trouble the directors of the club would ask the kung-fu club for protection. Tan Ka Hong would send his top students to go there for them.

Since Beng Kiam was so successful after three years in 1938, Lo Yen Chiu, also a ngo cho master from China, came to Manila and opened the Kong Han Kung-Fu Ngo Cho Club. Since his club was from the same style, a rivalry developed between Beng Kiam and Kong Han. Although it was not a public rivalry, the students of both clubs often compared skill against one another to see which club was the best. Even among the officers of Beng Kiam, they took pride in the fact that they were the first and the largest of the two ngo cho clubs.

This is funny because Lo Yen Chiu and Tan Kiong Beng were blood brothers in kung-fu and were real close to one another in China. But when Lo came over to Manila and opened a club, it's like he breached the unwritten code. In China there is a saying that you can't keep two tigers in one mountain or they will clash.

I asked Tan Ka Hong why when Lo came over the younger generation students always felt a rivalry existed between the clubs when they were so close in China. He told me the main reason was that Lo should have gone somewhere else and not Manila. Even if he stayed in the Philippines, he should have opened his club in another city, and not Manila. So, the moment Lo opened his club in Manila there was a breach of trust and friendship.

You say that Lo and Tan were blood brothers in ngo cho and had the same teacher, yet there is an obvious difference in the physical movements of the ngo cho they teach. I mean the names of the techniques and forms are the same, but they look quite different. How is this and why?

Well, actually, Lo Yen Chiu trained with the students of Chua Giok Beng and not with him personally. But Tan Kiong Beng surpassed the other students until he became a direct disciple of the founder. I don't know if the students have different moves or what.

Tan Ka Hong told me that when Lo Yen Chu was a kung-fu teacher by profession in China, Tan Kiong Beng was learning the art as a hobby. Some of Lo's early students were members of local gangs. One of the leaders who was a students had an affair with Lo's daughter-in-law, but Lo couldn't do anything since the guy was strong and powerful with great influence. After that, he sort of opened his mind and started teaching his kung-fu more openly to make him bigger. Tan used to go and watch Lo's class and Tan would say "Uncle Chiu, how come your ngo cho is different?" And Lo would reply "Shut up, kid. You don't know anything. This is the modern way."

So after Beng Kiam and Kong Han what other kung-fu clubs opened in the Philippines?

There was another club called Hua Eng, which also taught ngo cho. In the Sixties some Taiwan teachers started coming over. The first one was Han Ching Tang, who is featured in Robert Smith's book, *Chinese Boxing Masters and Methods*. He was here around 1963 or 1964. He stayed here for a while and Hua Eng started to adopt his styles, doing northern Shaolin, chin na, and Yang style tai chi. After Han returned to Taiwan one of his students, Sim Bio Hui, came to the Philippines.

Then some of the students from both Beng Kiam and Kong Han broke away and opened up the Kok Kong (from Kong Han) and Sampaguita and Kiak Nan clubs (from Beng Kiam).

As early as 1954 a group of students from Beng Kiam, who were searching for more knowledge, started studying privately under Master Tee I Ping. They studied choy li fut under Tee in Paco, a section of Manila. When Tan Ka Hong heard about this he got mad. You see, at that time cross training was unheard of and unacceptable. So Tan told them to choose to quit choy li fut and stay with Beng Kiam or quit Beng Kiam and go with Master Tee. The students decided to go out and support Tee and they opened up Hong Sing in 1954. Hong Sing is a world renown name used by many choy li fut clubs, although they are not related to one another.

I think in the early 1960s other Cantonese clubs started to open, like the Ling Lam Kung-Fu Research School. They don't have a formal master, but all of the Cantonese who knew kung-fu would go there and teach their own thing. One guy there who they looked upon as a teacher was Tiu King San. I think he was doing Choy-gar.

Actually before Ling Lam opened, the Cantonese, who were a minority in Manila, all knew one another and had their own association. So Hong Sing became more than just a kung-fu association. So besides Tee, Hong Sing also housed a Hung-gar master named Lao Kim. Even though the club had two kung-fu masters teaching in it, when one was active the other wasn't. It's funny.

In the late 1950s, when Lao Kim was teaching, Shakespeare Chan started studying kung-fu there. Shakespeare became one of Manila's best-known masters. Shakespeare studied for four or five years learning Hung-gar. Now the Hung-gar that Lao Kim taught was different than the Hung-gar they have in Hong Kong. So after learning everything from Lao Kim, Lao Kim gave Shakespeare a letter of recommendation to go to Hong Kong to study under Lao Kay Tong, who learned the popular version of Hung-gar that you see in the United States, like the style of Y. C. Wong, popularly known as the tiger-crane style.

That's interesting because I always thought of Shakespeare Chan as a teacher of northern praying mantis and Tibetan white crane, not Hung-gar.

Shakespeare was always fond of collecting and reading books and magazine about kung-fu. He knew about the styles of praying mantis from Won Hung Fan and from the magazine he knew a lot of different styles popular in Hong Kong at that time. He was able to travel to Hong Kong at that time because his mother's jewelry business took her to Hong Kong frequently. At that time traveling was not that convenient. Only those who were rich could afford to travel. So Shakespeare took a trip with his mother and started studying Hung-gar with Lao Kay Tong.

Shakespeare also went to see Won Hong Fan to learn the mantis, but Won Hong Fan was charging him per form, which he couldn't afford. So, a business associate of Shakespeare's mother brought him to Chiu Chi Man, who is actually more senior than Wong Hon Fan, but less famous as he hadn't written any books. Also, since Shakespeare was Cantonese, he could easily assimilate with the masters there. Chiu Chi Man ended up liking Shakespeare so much that he accepted him as an "in-door" disciple and gave him a crash course in all of the praying mantis styles. Since Shakespeare had a strong base in Hung-gar, it was easy for him to pick up another style.

I am not sure how it happened, but Shakespeare also got started in the Tibetan white crane style. He had a hard time learning white crane, though. At that time white crane was popular and most of the Hong Kong Triads were practicing it. In fact, there was a documentary on the triads, and their kung-fu style was white crane. There were various systems of white crane at that time. Although the grandmaster was still around, depending on how close you were to him depended on what version you were taught. So, Shakespeare learned from different teachers to find the one closest to the grandmaster, Go Show Chong. In his quest, Shakespeare was able to study under Kwong Peh Foo, who became the chief instructor of the White Crane Association of Hong Kong.

Shakespeare told me that he was training at three kung-fu clubs a day while in Hong Kong!

Did Shakespeare open his own kung-fu club when he returned to Manila?
No, when Shakespeare returned to Manila in the sixties he

brought with him the three styles. He began teaching at Ling Lam. You see, at that time, the clubs were sponsored by the local businessmen. So, the instructors taught for free and the students often stayed at the clubs. In wanting to make a name for himself, Shakespeare went into Ling Lam and said he would teach for free. They accepted him as a *sifu* there. And to make some money on the side he started accepting some private paying students. He would teach the paying students some more advanced techniques than those he taught for free.

This, however, created trouble within Ling Lam because the other members got jealous and started questioning why they are instructors in the club but Shakespeare's private students were learning more kung-fu than them. Shakespeare told them that he needed the money, and not to complain as they were getting lessons for free!

Shakespeare got disgusted and left the club. Actually he was so disgusted with the whole thing that he stopped teaching altogether and went into the travel business.

You became a student of both Tan Ka Hong and Shakespeare Chan. How did you first become interested in studying the martial arts?

Ever since my childhood, there were a lot of those old-time kung-fu movies in black and white—Cantonese, I think. You have Si Kien and Kwan Tak Hing and all those stars in them. Kung-fu was always a fascination to me. And I heard stories from my *lola* (grandmother), because my uncle used to practice a little bit of ngo cho also. So, it was all those stories about masters and people who could leap over walls and everything that got me started. Like in the United States, you have all those stories about gunslingers like Billy the Kid. In China, the stories are about kung-fu masters. So, I decided I wanted to learn something.

At what age did you take your first martial arts lesson?

I start my training way back in 1965. So at that time I was twelve years old. Back in the sixties it was hard to study under a master. Everyone relied on those big karate books for instruction. I started out following some karate books and kung-fu books. My brother picked up some style from his friends. I don't know what it was—just some self-defense moves. And my uncle was a football player and was always showing me those fancy jumps and butterfly kicks he picked up from some guys whose chiropractor was supposedly a kung-fu teacher. He took up a few moves and told me stories about how he was surrounded by some hold-uppers and did some fancy kicks and scared them away. So, he taught me a few kicks. That's how I got started.

When did you begin formal kung-fu instruction, and under whom?

During my high school days we had a group of friends studying kung-fu. And our friends who were studying in Beng Kiam used to teach me all the forms from the club—I learned some moves. After all my buddies stopped practicing—that was in 1968—a friend of mine who was also from Beng Kiam finally took me to the club so I could formally enroll as a member.

Weren't you also a student of Shakespeare Chan?

It wasn't until the Seventies that I met Shakespeare and started learning from him privately. Kung-fu was really big at that time and martial law was also declared. Since nobody could leave the country, Shakespeare had to close his travel business. With Shakespeare's help I opened up the Chin Wu school in the late seventies. Actually, the name was given to us by Chiu Chi Man, since he knew Shakespeare was fond of teaching different styles. Chin Wu is the name of the first kung-fu school opened by the *sifu* of Fok Yuen Kap, the guy played by Bruce Lee in the movie *The Chinese Connection.*

Basically, I learned Hung-gar and praying mantis under Shakespeare. Since I was his friend first, Shakespeare taught me everything he knew. He made his students prove themselves before passing on his knowledge to them, though.

How was Chin Wu different than the other clubs in Manila?

Chin Wu set a standard in Manila for kung-fu schools. We were charging more than the other clubs, and we were the first to make the students wear traditional kung-fu uniforms and also have testing times and an initial initiation period where they swear their oath of allegiance to the school. After about five years I closed Chin Wu since Shakespeare became tied up with his business again, and I was busy training at Beng Kiam.

About four years ago, Shakespeare opened another club. He was thinking about reviving Chin Wu, but decided to call it the Tibetan White Crane School. The reasons I couldn't officially teach at Chin Wu was because I was with Beng Kiam for so long. Tan Ka Hong never knew I was cross training.

Didn't you also go to Hong Kong with Shakespeare to study and start your own kung-fu magazine?

I began publishing *Martial Arts Magazine* in 1973. I think it was the same year Curtis Wong started *Inside Kung-Fu* magazine. I went to Hong Kong with Shakespeare in 1977. He brought me around to meet various masters like Chiu Chi Man. Chiu Chi Man was retired already and his students were the ones teaching. When we went to his house, I saw a photo of Shakespeare and Chiu Chi Man together posted next to the bed of the master. When they walked together and talked you could see how close they were. They embraced as father and son. I think this is why, before opening Chin Wu, Shakespeare asked permission from Chiu Chi Man. Chiu Chi Man gave him a banner and handwritten transmission scrolls for the mantis style.

I also interviewed a lot of masters and also studied briefly in choy li fut and wing chun. Shakespeare was able to negotiate with Yip Chun, a son of Yip Man, for me to be accepted as a disciple and train with him.

I was also able to meet the monkey boxer named Chan Sau. He was teaching five different monkey styles and when I went to him he thought I was rich. He told me the only reason he was able to learn the secret five monkey styles was because he married the daughter of the master. He said that if I wanted to learn the forms I would have to pay 30,000 Hong Kong dollars per form! I declined his offer.

You have played various pivotal roles in the promotion and spread of

praying mantis kung-fu. You are also the first person in the Philippines to publish a kung-fu book.

I had my first book published by National Bookstore on praying mantis. I believe this is the first kung-fu book ever published in the Philippines. I recently also signed a contract with Tuttle to write another praying mantis book. I told Shakespeare and he was happy about this, especially now since China has started to export wu shu teachers. Here in Manila, most of the younger generation don't even know much about the history of kung-fu. They think that just because it came from China, then it must be the real thing. But the seven star praying mantis I saw has already been influenced by modern wu shu. The former students of Shakespeare believe that what Shakespeare taught in the 1960s was not the original style brought over from China. I hope the publication of the mantis book will help support Shakespeare's claim on the origin of the seven star praying mantis handed down by Lo Kwang Yi (China) to Chiu Chi Man (Hong Kong) to Shakespeare Chan (Philippines).

In 1968 you began practicing ngo cho at the Beng Kiam Athletic Association. What was the teaching like? Did Tan Ka Hong actively teach, or did he sit idle by the side as so many Chinese masters do?

As early as the 1960s Tan stopped teaching already because there were so many students. So it was the students taking care of the students. It was so hard to get Master Tan to teach you since the classes were so big and there were so many members. You just learned from your kung-fu brothers. It was only in the eighties—ten or fifteen years later—that I was able to learn directly with him.

Wasn't there a lot of variation in form and technique among and between the students, since the master did not bother correcting anyone, and the students were left to their own devices?

Upon learning, just as with the regular group class at the kung-fu school, instruction is not really formal. Everyone came up with different techniques. So the eighties was the time that I was able to check out my form with Tan and I found out that a lot of them were wrong! I think one of the main reasons for this was because in the early fifties or sixties the first group that went up against him left him and opened the Hong Sing Club. He got disgusted with the students and decided to stop teaching and giving out the real thing.

If this is the case, then why did Master Tan allow you to become close to him and ask him direct questions when you were just a junior student?

When I was busy learning with Shakespeare I was not so active with Beng Kiam anymore, but I still went there whenever there was a celebration to do a demonstration and support the club. Then in the eighties, Master Tan called me back—I think he knew I was learning outside the club—and asked me to become a chairman of the club. As a chairman, I think I got special privilege and was able to get close to him. I talked with him a lot, and as time went on I think he started to like me. So that is the time I just started to ask him about kung-fu.

You mean that right in front of the senior students you were getting special treatment from the master?

No, because during that time we had class only on Tuesday, Thursday, and Saturday. When I started asking him questions regarding deeper ngo cho knowledge, he told me to go to Beng Kiam on Monday, Wednesday, and Friday, when the school was empty. And that is the time he started teaching me the correct way to practice the art.

According to Tan Ka Hong, he told me it is hard to teach just anybody because ngo cho is different than other styles of kung-fu. As you do your *chien* (tension) forms and everything, even without proper form you can get real strong. So, he was worried to give his true knowledge to just anyone since he was betrayed before.

Why, then, do you think Master Tan opened up to you?

After I became the chairman in the 1980s, I became quite close with Master Tan. I was helping him out in preparing the Association's anniversary. Master Tan was particularly happy when he found out that I liked martial arts books and magazines, and that I also published my own magazine. I featured his son Benito on the cover of one issue.

It is often difficult to become close to a Chinese *sifu*. And yet, aside from Tan Ka Hong, you were also able to become close to Shakespeare Chan.

I thought of how I started to learn under Shakespeare. I became close with Shakespeare because I approached him to publish a mantis book. In the course of helping him prepare the book, we became quite close. I was able to dig deeper into the knowledge of the mantis style as I started to question and analyze the style. Shakespeare took it lightly, like a casual interview for the book.

You must realize that in traditional kung-fu, it is considered impolite to ask the *sifu* questions, especially regarding the practical applications of the techniques. They take this as an insult, like you doubt the validity of the style. There was this incident, that Shakespeare told me, which I remember very well.

You see, Shakespeare was one of the real kung-fu masters who first started teaching kung-fu to non-Chinese. He got some private rich Filipino students, some of which were former karate students. They couldn't understand the sophisticated moves of the Hung-gar and praying mantis styles. So one time three of the students approached Shakespeare while he was at the house of a student. Shakespeare was teaching in the garden when the three students asked how they could apply these techniques. Shakespeare took this as a challenge. He told me that, in his mind, he was planning on how to dispose of these three guys. He positioned himself near the pool and asked one of the guys to punch him. He was planning on throwing him into the pool. The students must have noticed Shakespeare's serious attitude because they didn't dare ask him any further questions. From this incident, you can see how difficult it is to learn kung-fu. Imagine, Shakespeare is already considered quite modern and still he took it as an insult.

I also remember a similar incident in Beng Kiam. A senior student who had become a director in our club was asking Tan Ka Hong about ngo cho. He then made the mistake of asking how a technique was applied. Tan Ka Hong showed him a move and then the student asked how this move could be countered. Tan Ka Hong was not happy about this, then I saw Tan Ka Hong apply a painful *chin-na* (grab) on my senior's shoulder. He slammed down to the ground from the excruciating pain.

So from these experiences, I was thinking of how to break the ice, so to speak, how to start asking Tan Ka Hong questions without offending him. I asked him if he was interested in making a ngo cho book. Master Tan liked the idea and so I started asking him about the deeper knowledge of ngo cho.

You must understand that Beng Kiam had been established for a very long time and that most instructions were done by the senior students. There exists an unwritten rule that nobody would dare to approach Master Tan for explanations. I was given that special privilege to ask him about the art. To show you how secretive Master Tan was, when I was getting specific about techniques, Master Tan told me, "Alex, there's a Chinese saying that goes: 'You don't teach the art if there's six ears around.'" I didn't quite get his meaning so I asked Master Tan what he meant by that. "Alex," he asked "how many ears do you have?" Two, of course, I casually replied. Then he told me that if there was a third person around, that would mean a total of six ears. After that, I went to see him on Monday, Wednesday, and Friday when there were no classes. I was lucky because after some senior students betrayed him, he stopped teaching officially—that was around 20 years earlier!

I was lucky also to have read his *Ngo Cho Bible*. Master Tan told me that in his fifty years in Beng Kiam, not more than ten people were allowed to read the *Ngo Cho Bible,* which was handed down to him by his father. He treasured it as their family legacy. Master Tan told me that in the late 1950s, his first batch of student also proposed to him about making a ngo cho book. Some of the seniors who are still around approached Tan Ka Hong, and they were jealous and asked him why, this time, he allowed me to publish the book. Master Tan told them that he trusted me, besides I also had the experience in publishing. From making this book, it greatly enhanced my knowledge about ngo cho kun. From my private instruction with Master Tan, I came to realize the wonders within the art. Looking back, I guess I was just lucky. Many have tried to learn under Master Tan, but few had gained the trust of the old master.

I'm glad that you offered my book to be republished with Tuttle Publishing, Mark, because this way the ngo cho book will be distributed on an international level, therefore spreading the art on a much wider scale. I believe it is in this way that I can repay the privilege given to me by my teacher by helping to spread and continue his legacy: the art of ngo cho kun.

The Beng Kiam Athletic Association was quite famous in its day. In addition, the art of ngo cho kun as taught in the club. Who were some of the well-known karate masters that visited Beng Kiam in attempts to better understand their art?

Because of my interest in collecting martial arts books, I had since realized the close connection between ngo cho kun and Okinawan karate, particularly Goju-ryu and Uechi-ryu. During the 1970s, our club participated in the Goodwill Kok-Sut Tournament sponsored in Taiwan.

One Japanese Goju teacher, who had been going to Taiwan to research kung-fu, saw our exhibition. He was interested in the close resemblance of ngo cho to Goju karate. Later, he was able to find a foreign exchange student from Manila who served as his guide to Beng Kiam. He was lucky that the foreign exchange student happened to be the daughter of a wealthy and influential Chinese businessman who was a financial contributor to Beng Kiam. If not, I doubt if my teacher would have accepted them to interview us and take films of our style. At that time, I was only an instructor so I didn't have much chance to participate in the interview. But I was asked by Master Tan to help in performing ngo cho kun and particularly the *sang te pi,* which looks like the karate *sai.*

The name of the Goju karate teacher is Ohtsuka Tadahiko, who, by the way, wrote one of the many forewords to Patrick McCarthy's translation of *Bubishi.* After his visit, Ohtsuka published a book and gave my teacher a copy. After that, one of his classmates, I forgot his name already, also came to Beng Kiam in search for the roots of karate. After this visit, my teacher told me to tell them to stop coming to visit our association.

Later, when I attended an invitation from Singapore Beng Sing Pugilistic Association, I gave an exhibition of ngo cho kun. This caught the attention of a Shurite karate teacher who had been to Singapore to study ngo cho kun. He was impressed by my performance, and on one of his assignments to Manila, he paid me a visit to compare his ngo cho with our ngo cho. He wanted to become my student, but I declined his offer. Instead, I told him that we should just be friends. I would be happy to help him out. His name is Hiroshi Takamiyagi.

J. CHRISTOPH AMBERGER
The Evolution of European Sword Arts

J. Christoph Amberger is a regular contributor to American Fencing, *the magazine of the United States Fencing Association, and to the British fencing magazine* The Sword, *as well as the German* Einst und Jetzt, *Amberger founded* Hammerterz Forum *in 1994. He has been featured in the Discovery Channel's 1997 documentary series* Deadly Duels, *has been a consultant to the Metropolitan Museum of Art in New York for the exhibition "The Academy of the Sword," and is considered one of the foremost experts on historical edged-weapons combat in the United States.*

After becoming a member of the Corps Normannia Berlin and the Corps Hannovera Gôttingen, two of the most respected dueling fraternities in Germany, Amberger fought seven mensuren with the bell-guard and basket-hilt schläger between 1985 and 1987, and acted as a second in twenty-five more. His weapon of choice on the sports fencing strip is the saber.

The history of European sword arts is so vast, and your training in them so interesting, how did you became involved in the study of fencing?

It has been pretty much a lifelong obsession for me, with all kinds of swords—any kind of weapon. My parents let me have all kinds of toy weapons, from pistols to swords, in the hopes that I'd eventually outgrow them. Unfortunately, that was just one more expectation I disappointed.

I'm from a somewhat old-world family: as long as a particular physical activity, such as the martial arts, was concerned, one that is not part of the classic *bürgerlich* background, was automatically prioritized as peripheral to life. Fencing was outside of that background, both from the side of my mother and especially from my father's side. (My grandfather belonged to a dueling fraternity, and family rumor has it that he was actually excommunicated for a saber duel in the 1920s.) My father declined to join any kind of dueling fraternity during his youth—but I felt drawn the other way.

So when, then, did you begin your study of fencing?

I didn't pick up fencing until I went abroad to study at the University of Aberdeen in Scotland. It was kind of a double new beginning for me, as I both started fencing and I met my wife there.

You didn't mention where you were raised.

I was raised in West Berlin, Germany. I grew up in West Berlin and started studying in West Berlin. Let's say I'm a product of metropolitan provincialism. I left in 1984 when I got a stipend to study abroad in Scotland, which screwed up my nicely laid-out path in life.

How so, it sounds like it was really the best thing for you?

Oh, yes, you can say that again. I was originally starting out to become a dentist, like my father and grandfather and uncle and mother and brother. So when I reluctantly returned to Germany in 1985, the only thing I really got involved in my displaced state of existence was fencing. I dropped out of dentistry school and went on to studied English, journalism, and economics.

In early 1985, a school friend had introduced me to one of those dueling fraternities that had been so vilified in my youth. The thing that really attracted me was the dueling part—even though it's a completely different swordfighting system than the sports fencing I had been doing up to then.

Is there a name or school to which sports fencing belongs?

Well, I'd characterize my early training as generic Collegiate fencing. My main weapon then, as with every beginner, was the foil. I had also picked up on epee and saber. Saber is not very popular in Germany, so it was very difficult to get lessons.

What was the name of your fencing master at this time?

Quite honestly, in Scotland, I don't even recall my instructor's full name. He was a short, middle-aged Scot they called Dougie. Although he had a limp, he had really rapid, crisp, clean execution; an amazing fencer. I wish I remembered his name.

When I went back to Berlin I continued with foil and epee and was taught by a female instructor named Martina Gôdicke—a pentathlete with a strong fencing background.

Then in May of 1985, I got my start in the old German broadsword system, the schläger. My fencing master was Jurek Kaczmarek—one of those Polish fencing mercenaries of the pre-glasnost era. He was actually part of the 1970 Polish foil team that took the gold at the Olympics. He was teaching bell-guard Schläger to the Berlin corps.

What it a difficult switch for you?

It was something. I remember my first fencing lesson at the Corps house. In my foresight, I had brought my fencing jacket and fencing glove, which are both very elegant and very white. Then I entered the fencing loft in the attic of this turn-of-the-century building. So I found myself among raw brick and mortar and rafters, with a few bloodstained shirts and bandages hanging near the window, and there's is a bunch of guys standing in dirty, grimy, sweat-stained fencing aprons, which feel like they're made from padded burlap, with heavy helmets, heavy weapons, padded fencing cuffs over the elbows, massive gloves. (The bell-guard schläger gloves are like boxing gloves because the knuckle-guard only gives insufficient protection to the hand.) And picture me standing there like a moron, twiddling that pansy foil glove in my hand.

It was an incredibly difficult process to learn the first cut, the high quart, in the schläger system. It completely eradicates everything you have known about fencing before. You really have to get acquainted with the concept of attacking from continuous cover—and using the defensive angle of your arm and blade to guard and attack by shifting that angle in one continuous, fluid motion while always keeping your head covered. Any sloppiness, and you'll end up with a seven-inch gash across your scalp or face.

Oddly, one of the most difficult parts is to learn how to cut with the edge, not with the half-sharp or the flat of the blade, from a very odd angle. In the schläger system, a cut is executed from the combined rotational forces of shoulder, elbow, and wrist. When the tip of the cutting edge hits your opponent's head, your sword arm has to be straight, with your upper arm lying closely across your face, your fist pointing as high up to the left as you can get it. And to get that straight, and then actually return into guard position without providing an opening, takes about four to six weeks of daily training, just to master this one movement.

You need to get to viscerally understand the rhythm of the bout, because it is a very fast, very rapid exchange of cuts. When I was in good shape I was able to cut and parry about six times in less than two seconds. At that speed, you have to develop an instinctive grasp of what is going on. Your vision is limited. You see the basket of your opponent's sword, but the best clues you can get are from his face and the rhythm of the steel. The only way to hit someone who is cutting and attacking from a covered position is to break his time. It's like the stop cut or the time thrust in sports fencing. Unless you exploit a weakness in your opponent's form, you have to break the time by doubling your cuts, varying your speed, without letting up in your attack.

I had a hard time unlearning instinctive and conditioned reflexes—the reactive fencing that I had been trained in before. In schläger, you have to do your thinking before you actually start fencing, and control every small reflex and involuntary motion. It took me about five months of daily fencing—of two or three hours a day—just to be able to fight my first sharp bout.

Didn't you have your first duel fairly close to this time?

Yes. During my first full semester of membership I did my first three *mensuren*, that's the German term for these student duels. I got a little scratched up, but nothing major. Then I decided to drop out of dentistry school, and my parents suggested I should go to West Germany to do my thing. So that they wouldn't have to watch my decline, I guess. I went to West Germany and joined another fraternity.

Did you find there to be stark differences between the fraternities, fencing styles, and training in West Germany than in Berlin?

Most West German university cities use the basket-hilt schläger, which has quite a different technique. It is not quite as fast as the bell-guard schläger, but uses another subset of movements that takes awhile to master. I went to the University of Gôttingen. I fought my last three *mensuren* in Gôttingen. But since I didn't find an opponent for my fourth, I had to go back to Berlin on short notice.

That one was a complete massacre because I had been training on the slower weapon, which has a much more secure grip. You have a leather sling instead of an iron ring to hold onto the weapon. I think in the first five rounds I got hit three or four times. Actually, out of my seven duels, there were only two where I was taken out for medical reasons; the cuts had been accumulating a little too rapidly. That was the first one in which that happened.

Are you saying that these duels were carried out with actual, sharp steel blades?

Yes, the blades are sharp. But you're pretty well protected: you wear a full body plastron that these days is made up of a long kevlar shirt, with a chain mail shirt on top. Your neck is wrapped up to your jaw line and you wear iron goggles to protect your eyes, with thick leather straps to cover your ears. The targets are the head and the lower part of the face.

Do you have any type of protective mask or covering over your head during these duels?

None, except for the goggles.

So what happens when you get hit in the head with a sword during the duel?

You either end up with a nasty bump if your opponent hits you with the flat part of his blade. Or with a bleeding cut.

Isn't the sword fairly heavy and able to inflict deadly damage?

No. The weapon is indeed heavier than a sports weapon. But the blade configuration, technique, rules, your second, and your protective gear pretty much prevent any serious injury—apart, of course, from cuts. But your skull actually takes a lot more punishment than you think it would. There is only a remote chance of accident. So I did my seven duels and I was a second in probably twenty-five more.

What is the role of the second during a duel?

Your second is your protector and agent—who is right at your side and keeps an eye out for illegal cuts. He also protects you between rounds: sometimes people snap and continue to cut after "halt," which can be very dangerous, particularly if you're naive enough to go out of your guard too early. I heard about a case when one fencer during an intermission grabbed his sword, stormed over and just hit the other guy point blank in the head. Your second is kind of your insurance policy that your opponent is not going to do anything stupid.

Is there a significance to the number seven when one engages in fencing duels?

No. My Gôttingen corps required one duel to become a full member, and a total of three to become inactive. Inactive means you didn't have as many duties any more in the fraternity. My Berlin fraternity would allow full membership to the active corps after two *mensuren*, with a minimum of five to become inactive. I did two more just for the heck of it.

Why, weren't you damaged enough from the other five?

In a way, you know, you start not to care about the cuts and scars. They heal fast. And after your first duel, everything falls into a different perspective. It is a mental change. You wrote in your book *Filipino Martial Culture,* Mark, about the idea of sacred space and time, wherein certain martial artists wear their logo or carry their sticks to signify the crossover between the sacred and profane spaces and mind sets. In a way, I think the dueling scar is a kind of permanent manifestation of this. It's like a tattoo that you carry around with you for your entire life.

When my girlfriend at that time (she's now my wife) saw me after I had been hit on my cheek, she just looked at me and said, "I'm not gonna marry damaged goods." In a way, that is really how I felt, but not in a negative way. The scar was really just on the surface, but in a way my life had been going through so many revolutions: after dropping out of dentistry school, I no longer had any idea of "what I wanted to be when I grew up."

What year was this?

That was in 1987. This dueling thing is something that has prompted me to take a more philosophical view of life. If I look at the life of a man, I think there are certain phases in your life that you go through, and this is kind of the rambunctious young manhood phase that is or hopefully would be concluded at age twenty-four or twenty-five. And most of the corps students that I knew in my time stopped dueling when they hit twenty-four or twenty-five years of age. There is a certain point that separates the sublime and the ridiculous. If you have a twenty-nine or thirty-year-old still living that life-style, something is psychologically wrong with him.

So that is where my interest in fencing came from.

When did you relocate to the United States and what was the rationale behind doing so?

I came over to the States when I was twenty-five, in 1989. My wife and I had been in this long-distance relationship holding pattern for five years and just reached a point where we had to make a decision. I knew this was what I wanted—and came over with a big fencing bag full of stuff. I had all my weapons with me and a second set of clothes and a couple of books. I started to work and finished my master's degree in 1991.

What was your master's degree in?

I went to St. John's College's Graduate Institute in Annapolis, Maryland, one of the Great Book programs. So my master's in liberal arts, heavily focused on philosophy.

Were you able to continue pursuing your fencing interests after emigrating to the United States and during graduate school?

I didn't really have time to do much fencing while I was a grad student. I did fence saber afterwards for about two more years here in Baltimore, at Salle Pallasz under Coach Richard Oles. Actually, he is one of the old-school fencing coaches. I think he starts out with a novice class of about thirty people. By the end of the first three months, he has them down to about two who have the stamina to actually pursue something. This was actually the period when I think I actually learned the most about saber fencing.

What influence has your schläger background had on your life?

I feel something like a living fossil. This is really the modern remnant of a very old broadsword system that was practiced throughout Europe, England, even in America from the dawn of time until the 1840s. It only became more restricted and somewhat more rarefied in Germany after the 1850s and developed into this slightly degenerated form.

It lacks the athletic emphasis. There is a mental, a moral element in it. It is nearly a life philosophy: you consider your actions before you act and accept the consequences no matter what they may be. You take control of yourself and find out what's at the core of your personality. You have to develop an instinctive evaluation of a situation. And then of course the most practical of it all: don't attack unless you know you are covered.

This system sounds very practical from a realistic point of view. How would the techniques and strategies hold up in a sports fencing bout?

Of course, it's a restricted system and you can't really apply it to sports fencing. Your stance is static, you don't work with distance, and rather than avoiding a hit by a quick movement you actually stand and take it rather than break your pattern. The sports fencer would accumulate his five or ten points by flicking at my sleeve or dragging the flat of his saber across my vest.

But some schläger elements are still viable against sports fencers—some of the cuts and combinations no director will ever recognize in a sports fencing bout, but they are very effective. If I had to gamble my physical integrity, in a hypothetical bout with sharp weapons, I think I'd probably be better off using the fighting philosophy behind the broadsword and the schläger rather than the sports techniques.

When did your academic interest in fencing begin?

When my wife and I started to have kids, most of our spare time pretty much went up in smoke. I had to kind of funnel my obsession with swordplay into research that was helped by my different perspective. I could tell that some of the typical mythology in fencing just was wrong. So bit-by-bit I started scraping together all the shreds of literature I could find.

Is your research concentrated on the German schools in particular?

No, my interest now really is on the entire spectrum of Western edged weapons combat. I feel under qualified to say much about Asian systems because I have no training background in them. I had a few kendo lessons and a lowly belt in taekwondo, but I would never go out and say I have a background in Asian martial arts.

Now, the old European martial arts did combine all the wrestling, grappling, throwing, kicking techniques that you find in many Asian martial arts. But because of my focused—hey, let's face it: limited—background, I could never compare the effectiveness of the old European systems and the modern Asian systems because I really don't have the capacity to give a qualified opinion on that. My interest is predominantly in the Western systems.

My strength is putting phenomena into perspective by just the sheer number of sources I have accumulated. I can look at a passage in an eighteenth century manual and I say okay, this is a logical development of this or that predecessor, that one is related to a different system practiced in a different country, this is really just the same guard that this rapier master from the late 1500s calls by a different name. And I can see the continuations both on the artistic level and on the practical, self-defense level through the eighteenth and nineteenth centuries into the present. That's what truly interests me.

Also, part of it is trying to reconstruct some of those old schools. For example, in Germany, documented throughout the late 1400s through the early eighteenth century, there is that German wooden cutting weapon, called the dussack. Except for a couple of university students in Vienna in the 1880s, no one has really tried to recreate that system or tried to find out what all these maneuvers that are depicted in the manual were about.

You see, illustrations in a manual provide only a snapshot out of a combative situation—a pair of fighters, one in a classical upper guard position and the other in the lower guard. If we're lucky we have sequential images, where you have a start, middle, and finish—where the cuts lands. But that is very rare. If you were to make a movie out of one maneuver, you would have maybe a thousand pictures that go to describe the motions from the start through the end of the form. But you only have one frame of that sequence in these manuals.

So what are you going to do with that? How can you reconstruct how the weapon was carried from the guard position into the hit? Was it a flowing motion that maintained cover while cutting, like in the modern schläger, or was it just a direct cut and recovery? What did the weapon really look like? You have all these very various drawings. Some *dussacks* look like a wooden board with just a hole in it. Others are very specific: there's a broadening of the blade base that I have tried to reconstruct by building these wooden weapons. Based on these differences: where exactly is the balance point of the weapon? In the modern fencing weapons, it's very close to the hilt. In the old style cutting weapons, the balance point is farther down in the blade, which influences the entire way of handling the weapon. If there is no weight, you can make nice, close circular parries with one of those weapons. They just handle differently.

But no one has any real blueprints of these weapons. Finding the most reasonable compromise you can derive at by evaluating a number of sources, both images and descriptions, is what I like to do and what my ongoing challenge is.

There are so many old fencing manuals in existence. In a number of those manuals you see a lot of line drawings, wherein a gentleman has a sword and dagger with a geometric diagram in from of his depicting the cut angles and footwork patterns. Who originated this conceptual way of studying fencing?

I think a lot of the footwork and the striking patterns—the "magical circle" or "mysterious circle" as it is sometimes called—are actually used in different contexts. I think one of the images you have in mind is probably the plate of Sutor, a 1612 German manual, which is actually a compilation and plagiarism of a 1570s German manual by Joachim Meyer and another German named Hundt. They used the circle just to trace the path of the blade in the different cuts.

Then you have the Spanish school, which is based on geometric truths. In a way it is a very Socratic system. Socrates, in his dialogues, used geometry to illustrate a truth finding process toward absolute truth. The Spanish schools have a similar approach.

Geometry at the time the Spanish systems were perfected was very heavily drenched in alchemy and hermeneutics. The Spanish school is so complex I would have to say I feel unqualified to have an opinion about it—because I am completely outside of that philosophical circle. If you go through my book, *The Secret History of the Sword,* you will also notice the Spanish school by its glaring absence.

There is one guy who I know in New York, Ramon Martinez, who is still schooled in the remnants of that school and who has written several very good articles on the demystification of the Spanish school. I think that to understand the Spanish school you would have to have the full educational background of an Italian or Spanish nobleman at that time. If you look, for example, at Camillo Agrippa, his fencing manual was only one book that he wrote. He was into alchemy, he was into mystics, architecture, he was into geometry, all these semi-magical forerunners of modern science. What you really have here is nearly a lost world of intellectual background that is reflected in their systems.

The circles you see in Sutor or Meyer are carried through the seventeenth, eighteenth, nineteenth, and even the twentieth centuries. In the schläger system, we still learn the cuts by imagining the head as a circle.

The only practical application of this kind of circle I have ever found is in a 1798 English fencing manual by Roworth. Here, he actually incorporates exactly that same circle in his book, but uses it to illustrate the sequence of cuts you should execute with your cutting sword if attacked at night. You start with a diagonal cut from upper right to lower left, you follow up with a diagonal cut from upper left to lower right, then there is a slight break because it is a very unanatomical movement, you do the same from the downside up again from both directions, and then you follow through by two horizontal cuts, from the right to the left and then from the left to the right. And that is the only real practical application of the circle that I have seen outside of the Spanish schools.

If I recall correctly, at one time the Spanish school was quite feared. However it then became rather caught up in its mental masturbation and lost its focus on the practical, almost dying out as a result. Is there any truth to this?

I think, particularly in fencing, you always deal with at least two layers of practice: there's the geeky, overly cerebral approach that gets lost in its own rules and theories, and the no-nonsense, practical fighting skill that responds to a thrust by catching the point in your flesh while braining your opponent with a pommel strike to the forehead.

The Spanish probably developed the most esoteric system, which is reflected in manuals like Thibault's. But in how far those manuals reflected the everyday use of the sword is another question. Not everyone had the time or the inclination to learn the geomantic and geometric backgrounds of the system. Its practical use was probably restricted to fighting another guy trained within that system.

You also have to look at the distribution of power in Europe at that time. For a period, Spanish rapier schools were popular in Italy and the Netherlands, but that was usually in times that where Spain played a major power role in the overall cultural or political presence in those nations. Then you have the Italian masters that probably took a lot of the practical, hands-on Spanish applications, and incorporated or adapted them. They, in turn, heavily influenced the Germans—be it only by the fact that they managed to get German translations out very quickly after their original publication.

So you have all these cultural cross-fertilizations going on that reflect the geopolitical power distribution. And the more you dig into it, the more complex it becomes.

Is there one school that you would consider the forerunner of the more popular schools in existence today?

Well, I think the pedigree of modern sports fencing is probably as complex as the spread of the different national rapier schools through Renaissance Europe. It was probably influenced on nearly equal terms by the French small sword and the Italian small sword systems. In themselves they were renovations or innovations, or maybe just applications of the underlying rapier systems.

You also need to consider what period or what national brand of athletic fencing you're looking at. In Germany, the Italian influence always predominated. In Britain, and then in America, the French influence dominated. Later on, there are different impulses again from Italy, for example, on the sports saber; from the French on the foil again; and then the Italians on the foil and saber, which then is furthered by the Hungarian adaptation of the Italian innovations in saber.

This is really a continuous give-and-take that has only become standardized, at least in the weaponry, at the beginning of this century. In some of the early Olympics in this century, the Italians walked out on the other competition because the French, who dominated the Federation Escrime International, prohibited them from using the Italian-style epees, which were two inches longer than the French style.

Even the current brand of modern sports fencing is in constant flux. The Russians are very much different from the Italians and Hungarians and French. Then there's this one man in Germany, a former hairdresser by the name of Emil Beck, who single-handedly revolutionized the German approach to fencing after the war. Then we have a Hungarian, Kevey, after WWII, who emigrated to Poland and completely turned around the Polish style of saber fencing, which then is picked up by the Russians who in turn develop it further.

Today, China has become more visible in international competition. At first, they tried to copy the Italians and the French and the Russians. Now they are in the process of actually developing something on their own. It is new way to arrive at the same goal, which is scoring first, that may have been imported from the scientific insights they have derived over the last couple of years from sports that may even be derived from Chinese martial arts. I don't know where it is coming from because it is still very hard to get into the Chinese method of training. Obviously most of the written documentation is in Chinese. And hey, who reads Chinese....

You state that these individuals "revolutionized" the art. How can one person go about changing the face of a system to such a profound degree?

Look at fencing as a means of achieving a target. The systematic approach depends on what the target is. Did you want to kill your opponent? Did you want to kill him quickly? Did you want to kill him with style? Did you just want to have gentlemanly amusement? Did you want to score a touch? Did you want to score a touch in style?

Style was still a very important criterion like in the 1860s. There's all these beautiful calisthenics, the old form that you have your arm gracefully arched over your head and you throw it back while you lunge to get that extra stability and forward velocity.

Today, modern fencing is all about scoring a touch before your opponent does. Let me be more specific. It is about setting off the scoring apparatus first. Coaches like the Hungarian Kevey I mentioned looked at the intended result, and focused on what would get them there fast.

I am simplifying this, of course, but in athletic fencing competition, the revolutionary approach was to radically simplify. Cut the frills and take the stuff that the old masters were appalled by. Like the *fleche*, letting yourself fall forward with optimal linear energy projection and hit the opponent in the head with the saber (which, now again, is outlawed in saber after fifty years.) Kevey found it worked, looked at it in terms of "How do I do it best? Where do I look to get the best technique? Do I look at fellow fencers or do I look at other sports."

He looked at games like team handball, with its "dive throw." He looked at what the process of motion was and how to not only achieve the optimal transfer of energy but how to condition his fencers to do so without having to think about it. That's where the whole school of proprio-receptive conditioning and the modern sport sciences come in. These were only applied after the Second World War. This is when sports fencing became this athletic, high-powered activity that it is today.

If you look at high-level fencing tournaments with a classic's eye, all the pictures that make it into the fencing magazines worldwide show appalling form. The old masters would faint seeing people doing power jumps, dodging, being in the air with both feet off the ground.

Let's talk about a fencer like Aldo Nadi, for example, who has accomplished so much in the field.

I think Nadi is probably the most arrogant son-of-a-bitch I've ever read—but unfortunately there isn't a way of arguing with him.

I agree. I have read his book, *On Fencing*, and his autobiography, *The Living Sword*, and his arrogance comes across quite well.

You know, you have to admire him. I admire him because he is one of the few fencers who could actually back it up. At his level of innately grasping the essence of fencing, he is so far beyond not only the general grasp of the sport, but so far beyond the advanced and the coaching level that you find today, that very few people can ever reach that. I think he is probably one of, if not the most, perfect fencers of this century, and probably would have cut a good figure against most of the other masters in history.

Nadi did this one epee duel that I have picked apart, and he himself said that the duel is not necessarily a good gauge of a fencer's ability. But I think no matter what weapon he would have picked up, his grasp of the fundamentals of using a sword was such that it wouldn't have mattered what configuration it would have been.

Do you think his expertise was a result of superior genetic make-up or of a superior training regimen?

He comes from this fencing dynasty; his father, his brother were the upper crust of master fencers. And it is probably both nature and nurture in that regard. Let's face it, if you start fencing at four years old and have one of the best fencing masters in Italy as your father, then your direction is pretty much set.

Nadi was also an actor, was he not?

Well, he advised on a couple of movies. I think he consulted on some of fencing choreography in a bunch of them.

In his biography, Nadi really picked apart swashbucklers like Errol Flynn and movies like _Scaramouche_. There was one film I saw, however, that I felt had very realistic fencing in it. It was called _The Duelists_, and starred Harvey Keitel. What is your opinion of this film?

The choreography for that was done by William Hobbs, who is one of the best. If you read Hobbs' books and look at his choreography, you know where he takes it from. It is very hard to judge the stage and movie fencers or choreographers' work because the director really has the last word on it. William Hobbs, in my opinion, is one of the few who manages to get that compromise of authenticity and dramatic impact. There are very few who can do that.

In _The Duelists_ they have many dueling scenes wherein one of the participants get hurt, but not killed, and the fight is held for another day. Was this type of "honor fencing," wherein the combatants would only fight if both were at one hundred percent, standard for the time?

The duel is nearly like an unofficial court procedure, with the blades doing the talking. The active fighters actually have absolutely no say in the duel. They delegate their decision power to their seconds. And their seconds have to take the advice of the doctors into consideration to arrive at a mutual decision. So the duelist himself has no choice but to acquiesce to what his second is saying. He can try to influence his second, but particularly if an opponent is down, the dueling regulations, which are the framework and soul of the duel, really kick in...to say if one man is injured to a degree that the doctor says he can no longer fight, the duel is to be declared finished.

Sometimes, there is the option that the duel could be suspended and continued once both fighters were up for it again, but that would have to be arranged beforehand. At that point, the opposing party can say they relinquish their right to insist on a continuation. That still survives in the schläger *mensur*.

For the past couple of years, you have been publishing your own newsletter, *Hammerterz Forum*. What prompted you to begin this publishing venue?

It started after I got my third or fourth rejection of one of the articles I had written—a close analysis of Patton's 1913 saber system. But with fencing history, you pretty much sit between all chairs. The fencing magazines really care more about the ranking schedules. They will only occasionally run an historical article. The arms and armor people don't really care at all about fencing. They want to know about the weapons, how much they are worth, and the descriptive aspects of collecting. Military history is completely oblivious to sword fighting history. So, for me there was absolutely no medium to publish my hard-fought-for insights.

Since I am in the publishing business, I decided hey if what I learned had any practical value, and so I started self-publishing it. I started with eleven subscribers in 1994 and I am now at around two hundred. The point is to provide a medium for fencers who are interested in the history to (1) read about it, (2) argue about it, and (3) to further publish about it in this medium.

What I have noticed in the past couple of years is that the number of these researchers and the interest in this is growing. We are reaching a new generation. None of the leading researchers in the fencing field is really older than thirty-five. And there's a lot of different backgrounds and different levels of expertise, but there is the same obsession there.

A lot of them are also just interested in getting it as accurately as possible using the old manuals. Not only academically, as I have confined myself out of necessity, but also practically. What we have found is that a lot of the descriptions, once they are interpreted correctly and translated into movements and activities and sequences, are actually very effective fighting systems that have been dormant for two hundred to five hundred years.

So it's a challenge to get everything right. And of course even in that small group of researchers, there are amazing struggles and hostilities and identification with schools—who really share the same interest. But the one guy rips the other for using epee blades in his rapier recreation. The other guy says well you can't use blunt schläger blades because they are cutting weapons. The other guy says sticks are fine. Some do foil and others don't even touch one out of principle. So you have these very emotional and very personal grudges and hostilities in that small group. Now, everyone has accumulated a small following of sorts. And so you have a following running into each other and hitting each other about the head.

So how do you feel about all of this bickering and confrontation?

I usually believe there is a lot to be said for confrontation. Some of the best progress is derived from confrontation. But it gets annoying as hell after a while.

I think the best thing you could use this rivalry for would be to have these guys put their opinions to the test is a kind of *kumite* of Western swordplay. Given the lack of sponsors, I guess this won't happen anytime soon.

I heard that you were actually kicked off one of the on-line history recreation groups because they disagreed with you. What happened?

Well, I have a big mouth. I can be very insulting, particularly to those flaccid egos who limp around as sysops.

Let's talk for a bit about your book, *The Secret History of the Sword*. It is truly an impressive piece of work. An opus magnum, actually.

My book is great. Buy my book. Please. *The Secret History of the Sword* pretty much reflects the status I have arrived at with my research over the last seven years. It's the quintessence of my approach, very detailed detective work piecing together ancient edged weapons fighting systems from the function and morphology of the weapons, wound descriptions and pathology, as well as a close interpretation of whatever shreds of sources have survived. It's amazing what stuff you find in the oddest places.

But I always attempt to balance the egghead academics with the entertaining, by providing the original sources, the stories, the adrenaline.

So, in a way it reflects the contents of my brain…kind of scattered and scatterbrained and frequently going off into tangents that I hope I have confined to the footnotes.

For me, the world and fencing history is not the sum but the product of a thousand different factors from a lot of different aspects of life. So many things interlink—cultural phenomena, intellectual and philosophical currents, raw power politics. I'm trying to reflect this in the structure and the general approach of this book.

Do you see an intimate connection between the philosophy of fencing and life?

Yes, actually. There is a German writer, who also happens to be a fraternity brother of mine, who died in 1943, Hanns Heinz Ewers. He subtitled one of his books *A Novel in Shreds and Colors.* I think that's pretty damn close to reality: shreds and colors. Who was this *Biblical* figure? Wasn't it Joseph who was given this coat of many colors by his father? In a way that is my image of life and history. It is a texture of elements that you don't really know where they came from, you can't even guess where they came from, but overall they provide a nearly psychedelic reflection of what life can be all about. Hey, sounds like a new meaning for Fabric of our Lives…maybe the U.S. Cotton Association should buy a pallet of the *Secret History.*

PART TWO

ON INDIVIDUAL SYSTEMS AND STYLES

CHEONG CHENG LEONG
Chuka Shaolin:
Art of the Phoenix-Eye Fist

Cheong Cheng Leong is the current grandmaster of Chuka Shaolin, more commonly known today as phoenix-eye fist kung-fu. He has co-written two books on the art, Phoenix-Eye Fist: A Fighting Arts of South China *(with the late Donn F. Draeger) and* The Secrets of Chuka Shaolin *(with Mark V. Wiley) and has appeared in multiple martial arts magazines around the world. Cheong resides in Pulau Pinang, Malaysia, where he makes his living as a tourist gift shop owner, and where he teaches Chuka Shaolin and works as a natural healer.*

Mr. Leong, at what age, and under whom, did you begin your study of Chuka Shaolin?

I learned from Master Lee Siong Pheow, in 1951. I was eleven years old. Master Lee was famous in Air Itam, a section of Pulau Pinang, Malaysia. Someone told me he had a very special type of fist that is very strong and can kill somebody. So when I was a boy I went to him with a young friend of mine. Actually, during that time he only taught Cantonese students of Hakka status, no Hokkien.

I started learning because I liked to fight. There were a lot of boys in our group and we fought near the Air Itam River. Nice water, fish, and fighting. After training started I stopped fighting. No more. During the next few months from that day, I had a fight with my co-students again. So from that time onwards, the master said if we fight he will kick us out. The art changed my character. I have not fought since.

Why, then, if you fought frequently, did Master Lee come to accept you and your friend as students?

Master Lee was interested in us because we were so young. He asked us if we were interested in the art for fighting. I said "No, no fighting." Then he asked why I come to him to learn kung-fu? I stayed quiet. He then said, "No fighting, really?" And I said, "Yes, yes, no fighting." But I really wanted to fight. "Good, good," he said, "no fighting so I accept you."

Was there a formal initiation ceremony you had to go through to officially be accepted as his disciple?

No. The training fee was five ringets per month. It was expensive, because if you joined one of the other martial arts associations in Penang, like the Chin Wu, you only had to pay something like one or two ringets. Some people who could afford it paid Master Lee fifty ringets. So he taught them special techniques—without us, closed door. But I don't think what they learned was something special.

What was your training like under Master Lee?

The classes were held walking distance from here, in his back-yard. He taught all week, every day—one session in the morning, afternoon, and nighttime. Sometimes I did not practice a night. In the morning or afternoon I would go because in the nighttime I would help him teach. I trained for two or three years and became very good.

When you go to class you cannot just sit and talk. At least you have to do your stance, stand on your horse. Then if you want to talk, you can talk. The Chinese style of teaching is that class is two hours but everyone is doing their own thing. When the master is free, he'll come over and say "Okay you do this form and you do that form."

I went six or seven days a week for three years. Each class was two hours long. I used to go there and Sifu would say "Come on, do this form for the students." Then after three or four years he told me I didn't have to pay the training fee anymore. So I helped him with class.

How old was Master Lee when you started training with him?

I think he was sixty plus. He died in 1961, when he was seventy-seven years old.

How did you come to inherit the head responsibilities of the Chuka Shaolin system?

Yes, yes. So after he passed away we had a discussion. All the students said that I should be the head since the master passed away. I learned the most things, you know. Some of the senior students, they had come to me for some time already to learn more techniques. So I used to go there to teach them so many times a day.

I have been training now for forty-six years, since I was eleven. He passed away in 1961, so in 1964 I started teaching.

Why the three year wait?

I don't think of teaching, you see. But people say I should teach something of this art before it gets lost. This kung-fu is very special, you know. You can't find it in other places. Slowly, slowly, bit-by-bit you know, I try to pick up some forms from his other disciples. Some of them, they learned only one form and then they go their own way. I would tell them okay, okay, teach me what you know. I learned their forms, too. I learned two or three forms from the senior students.

You began teaching in 1964. Was that in your current location on the steps leading to the Guanyin statue here in Penang?

Yes, yes, this is the place. I opened my tourist gift shop in the 1970s. Before, I used to have the local product shop. In my shop now I sell clothing, souvenirs, toys.

When a student first comes to you and wants to learn kung-fu, what is the first thing they are taught?

Horse riding stance, all of the foot movements, how to move forward and then the dodging stance, and then after three of these they start on hand movements. For hand movements, they are taught how to hold their phoenix-eye fist and then how to punch with it. Once they learn how to punch they put it together with the footwork. So, step forward one step and do one punch. Then combinations. After they have learned this they begin to learn the first form.

How long do the students spend on each form before they move on to another form?

Beginners take about one month to finish a form. This includes the basic movements. But they have to come three times a week to class and each class is two hours. Then they learn another two forms and then start the two-man sets. There are seventeen solo empty-hand forms in our system.

What is the purpose of forms training in Chuka Shaolin?

Forms are good for stamina and flexibility. Also for learning and developing combinations of movements.

Does your style advocate the practice of free-sparring?

No. In sparring we cannot use the phoenix-eye fist because it is too dangerous. But it is our main weapon; so how can we spar? So you cannot show or perform your real talent by holding back in this way. Chinese kung-fu doesn't do free sparring because we don't have certain targets, we hit everywhere. You can't see real kung-fu in free-sparring.

Is that why you have two-man sets, to practice the fighting applications from the solo fist forms?

Yes, you learn how to do the movements and how to counter them. Two-man forms also train your courage so you won't be afraid when you face an opponent. They also train timing and distance. Having proper distance is very important.

The best is for the students to do the two-man sets all the time with the same person. When you change partners the form changes sometimes as your speed and distance will be different.

But if you are attacked on the street, you will not be in cooperation with your opponent. So isn't it best to learn how to apply the art against a variety of opponents and body types?

Yes, but that is fighting. Fighting is a different story. The two-man forms are for training. So, for demonstration it is nice to have practiced with the same partner. Of course, for fighting, we train applications with different partners all of the time.

Within your empty-hand art, do you also have *chin na* or joint locking techniques?

Yes, yes. It is for advanced students. We also have leg sweeping, but not ground fighting.

Do you have empty-hand defenses against weapons, such as the knife, in the event that someone should attack you with such a weapon?

Our techniques are mainly hand-to-hand and weapon-to-weapon. But it's also practical. I tell my students that if someone comes with a weapon, they better run or find a weapon to counter—don't go in empty-handed, don't follow the movies. It's quite nice if you do empty-handed against knife for demonstrations, but not for real life.

How long does one have to train the empty-hands until they can learn the weapons of Chuka Shaolin?

They must train for at least one year. They then begin their weapons training with the *koon* or staff. It takes one month to complete the first *koon* form, called six-and-a-half point staff or plum blossom pole. The practitioner's staff is set to the individual height of the practitioner, above the head. Also, we hold the *koon* with both hands at one end only. Sometimes we use the butt end for striking.

After the first staff form I teach them a pre-arranged two-man set with a partner. Again, as with empty-hand pre-arranged sets, it is best to maintain the same partner in an effort to master the form and its movements.

The second *koon* form I do not teach. It is my personal form. Usually we have this private form. Maybe when I become too old I will teach it. I have one staff form I don't teach them, and a spear form, and three empty-hand forms I keep for myself.

After that, do they have a choice of which weapon they can learn next?

Yes, but it takes a long time, at least two or three years, before they can learn the iron ruler *(sai)* or twin knife. We teach five weapons. First the koon, then the long spear, then iron ruler, twin knives, and hoe. All the weapons have four basic movements and a pattern. The staff and spear have two forms each and the staff also has a two-man set. Then we have so many empty-hand forms again, two-man forms, and we have to teach them how to kick—not to mention all the applications.

How long must a student spend on a weapon until they are permitted to move on to another?

Each student must practice a weapon for two or three months before moving on to another. But usually they don't master the weapon. You teach them and then ask them to do it later and it looks very bad. So, you can't teach them a lot of forms. If a student is very hard working, you can teach him another form in two or three months.

Do you then learn applications of the weapons after the forms are mastered?

Yes, and there is one two-man form for the *koon*. Before we had a double knife two-man set against the empty-hands. I discarded it because people would laugh at us during demonstrations. It is impractical.

Why does your system have these five weapons and not other classical kung-fu weapons such as the three-section staff, chain-whip, kwan dao, and so on?

You see, different styles use different weapons. We are of the southern Chinese styles so we are mostly farmers and use the hoe and iron ruler. We also had the nine-section steel whip, but it is hard to train and so we do it no more. I only learned a little bit of it before.

How do you teach the weapons to students?

We don't train like the Japanese do. We don't train in large groups, only one-on-one. The master will tell a student in private what a movement is for, and then he won't show him again—the student will have to do it himself. The master teaches you the form and then the two-man set and then you learn the application that way.

Is there a ranking structure in the Chuka Shaolin style?

No, no rank—just student, teacher, master.

Are there a set of fighting principles your art adheres to when applying its techniques?

First you must decide if you are going to fight. If you want to fight, you have to learn how to move fast. If you decide to fight, then you must fight. You mustn't think "Oh, this guy is bigger or stronger and I don't know if I can beat him." No, if you are going to fight, go in as fast as you can. Our style is short range, you know, so once a punch in thrown you have to go in immediately. Once we go in we can get our opponent. Another thing is that it's not so risky to go in if he doesn't have the kicks. For other styles, you move in and their punch becomes less powerful. If you stay out, their techniques are powerful. But if you go in, they're not so powerful. Our style is that we hit close targets so we have to move in as fast as we can.

When somebody comes in on us we step sideways to their blind side. We always go for the temple. It is the first target we strike for. The best targets are the sternum, the ribs, throat, eyes, temple. We use the phoenix-eye fist to strike with. We also have open hand strikes, like the chop and finger thrust.

Is there a set of supplemental training that practitioners of your style engage in?

We have *chi* and power training. We use our *tan tien*. We focus on our *tan tien* while standing, with feet a shoulder's width apart, knees slightly bent. We use our mind to visualize the *tan tien* moving from our navel to our hands. We then move the *chi* by scooping our hands up, like scooping rice, and then pushing down, like washing the face. The *chi* feels like water.

We train the *chi* but not during class. Students are supposed to do it everyday in the morning in their house. It takes three years to properly develop the *chi*. But it is an exercise that gives them the extra power.

We also have the phoenix-eye fist post for hitting. It is used to develop accuracy, conditioning. We also use a sandbag.

We also have many kinds of two-man arm-conditioning exercise, which we call wrist banging. It develops strong forearm bones used for blocking hard strikes. We use the forearms to block with, so it injures our opponents upon impact. Also, the blocks are not force-on-force, but twisting. We don't feel the pain from the impact, but our opponents do.

Chuka Shaolin also encompasses a healing art. In fact, you used your healing skills on the late Donn F. Draeger and on my old back injury. Can you tell us a bit about this dimension of Chuka Shaolin?

Yes, I have a practice for that. Healing is done by my senior, Master Tan Hun Poey. Only for close friends and my students do I do it. Otherwise I ask them to go and see Dr. Tan. This is the work of him. I am doing the teaching and he is doing the healing.

But now you can't get one hundred percent of the herbs. So we have to get something else from the Chinese medical shop. Because from the hill they are very hard to get.

When did you begin learning this aspect from Master Lee?

When I was quite advanced in kung-fu already—eighteen years old. Sifu asked me to help him pick the herbs on the hill. After gathering them, we would cut and dry them for him. After the herbs dried we would take them to the Chinese medical shop and they would grind them for us.

Did Master Lee allow you to assist him with healing patients, like an apprentice?

When the patients come, I just watched Master Lee. He would tell me what is this and what is that and what to do. Then, after a while, he eventually let me work on the patients.

Is there a specific name to this healing tradition that you do?

No.

What types of illnesses or problems can be cured with this healing art?

Our healing is good for old injuries, like an old back problem. Straightening your legs and arms from hurting, anybody can do it. But with old injuries, suddenly you feel pain. That is from when you were young and you didn't take care of it at the time. Then when you get old your *chi* is blocked in your muscles so you feel the pain more. Our treatment is good for that.

It is not used to cure diseases, then?

No. But if they have pain in the whole body it is affective. If you have the flu, no.

What are your specific healing techniques or methods?

We use banging and massage. Mostly we use banging with the back of our hand and fingers to the injured location. If it is a new injury, a massage will do. But if it is an old injury, you have to bang to get through the muscle and injury, which is quite deep.

So, if somebody has an injury on their forearm, you would just bang it?

If it is an old injury, yes. But it depends on which part of the arm is injured. If there is injury we feel a lot of heat when we are banging the area. When you feel the release of heat you stop already. You can't hit very hard so you project your *chi* into the injured spot. After hitting, if there appears a lump, the *chi* will then flow. The blockage is open.

How many treatments does it take to heal an old injury?

It depends on the seriousness of the injury. Sometimes you need only one treatment. One whipping treatment is better than ten massages.

So how do you know if you have slapped enough to have actually healed the injury?

We can see the wound come up and the veins. That means the blood and *chi* are flowing properly again.

Do you apply the herbs before or after the treatment?

Before and during the slapping we apply the wine herbs. After the slapping we put the ground herb paste. You apply the herb paste to the entire wound and then cover it with a cloth for one night. The paste hardens and can easily be removed the following day. The medicine has seeped in by that point.

Do you see a connection between the martial arts and healing arts?

If you know Chinese kung-fu, you should know something about this healing. The good kung-fu is also about healing and *chi*. Otherwise you practice how many kung-fu but when you get old you have nothing. So, if you learn this, at least you can help people, you can heal people. And then, if you have *chi*, when you get old you can feel better. Without *chi* you have nothing. Some people study Chuka Shaolin without *chi* and if they stop for three or four years, they have no more.

Is there a philosophical rationale behind this?

Yes. If you now how to hit people with a punch, you should know how to treat people. We have a book with what vulnerable points on the body to strike at what time of the day, but we don't use that anymore. To do that, you must also be able to heal the person you strike. We don't like to kill. In Chinese kung-fu chi and healing are very important. Most of the kung-fu masters are also Chinese doctors.

Are you teaching this healing art to any of your students today?

If you want to learn the art it should be from Master Tan. He is taking care of teaching that part of the art and I am teaching the kung-fu part.

So won't the students today, if they don't wish to learn the healing art, end up developing incomplete kung-fu?

Yes, but most of the students who want to learn kung-fu come to me after one year and already want me to teach them how to heal people. But my brother-in-law, Ong Tatt Lin, I tell him he should learn the healing art. I tell him it is very useful, but after more than twenty years of training he is still not interested. He is really into his forms. He can do them every night, but he doesn't want to learn healing. He also doesn't like to teach. He just likes the exercise.

In the 1970s you wrote a book on Chuka Shaolin with the late Donn Draeger. How did that project come about?

Yes, yes. Draeger Sensei came to me in 1972 after watching our demonstration. You see, in Penang every year during this festival season all our kung-fu clubs were invited to demonstrate there. So each demonstration is one hour. Draeger Sensei came and asked a man "Oh, these are quite special movements, you know. Do you know the master? Will you ask him if he would like to do a book with me?" So he asked me about a book and I told him I would first have to ask my senior and my master's wife, because our system is very special and they don't like it in publication. So I asked my master's wife and she said I could do it as long as there is nothing secret in it. So two or three years later we started on the book.

Aside from your classes and writing the book, what other types of things have you done to promote the art?

I have taught the art in Penang and Venezuela. I give demonstrations at the festivals, but not every year because the organizer of the festival doesn't want every year to be the same as the last. We have stopped for many years already, only last year (1997) I did another demonstration. But last year was a demonstration for all the chief instructors, the older ones. The older the better.

Wasn't the demonstration held in part as the beginning of a new government-sponsored martial arts organization in Malaysia?

Yes, yes, but it's Penang only. It is the Malam Seni Silat Malaysia Sempena Pesta Pulau Pinang (Penang Government Kung-fu Society). All the styles from Penang demonstrated, and one or two from Johor. A lot of them, four or five, are jow-ga style.

Is there anyone else teaching Chuka Shaolin in the world?

Here in Malaysia, we have three Chuka Shaolin groups. They all have different patterns and do the art in different ways; three Chuka with three different lineages. The reason for the different styles is because Chuka stands for both the Chinese surname Chu, and also for South China. Our art is from the Chu sisters.

In recent years you have gone through heart surgery. How has this affected your kung-fu?

Yes, twice they replaced three arteries. Now I seldom practice kung-fu. I mainly practice chi kung.

Where do you see Chuka Shaolin heading in the future?

I don't know. Of course I wish the style will spread and grow bigger. But I don't think this will happen because even the people here who learn are lazy. Because of work problems, and if they are a school student they have too much homework and video games to play.

Nobody cares about kung-fu anymore.

HAWKINS CHEUNG
Fighting Theories and Principles
of Wing Chun Kuen

Hawkins Cheung is one of the world's leading authorities on wing chun kuen, an "in-door" disciple of the late famed master of the art, Yip Man, and the former best friend of the late Bruce Lee. Cheung has written and appeared in dozens of magazine articles around the world and is prominently featured in the book Complete Wing Chun *as one of the leading authorities on the Yip Man style of wing chun kuen.*

Hawkins, it's a known fact that you and Bruce Lee were good friends and training partners in wing chun under the late Yip Man. Can you tell us a little about your relationship with Bruce and Yip?

There was no formal training under Yip Man, really. Bruce and I were classmates in school from the age of fourteen. We both had drivers who would take us places together. During our time under Yip Man, Bruce and I were young and respected our seniors in wing chun.

Didn't you and Bruce train alone on the rooftops in Hong Kong to try and develop your skills to a higher degree?

That's right. After school we trained. We went to a particular rooftop. He used to do the gymnastics, weights, or whatever. Bruce had to pump up his body, you know. When we were training, Bruce's personality was very emotional. He emphasized attacking, since he was very emotional. He used his emotions to speed up his attacks. He emphasized closing-the-gap and was faster than me— pretty athletic type of movement. Yeah, he was fast. But as we were partners, it made me have to practice more to defend against him. Once I could handle one attack, he would have to make up a new method of attack. From this, I could see his character.

Despite the fact that the two of you were close friends, there seems to have been some rivalry when it came to who was more skilled in wing chun.

Right. One day he would go to Yip Man and ask how to defend against a technique I hit him with. And then the next day I would go to Yip Man and ask the defense to what he just taught Bruce. When Yip Man taught us, we were taught privately at different times. When Bruce went, I didn't go. When I went, Bruce didn't go.

You know Yip Man was just like a coach for us. He would teach me how to counter Bruce's technique and how to counterattack. The next day he would teach Bruce how to get me! We didn't care about forms or that sort of stuff at that time; we only based our training on applications. We didn't care about the forms; we just wanted it to work in the street. So when we trained, Bruce was always at high speed, so Yip Man taught me how to be defensive. Eventually, it benefitted me because Bruce's high speed developed my ability to handle high-speed attacks. It would be like today Bruce beat me, but I learned how to solve the problem. When I solved the problem, I give Bruce back another problem. That then forced Bruce to come up with a solution. We were always like that: giving each other problems and solving them.

But Yip Man did have a formal class that he taught. Didn't you and Bruce also attend this?

Everybody starts training and wants to become better. So okay, when we went to Yip Man, he is really funny—he wants to attract the students to stay with him. He won't teach students how to get him; he would only teach them how to get the other guys or me. We mostly learned separately. The form, he didn't care about correcting it. He would just tell us, "You have a problem? Solve it this way or that way."

Without the forms, how did you learn the techniques? Don't you have to first develop and understand the techniques through forms practice before you can use them to fight with?

No, we didn't care! Look, we just wanted to learn to fight. We just asked Yip Man to teach us the way to use the techniques right away. That way, we knew how to fight. That is how we developed timing. We changed, we developed. We learned the form from the application. So that means we survived on the streets.

Didn't you and Bruce go your separate ways about this time?

We parted. I went to Australia. I was there for four years for college. I had a big fight with a Thai boxer. Later another fight, where it was me against six. Then immigration investigated me. I was okay, because I was a small guy in Australia, and it seemed unusual that I had fought against six people. At that time I wore glasses, so I guess people liked to pick on me.

After college, Bruce Lee wanted to help me out of my problems. So, he asked me to come to the United States in 1961. I knew his character. I have a strong personality, too. I said, "Look Bruce, if you take care of me that means I can't do anything. No, you are my compadre and I'm not going to take anything from you." He intended to invite me over to the USA to take care of me. That was his character. But my character, on the other side of the world, was like, no, if I come, I will do it myself. So I went back to Hong Kong first.

Did you open a wing chun school upon your return to Hong Kong?

No, I didn't want to teach. And at that time, you know, a lot of people they learned techniques of wing chun. Wing chun is actually never finished. Many finish the three forms and the dummy set, okay, and they go and open a school. Actually, some of these instructors I didn't even know. When I left Hong Kong for college, they learned from Yip Man, and when I came back, they were already teachers! Once you're finished you can teach whatever you can dream up. But, if you don't actually train how to use it, or apply it, it's just like when you get your license from the DMV, you only feel comfortable driving in a twenty-five miles-per-hour zone. If someone is a beginning driver, you can train some beginning drivers, but you can't instruct others in becoming competitive racing drivers.

How did Yip Man teach?

Yip Man was, like, if you open a school he doesn't care. He would just stop teaching you, that's all. Now you are his competitor. He can't stop you from opening a gym. All martial artists are the same. If you have someone you want to teach and you teach them and they open a school, that's okay. You just stop teaching them and go teach someone else. That means, who got it better?

Bruce and I got it better.

Is that because you went to Yip Man with the correct questions of how to defeat this or that technique, and you didn't open a gym in Hong Kong and compete with him?

Yeah, yeah. Okay, when I went back to Hong Kong I didn't like to teach martial arts. Martial arts are kind of a hobby for me. I went to see Yip Man all the time. But when I see him I usually don't ask him to teach me. You see, this is the trick! I always give him money first. I put money in his pocket. I tell him here's some tea money, all right. Then eventually, I see him again and give him some money, but I act like I don't want anything from him. My method was to trick him: he owes me something. Get it? When I need help, he definitely will give me help. When he teaches me, it will be the real thing because I didn't ask for anything. The trick is, he owes me a favor.

How do you know he actually gave you the real art? Didn't you learn the system many times?

Before I went to Australia I learned, and when I returned to Hong Kong I relearned. At that time I found out a lot of things were left out the first time. When I first learned, I was too emotional—I just wanted to fight. I was young, I couldn't sit still. So the second time coming back, I'm more mature. I saw the world, I had a lot of fights, so that time I really concentrated on why the form is the way it is. Why it looks like that, why it works like that.

Yip Man, you know, he thinks I'm not teaching, I'm not his competitor, right? And then my size is small. So mostly, when he teaches he is always on my side. Yip Man was about my size. There was a lot of complaining by the other students. A lot of people complained that Yip Man never taught and never stuck hands with them. Yeah, it's true, in the group class he never did sticking hands.

If Yip Man wouldn't touch hands and play *chi sao* with his students, how did they learn and develop the skill?

With a big sized guy, Yip Man would just show them or give them examples. He never took pressure during *chi sao* practice, he just told a student to *chi sao* with you. Looking back, I can see that a sixty-year-old, small old man teaching doesn't like to stick or hold up against an eighteen-year-old's hands. When you're teaching, you cannot use your advantages and skills. Yip Man always brought one or two extra students when teaching privately. This was because teachers in the old days never allowed the student to know their standard or condition. *Chi Sao* is a fair game of questions and answers; Yip Man wouldn't show how to solve the problems. When it came to learning how to relax, how to soften the hands, you never saw the old guy do it. Now that means that a young guy had a hard time learning from the old man, right? So, you know, Yip Man wouldn't bother with that. If you don't teach and your student doesn't touch your hands, your student will either get something from your concepts or merely mimic your body. How you do this or that, would be like most karate training. But in reality, with wing chun you need to feel. If you don't touch hands with your *sifu*, you don't feel. You don't know your opponent's center of gravity. You don't know how to react, avoid jams, free yourself up, or how to respond. That's the key point.

So how is your wing chun different than that of the other masters?

You see, I never changed the tools or the forms. I upgraded the power, speed, and combinations in *chi sao* and distance fighting. There is no difference. The way I practice, I differ only with power and control. I just found more ways to use the same tools. Let's use *bong sao* as an example.

In practice, *bong sao* is passive, but I have many variations. I can put more emphasis on hand strong and body weak. Sometimes, I like to have the hand soft and the body soft, like water. Other times, I can also have it so my hands are soft and my body strong so that I can hold pressure and direct my opponent. If the hand and body are both strong, one cannot feel. Nowadays, many wing chun teachers have the mechanical forms, drills, and exercises, yet ignore the functional aspect. Mechanical: that's where all the politics always come from. They say, "Oh, my hand is too high, my hand is too low!" Everybody talks about the way Yip Man looked with his wing chun. But at the high levels, this is not correct. I have no wing chun. The art becomes second nature.

When I came back to Hong Kong from Australia and relearned wing chun, I found out a lot of things—more details. One of the more important things was to concentrate on not how to fight but how to adjust myself, how to know myself. When you know yourself, you compare with your opponent and learn how to reach your opponent. When you reach your opponent you're already one step ahead and know how to adjust yourself. It's the feeling. That feeling you have to develop; you can't learn it.

Would you care to elaborate on this idea for us?

You have to adjust yourself to fit in with your opponent. You have to know how to get in. You see, this kind of thing you can't teach in a style. You have to learn a system to trick or to trap or to make way. Make your opponent pay attention to you, and lead your opponent to your trap. Not just trap your opponent's hands, but to trap his mind and his personal activity. What you like the most or what you don't like the most, everything comes from your head; touch the guy and you will know.

Sticking hands or *chi sao* is an insider's game, whereas distance fighting is a universal game. If your *chi sao* is good, it doesn't mean your distance fighting is good. In distance fighting, you have to develop your speed and timing, eyesight for reading an opponent's intentions, power for the delivery of your tools, and your confidence. Your experience is more important here, not politics or who you learned from. Can you do the job? Can you solve my attack? Once you walk out of the school, you are in the real world, not the wing chun world, and you'd better be prepared. In Hong Kong, people would punch to the face with a snap. In the USA, everyone here is taller, one has to punch the body, throat, chest. You have to drop your elbows here to prevent against kickers. A small guy like me, once I'm in, I don't like to move back. Many people use one shot, then follow up. What I do is different, with one shot, I interrupt the center of gravity. If the opponent has a bad stance, he flies out. If he has a good stance, I make an adjustment, then counter his answer and apply pressure. I never let them reset to the beginning. Since no one plays sticking hands in the street, you're the one who has to be in control. Wing chun has no problem in close range because of it's defense, but there is a problem when you use it at a distance, against hit-and-run fighters. In distance fighting, you have to walk in against an opponent's strike and jam it—maybe lessening it to sixty percent of its power. In this way, I take one shot, but I can deliver at least five. Wing chun people may overemphasize sticking. Some can fight, but can't *chi sao*—they don't care to feel and adapt. Some can *chi sao*, yet can't fight—they don't know how to close the gap. Actually, you need both and must be able to flow from soft to hard to soft again. How many people can put it all together?

In wing chun, one requirement is to chase the body, not chase the hands. This means to destroy the body structure and take control of the center of gravity. You don't make it like a question and answer where you give me one and I answer it. One should never let the opponent have a chance to ask a question. In this way, you don't have to answer it. You have to control the body's center of gravity; if you don't, you will have to answer another question that the opponent throws at you.

A lot of people when they do *chi sao,* they roll, do one or two exchanges, stop, then reset and roll again. They never develop the continuous combinations, where you can strike an opponent multiple times. If you stop and reset, you give the opponent a chance to come at you again. Developing the skill in combination attack is hard to develop. By attacking the opponent's center of gravity, you make it so that the opponent has to concentrate on your attack coming in, and also has to deal with his loss of balance. In order to affect his center of gravity, I must use my body power so I can create another attack without leaving his hands. You are the one in control and you have control of the opponent's mind. In this way, you are always a half-step ahead of his timing, so I know ahead of time what the outcome is going to be.

So the fact that you learned wing chun several times under Yip Man is what afforded you a deeper understanding of the art?

I relearned wing chun so it would be another matter to look for other things. I personally went back three periods to learn from Yip Man. As far as I know, of all my generation, nobody went back to study a second time. Who is gonna go back a second time? Everybody thinks, "I learned it, I practice, I teach, whatever." No, they never go back to Yip Man. I went back three times.

The second time I got some extra things. The third time I went back, wow! So the wing chun, the art part, you can say I learned. Because I'm a small size, I'm one hundred and six pounds, I can do the job. That means my information and skill has to make up for my physical disadvantages.

But wing chun people don't care about that. They all say Yip Man taught them this or that. But I tell them Yip Man is Yip Man and that has nothing to do with you. Yip Man does not exist now.

Even now they talk about Bruce Lee and jeet kune do. Bruce Lee does not exist now. What I am saying to people is that you are yourself and can you, personally, do this or that? I don't care if Yip Man could or if Bruce Lee could; can you?

So, you have to go back and look at the whole thing again. That is because you are the guy who will use the art, not Bruce Lee and not Yip Man. Then you will find out for yourself what is your weakness, your advantage, and your disadvantage. Then you will reach your opponent and what happens? Never give him a chance. As far as my generation goes, no one in my generation, nobody, went back a second time to learn from Yip Man, except me.

So none of your contemporaries returned to Yip Man for fine-tuning or corrections of their techniques after completing the system?

Nobody went back.

Did Yip Man teach his students the same way with the same techniques, or did he teach them all differently to accommodate their different body types and psychological characteristics? I mean, after all, each of the masters all teach the art in a different way and certainly look different when they apply its techniques.

Yeah, they all look different. You can say that. No matter different or not, no matter what they all look like, everybody looks different when they do wing chun. The form is the same. But that I call "mechanical" wing chun.

"Mechanical" means you learn yourself. But fighting, how to fit in with your opponent, is different. Even though everybody teaches the forms differently, and some complain about the precise way of doing them, they are missing the point. The form is mechanical and the form doesn't teach you how to move your steps. Does the form teach you how to move aside? Does it teach you how to do this or that? No. Did it teach you how to apply the whole system? No. The only person who can teach you these things is your instructor. But, if your instructor never had a fight in the street, how can he teach you to move? Tell me!

Others say they have sticking hands and move their steps. One step or two steps? But sticking hands is still a game, it's not a fight.

Fighting is a real thing. It teaches you footwork and everything, you have to go in to the active battlefield and then you'll learn about that. Do you understand what I am trying to say?

Sure. But are you saying that mastering the three forms is a waste of time?

You see, there are only three forms in wing chun. A lot of people they think they know the art because they know the forms. They really only know the mechanical side of the art. They don't know the attitude or how to make the forms free. The first form, *siu nim tao,* develops the hand tools. The second form, *chum kiu,* teaches you to develop spinning so that you can use it any second. Once you're in, you don't retreat, you can spin to the opponent's side. It also develops the body to soften the hands, coordinate the hands and the body, and transfer power from the body to the hands, and *vice versa.* The third form, *biu jee,* is used when your structure or balance is destroyed. It teaches you how to regain the centerline from the outside in, not to use finger strikes, as the name may imply. The third form's requirement is to use the first form's hand tools and the second form's body development and trains you to use balance. The third form teaches you to utilize space to handle emergencies.

A lot of people think they can spar and then they realize they can't do this or that. They suck. When you meet them, you can handle these guys with a *jut sao,* even if he's bigger. If he's twice as big, no *jut sao* will fly now. Many think they're smart and if they use it this way it is correct. Yeah, for a small guy it's correct; for a big guy, it may not be correct. For wing chun, for the big guy, they feel jammed up so they try a shove their opponent. They try to do the second form. They want to do that because when the pressure's coming in, you shift. Actually, it depends on timing.

Can you explain this in more detail?

Unlike most who turn to avoid a strike, we turn into the body in reaction of a strike. We spin the body, borrowing our opponent's momentum and pressure. When we feel pressure, we hold it, then turn once we feel the body is committed. Most use the *chum kiu* attributes wrong. You need to eat up your opponent's space and move his hands. That means to say, if a bullet train is coming you try to knock the bullet train away. That's impossible, unless you have another bullet train bigger than this bullet train. But most wing chun people, they don't train the physical part. You can't move the bullet train, no way, that's because the bullet train will rebound your arm. When force rebounds on your arm, the pressure's still coming. So everybody says "Oh no, the guy won't let you adjust this from the second form." No, you need to adjust just one thing: you give your opponent the kind of pressure for him to watch out. That's in the first form, which is basically in and out. You jam me up, I step out; you give me a jab, I step out. That's it.

All three forms deal with in and out, in and out, until you learn your timing should be a little bit ahead. When you are a little bit ahead of your opponent, I step back first before you step in. You need to be one step ahead of him. Once he starts to do something, you are already waiting for it or expecting it.

It is essential, then, to be one step ahead at all times. Timing is the key.

This is the first form requirement. Let's say we're playing a game of dodge ball. You know ahead of time and are waiting for your opponent to throw the ball at you, so when he does you can hit the ball away; that's like the second form. I go forward and I don't step back any more. But I already know, and I automatically move my feet to come in. That means to say that in reality, you don't look at me until the ball hits you. Your timing is slower than my ball. And you know the guy, you watch the guy, he throws the ball to you, and you look at the ball coming and what are you going to do to get it out? Then you can get it out.

So the second form's requirement is this: if you are not one step ahead, the ball will hit you; if your timing is one step ahead of the ball you watch the ball coming and you can hit the ball away. That's the second form. You're not in my way, so I'm gonna step away from the ball. What does that mean? Timing wise, you are all upset. But I can spin the ball, follow the ball, hit the ball. When you spin the ball, it uses momentum and you can easily follow up and it works. If you step forward, the guy will step back and his balance upset.

How many wing chun people know how and why to use the second form? If a guy comes in and you just step back to do the *bong sao,* you didn't feel it, you only did the mechanical. So that means you used a mechanical one against a mechanical one. If you, feeding one to me, throw me a ball, I sock the ball back. When I sock the ball, your body will cut my spin. That means I forced you to come at me, I checked your ball.

Did Yip Man teach the application of these concepts along with the form, or just the mechanical aspect of the individual movements within the forms?

It has nothing to do with whether Yip Man held his hand like this or that. It's the same thing when you go out and fight with any other style. The first thing you develop is your eyesight, your ability to read your opponent quickly. When you start to make a move, I already stopped you. That means to say, like I'm talking with you, I watch your mouth and when you are about to talk I say "Shut up." I cut you off. That's called going in with timing.

A lot of people say it's Bruce Lee's intercepting. But intercepting is intercepting. Here I am watching you and reacting to you with proper timing. So, to intercept is not a style, it's not mechanical or the way you do it. If you can do intercept, that means your timing is super fast. A lot of people say I don't talk much about Bruce. Yeah, because I'm his lifelong competitor, whatever he attacked with, I know. I could read Bruce's timing. I can show you, no pressure, no reaction. You give me a punch and I can intercept it. Intercept comes from emergency. If suddenly a guy gives you a punch and your reaction is that you can intercept him with no problem, it means that you can counter-react.

All martial artists are looking for that type of timing. It has nothing to do with what style, wing chun or karate or whatever. Everybody is looking for the same thing. So the second form, it plays on this. I give you the pressure and you return the pressure and keep it up. But if you don't have this set-up thing, your shifting will be useless, because you can't control your opponent's momentum. I have to answer your pressure. When you exert pressure on me, I neutralize the pressure. When you answer my pressure, I then counter your pressure by spinning it away. That is the second form, *chum kiu.*

What is the essence of the third form, *biu jee?*

In my opinion, the third form is useless. It's useless. If you have the second form where you can destroy the opponent's body structure, you don't need the third form. The third form is used when you become disengaged. If you concentrate on the third form, it's because your understanding of *chum kiu* sucks. The famous saying, *"Biu jee but chut mun"* (*biu jee* does not go out the door), means one does not need to use the third form if you have mastered the second form. You don't have to gamble! The saying doesn't mean the third form is a secret. Throughout the third form, you see second form bodywork, and when the body structure is destroyed, you'll have to gamble to regain it.

Many people who do the second form don't really know how to use it. To me, the first form and third form are almost the same. For example, if I give you a punch or if I extend my fingers, or I follow the extension from the shoulder, it's basically the same thing. It's still going forward, just extended. To me, the first form and third form are basically the same. In wing chun, you don't need the third form. We say if you have the second form, you don't need to use the third form. You think the third form is the high level? It's not. Some people have this impression that the third form has an emphasis on finger strikes. If people actually use that, they'll see that the human body is already programmed to protect against finger strikes to the eyes, axilla, and groin with natural reactions.

So you're saying that the third form is useless since it teaches you nothing different than the first form? Why not just discard it, then?

The first form teaches you "in and out," but not how to extend. If you want to extend the hand you don't need to do it from the shoulder; you do it from the step. That means to say, lock the shoulder, don't extend it. When you extend the shoulder, that becomes rotation. People have a chance to keep the rotation back. You see, once you extend the shoulder your center of gravity is on your lead-in foot. And the lead-in foot becomes the center, so if I spin it and do the pak sao, you will start spinning. If you can do that, then wing chun people can use one hand at a time, or two hands at a time.

A lot of people who know wing chun can tell me a lot of ways to do that; I don't have to tell them. If you are in and out, and in and out, your body is in the center. If people deflect this one, they don't deflect that one. If you do like that from an emotional way, that means you throw me the ball and I sock the ball back to you. The returning force is double. That means if you have a ball and throw the ball to the wall, it travels faster and farther back to you.

I think, again, that this comes back to timing and also proper body structure.

Yes, you have to learn the body, the so-called framework. Within the framework of wing chun, my mind is not focused in my right hand or my left hand; my intention is in the middle. When I have too much pressure, I'm not effective. It's psychological. You hit me, you push me, okay, I'm centered. I, myself, am not just defensive. I can hit you. Then if you do this or that, this will hit this hand back, right? Because they don't know where the center is. They think the center is on the center line.

They think "Oh, Hawkins, you tell all the secrets out." But the thing is, can you do it? I have nothing to hide. You see, if you haven't trained to do that, even if I give everything to you, you still can't do it because it's psychological. So if you have that center on the body, not on the head, then you're psychologically calm. When you move forward, and give your hand, I slap your hand and I hit you. So you don't have to use your emotions to double your speed, like what Bruce Lee did.

How so?

Bruce Lee had problems applying his wing chun in the United States, so he changed his way. I know his problems: he was emotional, small, and had these skinny chicken legs. It was hard for him to root, his center of gravity was high, and his profession as an actor made him fearful of messing up his face. Whenever you punched him, he wouldn't shuffle back. Wing chun is straight forward. Stepping forward to a small guy is okay. You can run over a small guy. But a bigger guy, when you go to him, being emotional won't allow you to step back.

You see a lot of people are emotional in the ring, and they don't want to release, they fight head-to-head. Bruce Lee also had a problem with controlling his emotions. He didn't want to do the wing chun this way, that's why he changed in the United States to a hit-and-run style. So, you gotta train your speed before the guy realizes your punch is coming. Bruce had the character. He trained hard. He used high speed to come at you and power to cover up his disadvantages. In reality, people don't know his weakness because he covered it up so well. He covered up his lack of infighting skills. Yet, on the other hand, how many developed his high speed?

I knew him for many years. He had speed. A lot of people would think wing chun had problems or limitations and that's why he changed. I don't agree because his psychological profile didn't change; he was still there with his center line in his head. When you put your center, your emotions there, it's all there on your lead arm. When people hit your lead arm, force reverberates back to your body. When it goes back to your body, you have a hard time stopping it. He didn't know how to redirect with his body, to use structure for infighting. Traditionally, wing chun is not used for distance fighting. I use my tools as a shield to absorb and protect and press. It's not high speed, but it does the job.

Wing chun, then, is best applied with lack of emotions and a centered mind. It appears to be another example of the state of "no mind" that is often attained after years of diligent practice.

That's wing chun. Everybody knows the wooden dummy set and thus how to use both hands. They say wing chun teaches you to move simultaneously. So what? But when they stop the hand, this time the emotion is what? Because you use the emotion to pump it up, the small object you get out. The big object, it returns back and will destroy your path. So that means your center is in our mind. That means you're not involved with it, you just let it go. So that means I fight you, I go in, I touch your hand, you will swing my hand. When you swing my hand, I shoot my other hand in because these are two different things. Two hands can do different jobs. If you're emotional, you can't separate the two hands.

Just like the president of the United States, he can head millions of people but if he's emotional everybody will kick him out. Why? Because he's supposed to be at a high level. You have to learn how to manage, how to use the skill, and in what manner. It has nothing to do with the style. Like if you have two girlfriends to handle. If you treat one pretty nice, the other one is not going to be happy with you. You are in the middle and they should be apart. So, your left and right hands should be separate. That way everybody understands. Is this an easy job? No. Just make sure the women never meet, and your hands never cross.

You spent a great deal of time training with Yip Man privately. What is your opinion of the so-called "secret footwork" that is being taught by some of your contemporaries?

Come on, give me a break! Everybody talks about footwork. I don't want to criticize anybody, okay. Wing chun has a high stance. When you use a high stance for fighting, when your body moves away, your footwork moves away. We're not like those arts that use a traditional deep horse stance, where when a guy comes, you have to stand up or you have to step back. That's what you need the footwork for. For other so-called mechanical kung-fu or karate you need the footwork. In wing chun, it's a high stance. If you are in a high stance, when the body leans backward your foot will go back because you want to maintain your body upright. If you move the footwork first, that means your body better move with it.

Your energy is on the high portion of your body. If you do your footwork without your body, that means your footwork is mechanical. That means you are doing everything not based on feeling. If you have a fire in your master bedroom, who teaches you footwork? Nobody! You just run! You instinctively know how to move. It is natural. So, in fighting, when pressure comes, I have to maintain my body upright. It's automatic. It goes back naturally so you don't need the footwork. Who taught you how to run from fire? Your human nature.

You speak about the essential aspects of wing chun being timing, feeling, and a centered mind. But, aside from those things, wing chun has a set curriculum and forms to which its practitioners must adhere or the techniques will not work. How, then, would you describe the proper mechanical structure and footwork of wing chun?

Wing chun's structure is a triangle. That triangle, your upper body goes and the bottom will carry you. If you need to run, then you run. If you need to step, then your opponent teaches you how to do the step. If you step out, then you have to come in again. In between that step, suppose there is pressure on the guy. If you step out, that means you released pressure. If you release pressure, it means you released the opponent. This is not correct. If you push me, I should still stick with you. Footwork is just like dancing with a partner. If the partner steps forward, you step backward. Who teaches you how to step back? Your partner. If you step away, the partner doesn't like it. If you step with the wrong foot, you will step on your partner's toes.

Look at wing chun. They seem like they don't teach you how to do footwork. People ask why we don't add some footwork? But wing chun is based on the same simplicity when you go back to the mechanical. If you press forward and make me move back, the gap between us is the same. If I step out and you step out, that means our fighting distance between us or the gap is far away.

In the wing chun system, if you come in on me I make you stay. If you go back, I run forward twice as fast as you. Wing chun teaches you like that. If you come at me and I step back, I have only used the mechanical to handle the pressure, handle the movement. You use the space taught in the first form. You step back and you come forward. In sticking hands, when I touch your hands I step back like a dancing partner. But when distance fighting, if you come forward, I step back. Maybe the distance is accurate—one foot. You might step forward one-and-a-half feet. But if I step forward and the guy also steps forward, in timing you are lost. That means if you adhere to the mechanical, you may not have met a guy who know hows to fight. Don't pay attention to the footwork, just pay attention to the opponent.

In a general sense, this redirection principle sound similar to tai chi's pushing hands. Since you also practiced tai chi, do you see a similarity?

No. It's different than pushing hands. Push hands is yield; wing chun is not yield. Wing chun is just go in. Wing chun is just like a pinball: when you hit the pinball the pinball turns. You cut the pressure down. The pinball is not going back. Not like in tai chi when you come forward I roll back and then I come forward. No, wing chun is totally different.

Wing chun is like right ahead forward. If you come I spin you, I still go. That means, how can you do the form? Why do you do the footwork? If you're doing the footwork, that means your pressure is not strong enough to go against him. And then if you step back, that means you didn't know how to follow your opponent's pressure. If I press you and you press me back I will take it away. That's the second form. If you step back, you go back, okay, keep the momentum.

Again, we get back to the discussion on footwork and pivoting and pressure—an alive wing chun rather than a mechanical wing chun.

Yeah, yeah. If you have no pressure and you use the second form, is it mechanical? You use the mechanical, not reality. That means when you fight, your fighting comes from the memory, not from feeling. This is not the real wing chun.

Okay, so people say Bruce Lee changed wing chun into jeet kune do to cover up his weakness. Bruce Lee didn't dare to go in fighting. Bruce didn't like to use that pressure. I'm a small guy, and if I step back, my opponent will make me step back again. If I step back, I will eventually be backed up against a wall. Facing a bigger guy for me is like facing a wall. I have to know how to meet the wall. The wall is there, so I push the wall. Because I am small, I have to do more in-fighting. More in-fighting means I have to have a means to fight back against pressure, I can redirect the pressure, like spinning a wall away. A small guy has to stay inside, not outside.

A lot of wing chun people, they stay outside. They say, if you give me this technique I will give you that technique. It's all mechanical, they don't understand. The opponent answers their attack, then uses a technique. I'm small, one hundred and six pounds, against a big guy. You give me a punch, I do the tan sao. Your punch is two pounds, my punch is only eight ounces. How can I get it away? I go in and stop the attack. Let's say the distance from you to me is two feet. I don't take the two feet away, only a few inches away. I make it so that my physical start is where your physical ends. Understand now? A lot of people they punch at you and then you handle that extension. But if you're smaller than your opponent, you're in trouble. If you step away, returning will require more timing. So, I have to stay close.

The second form in wing chun deals with redirecting. The whole body moves or just the top body moves or just the arm moves, or your whole body's weight just sits on the floor or braces on the floor to redirect. In the beginning of the second form, a lot of people spin on both feet lightly and their energy is up in their chest, so they can do the turns easier. When you can spin easier, you'll be in trouble when pressure comes, as you will have to lower your center of gravity. If you have to do this it means you're already uprooted. You want to redirect the guy, but the guy actually redirects you. If you talk about structure, the muscle part, it's as if you're really stuck onto the floor. It is as if there is a large motor under the ground turning you, which is stronger than turning on top of the ground. Everyone wonders, "Hey, how can you do that?"

If you can't do that, you had better psych yourself up to get what we call the focus. In the soft arts, they call it *chi* or intention. That means, when your mind has the thought to do this or that, your body has already done it. You send your *chi* down to the ground and project it to your opponent. All the *chi* and movement we call intention of the focus. It's imagination and projection. Just like if you sit over here, and I say you look like a skinny little kid. Automatically you will droop and feel like a skinny kid. Then if I tell you you look like Mike Tyson, you will feel your muscles growing. Now this thing is called imagery. Your attitude will change. So when I do the second form, I spin you out, like I am a giant. I am confident, not like a little scared kid. It's like bluffing or psyching myself up. But how many people know that?

You see, I am a small guy and everybody tries to trick me and take advantage of me. So I had to develop myself into a guy who is not afraid. That will help your psychological center. If you are calm, you will be centered. If you are chicken, your center will move. People say wing chun traps hands. No. They don't know why they trap hands. One punch is one punch. Everybody knows one punch going in. Everybody knows how to handle one punch. But if my punch comes in, it is very solid and you can't handle it. If you already figured out your physical condition and the way you handle the movement, you can't get it away. Because once you do the *pak sao* and deflect it, I know you are going to do that. I know. That means when I extend, if you haven't touched me yet, I didn't lower any pressure. Once you touch me, I lower pressure. So, once you *pak sao,* I don't do another punch, I redirect and still go in with the same punch. Each punch originates the next movement. I don't need Bruce Lee's high-speed punch because you answer my hand. When you touch my hand I redirect and go in.

It appears that your practical fighting experience on the streets is the key component of your ability to understand and apply wing chun. Do you see many specific differences between your application of wing chun and that of the traditional masters, many of whom have never fought for real?

In traditional wing chun, two hands handle one hand. If you give me a punch, I use two hands to handle your one hand. No, that is wrong. One hand should handle the punch and one hand should hit the opponent. But, because many of the other masters use two hands to handle one hand, it's overkill.

They use the wooden dummy to develop powerful arms. This, too, is wrong. Wing chun is about proper body structure. That means, the way I do wing chun is opposite the way many people do wing chun. Where they use two against one, I use one against one, so I have the other hand free to hit my opponent. This comes from my experience in fighting for real on the streets of Hong Kong.

Has wing chun evolved differently, or is it practiced differently, here in the United States than in Asia?

A lot of outsiders criticize wing chun, saying that it is too classical. Yeah, wing chun is a classical style. Okay, but in the United

States the way you use the wing chun is totally different than in Asia. A lot of people don't realize that. Traditional wing chun is used against a lot of Chinese martial arts. They fight with the bridge hands as the opponents come out with blocking and swinging motions. Originally, it was like that. But when you come to the United States, you don't see the swinging or bridge arm movements, you see boxing. With boxing, the punches are here one second and gone the next. So, if you put the block out and then counter, you are too slow. How many wing chun people realize that? If I didn't have experience I wouldn't have realized that. It's like an amusement park game where heads pop out of holes and you try to hit them with a hammer. If you always wait to get them, you will miss every one. Wing chun is not about blocking; it is about timing, placement, feeling, adjusting, and structure.

So how, then, do you define real wing chun?

The challenge of every wing chun student is to make the wing chun art come alive for them. The classical wing chun system doesn't teach you how to fight; it's up to your own experience. The three forms, *chi sao,* dummy, pole, and knives sets are there for reference material, but it's up to you to put it together in application. Many create wing chun patterns to sell, but wing chun has no pattern. Many sell their patterns as wing chun, but wing chun is beyond these patterns. Real wing chun is formless. We can create patterns based upon our opponent's pattern. We study forms to reach a formless state. When one has reached a high level in wing chun, one discovers the variations in timing and changes in position that are possible in application. In Chinese, we call this *bien fa,* variations or changes. How many spend the time to research and develop their wing chun to this point? Yet, it is essential.

JOHN LITTLE
The Art and Philosophy
of Jeet Kune Do

*John Little is the world's foremost authority of the life and
work of Bruce Lee, his training methods, and his philosophy. Little is the only person ever authorized by the Bruce
Lee estate to review and use the entirety of Lee's personal
notes, sketches, and reading annotations. He is currently
the associate publisher of* Bruce Lee *magazine, the man-
aging editor of* Knowing Is Not Enough, *the official
newsletter of the Jun Fan Jeet Kune Do Nucleus, and a
director of the non-profit Bruce Lee Educational Foundation (http://www.bruceleefoundation.com/). In addition, he writes books and magazine articles on men's
health and conditioning and is an award-winning documentary film maker.*

John, it's obvious that you have spent much of your life on a quest to promote the philosophy of Bruce Lee. When did you first become interested in Bruce Lee?

In 1973, at age 12, when *Enter the Dragon* was just about to come out, I purchased a magazine in August of that year solely because it had an article on the "Kung-Fu" TV series, which I was enamored with, as were most people in North America at the time. On the cover, and within it, was extensive coverage for this forthcoming film from Warner Bros. called *Enter the Dragon.* The irony of it was that on the very first page of the magazine was a memorial to Bruce Lee, the star of the movie. And I thought to myself, "Who was *this* guy?" Then I read in the magazine that he had played the role of Kato in "The Green Hornet" TV series, and I remembered who he was.

Anyway, when I read the profile of Bruce in the magazine, I was fascinated. Unlike a lot of the "Kung-Fu" TV series, which was all esoteric Taoist discussions, Bruce Lee was very down to earth. In addition, unlike David Carradine, the star of the "Kung Fu" TV series, the magazine revealed that Bruce Lee was a real martial artist—and an exceptionally talented one. Plus, he had an absolutely tremendous physique.

I was twelve years old at the time, and Bruce became a role model right away for me: he was well built, good looking, intelligent, successful, he could look after himself in a fight, and he seemed to personify all the things that someone might aspire to. So, I became very interested in Bruce and went and saw the film as a result of that magazine article—and I was hooked.

Were you training in the martial arts or weight training at that time?

No, and I wouldn't have considered myself an athlete at that time either. At the age of twelve I was having fun, hanging out. I spent that summer at a cottage on a remote lake that left a lot of time on my hands to read and re-read that particular magazine. But after reading it and later seeing Bruce in action; seeing what a human being was fully capable of achieving—particularly physically—I became very interested in physical fitness, body development, and muscle physiology.

I became very interested in how Bruce built his body because he had a physique unlike any I had ever seen. I bought all the maga-zines I could that featured articles on Bruce Lee. I went to Chinatown in Toronto just about every weekend to purchase Chinese-language magazines on Bruce Lee, and brought them back to where I was living in Agincourt and had people translate them for me. But none of the magazines—or any of the books that came out—explained his training methods or how he developed his body. They just said "he lifted weights" or he "ran," and that was an awfully inadequate description of how he built his body.

Having grown frustrated at the paucity of information on how Bruce trained, I eventually started digging into physiology, finding out how muscles respond to the stimulus of exercise, the various mitigating factors there are that attend a muscle's growing bigger and stronger, and how a whole body becomes more defined.

And you were still twelve years old at this time?

Yeah. And this went on until I was in my mid-twenties, all of it a direct result of the impetus of Bruce. And when Linda Lee's books came out in 1975, I absolutely devoured them.

And what books were those?

There were two: *Bruce Lee: The Man Only I Knew,* which was her biography of Bruce, and *The Tao of Jeet Kune Do.* But *The Tao of Jeet Kune Do* was very confusing for me because it had a lot of Zen precepts in it that, to an initiate like myself, made no sense at all. I wanted the nuts and bolts: "How did Bruce kick?," "How did Bruce punch?," "How did Bruce train?"—and could any of it be applicable to other people? And although I liked his philosophy on a perceptual level, without any comprehension of Zen thought, there seemed to me to be scores of contradictory sentences. It was only years later, when I started going through Bruce's collection of Alan Watts audio recordings that I came to fully understand what was written in the *Tao of Jeet Kune Do.*

As a result of Bruce Lee's philosophical writings, I went on to study philosophy at university. And as a result of his physique, I poured into anatomy and physiology and eventually came to do research in the field of exercise science and to work for Joe Weider in California. So you could say "all I ever needed to learn" I learned from Bruce Lee.

So how do you see the importance of Bruce Lee in the world martial arts community?

I see Bruce Lee, without question, as the most significant individual of all time—both in terms of embodying the highest spirit of the martial arts and as being its foremost ambassador. And there's been a grudging giving of ground over the years in terms of the credit that is due Bruce Lee for his contribution to the martial arts by the martial arts community.

When Bruce first passed away, most martial artists who were "champions" suddenly wanted to become movie stars, like Bruce. They quickly flooded the Hollywood production offices and said "Bruce Lee was only successful because he was a martial artist"—forgoing completely his own charisma and acting ability. They actually thought that if you put them in a film, they could do better than Bruce because they were, in some instances, "world champions"—as if this meant something. And so the producers took these guys at their word, put these guys in films, and with the exception of Chuck Norris, not one of them could make a career out of it.

I think that Bruce's contribution was massive. Since Bruce Lee passed away, people have read his philosophy of liberation in the martial arts. You see all sorts of new styles and hybrid systems cropping up that never existed prior to Bruce coming on the scene. You now have these no-holds-barred competitors and lots of self-expression guys who take what they consider to be "the best" of different arts and melding them into their "own style."

These people think that is what Bruce did, but it really isn't. Nevertheless, as Bruce said in his interview with Pierre Berton, "through the contrast of comparison some new thing might grow." And this has happened in the martial arts community as a result of Bruce's contrast with traditional martial arts.

At the time Bruce was coming out with his ideas it was very much looked down upon by the Chinese community.

Oh, by all communities. Bruce stood alone. That is the thing people don't often grasp. For example, it's one thing when a Muhammed Ali stands up against, in his case, the United States government by refusing induction in the draft. A lot of people in the sixties were against the war in Vietnam and a lot of people were for it. A lot of people said that Ali stood alone when he stood up for his convictions. Well, the truth was that Ali had the support of the entire Muslim movement. The Nation of Islam was backing him. So he wasn't alone by any stretch of the imagination.

However, when Bruce Lee stood up against traditional methods of Chinese kung-fu and traditional martial arts in general, he truly did stand alone because the Chinese community did not back him one inch, and his American friends who were trained by Asian martial artists didn't back him because he bucked the traditional systems that they were a product of. So he had no allies at all. But Bruce wasn't just simply a reactionary, he didn't think that just because something was traditional he was "against" it. Instead, he was deeply rational and philosophically minded; he wanted people to tell him the reasons they were doing the things they were doing. And if you couldn't give him a reason apart from "Well, hundreds of years ago it was performed this way," and couldn't prove or justify why it worked, he wouldn't accept it as a valid way to approach the practice of martial arts.

That way of thinking is what directed Bruce to search for the fundamental truth or "essence" underlying efficient human movement. This led him to study the science of physics. In turn, he researched anatomy, physiology, kinesiology—and applied their principles to martial art requisites such as body alignment, balance, recovery, speed, power, and coordination. Bruce Lee certainly blossomed as a martial artist once he went in that direction. To actually look to science—as opposed to tradition—was considered a novelty at the time.

What do you think was his impetus to analyze different fighting systems? Was it from his Hong Kong street fighting days, or when he came to the United States and faced larger opponents?

I think primarily to read their "play books" ahead of time in the event that a martial artist from one of those styles should ever challenge him. Certainly in Hong Kong, by some reports, Bruce had over one hundred street fights. That number seems high, but it's not improbable.

Bruce came from an environment where he knew what worked in a "real fight" because he had been in a lot of "real fights." So when Bruce saw a lot of the technique and "systems" that were being handed down as "street lethal," particularly in America, he realized instantly that these things were inherently impractical and would never work in a real street fight. Bruce really had a disdain for people who were handing their students "black belts," based upon the student's ability to perform techniques that were impractical and actually dangerous to the practitioner if attempted in a real street situation.

Bruce's well-publicized fight against the Chinese martial artist in Oakland was another pivotal point in his formation of jeet kune do.

That was pivotal in terms of how Bruce viewed the importance of endurance and conditioning. It also opened his eyes to another aspect of martial reality. Until then, Bruce had been practicing what he called "nonclassical gung-fu"—primarily a quick close and the straight blast from his earlier training in wing chun gung fu. That is what he had used to win an earlier altercation against a Japanese karate man at the Seattle YMCA. This technique is great for dealing with a martial artist who is coming directly at you— like in arts that tend to be rigid and linear—but for someone who takes off in the opposite direction, like the martial artist in Oakland did, the technique didn't work as well because the guy was moving away from the force of Bruce's blows—coming at him as they did in a straight line or linear direction.

According to the people I have spoken with who witnessed the Oakland fight, as well as others that Bruce spoke to about it, the gung-fu man was running away from Bruce—in fact, Bruce would thereafter refer to this man as "The Runner"—and sort of flailing his arms behind him as he ran, which meant that Bruce not only had to be alert defensively but also had to press the attack. As you know, you can certainly do hundreds of punches in a span of three minutes—which is how long the fight lasted. And this evidently was what Bruce did. Bruce was exhausted, but eventually took the guy down and forced him to give up. But as the guy went down, he attempted to foot sweep Bruce. Afterword Bruce revealed to Linda how lucky he was that he hadn't been swept because he was so tired, it might have turned the course of things right there.

The big lesson Bruce came away with from this fight was, if you go into a fighting situation with a set method of dealing with an opponent—such as a quick close and a straight blast—however efficient this set method may be, you really are handicapping yourself. You can't go in there with a game plan because the other guy isn't always going to play to your strong suit.

The other thing Bruce learned was that he needed to improve his conditioning, because if another fight ever went beyond three minutes he wanted to be able to finish it at full power. He realized that a fighter had to be able to adapt to any circumstance, including one of high endurance. Boxing champion Roberto Duran once said that his toughest fight wasn't in a ring but an hour-and-a-half brawl in the streets of Panama. You never know how long a fight is going to last—which is why you can't have a fixed game plan entering into it. If fighting is your game, you have to be able to mix it up in any situation. That means you need the endurance to go full out for as long as it takes; you've got to have the power to put a guy away quickly if the opportunity presents itself; you've got to have the coordination and dexterity to get out of trouble if you're in trouble, and also to seize an opening should one present itself. You also have to have dexterity so that you are not a one-dimensional fighter, which is what many martial arts styles produced during Bruce's era. Instructors had these systems that were little sausage factories. Students would go in at one end and get all of this patternized conditioning and methodology, and they would come out the other end as these little patternized robots. They might be very good within a certain segment of combat, but once the parameters changed they were lost.

Take, for example, an art like wing chun. Wing chun is primarily a passive art. By "passive" I mean it requires you to react to what your opponent offers you as soon as he comes into your range. Bruce's writings, during his wing chun period, are loaded with sayings like "You must complete your opponent's energy; and "Never oppose your opponent's force head on." This is the antithesis of "interception" techniques such as stop-hitting—the founding principle of jeet kune do. But if your opponent doesn't come into contact with you, you are going to be waiting a long time for the fight to begin. And if he's quick and doesn't allow for that kind of contact, you are also in trouble. So, while Bruce realized that wing chun was a wonderful art and a great in-fighting system with its economical movement, sensitivity training, and centerline theory, it still represented only a piece of the fighting puzzle.

At what point did Bruce Lee start bringing weight and cardiovascular training and other conditioning and training regimens in?

Well, according to people like Jesse Glover, who trained with Bruce in his early days, Bruce was doing strength training in the early 1960s. He would roll barbells up and down his forearms, he would do isometrics. It was after the encounter with the gung fu man that Bruce began to take a closer look at cardiovascular training and incorporating exercises like skipping rope and progressive barbell training into his daily fitness activities. Bruce had a gripping machine made for him by George Lee, a student of his in Oakland, and he would load that up with about seventy-five pounds and keep going until he hit exhaustion in his forearms. Bruce also did a lot of abdominal exercises to be able to take a blow, and he also recognized that the abdominal area was the central region or nerve center of the human body—responsible for everything from torquing your hips to throwing a punch. So it was after that fight that he really keyed-in to the supreme importance of physical fitness to the martial artist.

Bruce purchased hundreds of bodybuilding magazines because at that time they were the only publications that catered to physical fitness by any description. He had at least four or five folders with articles that he had clipped from the magazines dealing with everything from diet and nutrition, to muscle development, cardiovascular training, yoga, and hard-core bodybuilding.

Is it at this time that Bruce also started to research martial arts other

than those of Chinese origin?

Before this, Bruce was really primarily interested in creating an ultimate gung-fu system. But then he realized that even the Chinese martial arts represented only a segment of the totality of combat. He began to research some of the more popular Japanese arts at the time, such as judo, karate, and jujutsu. His interest in martial arts just continued to fuel itself. He could look at things from his scientific vantage point and know right away whether a technique was efficient or inefficient, not based upon some nebulous category of which technique was "the best" in any given style, but in terms of scientific pragmatism.

Bruce realized that techniques, for the most part, had to be simple, direct, and efficient to work in combat. And if you read Musashi or the writings of other martial artists who have been involved in real combat, they all come to the same conclusion. Again, Bruce looked for balance, coordination, and body alignment so he wouldn't hurt himself when delivering techniques, and he looked into maximizing his kicking and punching power.

Look at the way Bruce threw a side kick, for example, or the mechanics of his lead punch. It's all geared to put the entire body weight in motion behind the strike. It's not a side kick like you would typically see in karate, where the *karateka* would chamber his leg, deliver the kick, and then quickly withdraw his kicking leg and return to his horse stance. If Bruce was kicking with his right leg, his left leg would be the impetus and it would cross behind his right leg so that now the gluteus maximus muscle of the right leg would be activated, in addition his body weight had now been set in motion behind the kick. It's almost like a rear kick when Bruce did it, but it's a far more powerful kick because of his moving body weight plus the force generated by the muscles of his left leg, the rotation of his hip, and the extension of his right leg all together. It's a more powerful kick than the regular side kick, but again, that's physics—the science of motion—and kinesiology, of course.

Aside from using equipment for training purposes, Bruce also had his students like James Lee making him specific equipment to train specific techniques, like the headlock machine, finger jab machine, and so on.

People don't realize that Bruce viewed his body as the machine that drove his technique, so he was constantly researching ways to make his "engine" more powerful and efficient. And one of these ways was an on-going attempt to bring more realism to his training. The problem was that he had to do this largely on his own because no one wanted to stand there and have one of Bruce's full-force kicks delivered to them. So, Bruce had his students and workout partners hold heavy, foam-padded kicking shields of about three or four feet in circumference. Later, this was supplemented with an "air shield" for football training made by *Rawlings*™. The thing with the air shield is that it also gave the person holding it better mobility than the foam shield so they could be a moving target for Bruce, which allowed Bruce to further improve his coordination, power, and timing. Bruce also employed a smaller foam pad for high hook kick practice.

Bruce was the pioneer of full-contact martial arts in this country. He was using chest protectors and shin guards from baseball, as well as boxing gloves and naval headgear. It was his idea to bring reality into the way the martial arts were being practiced and instructed. At the 1967 Long Beach Internationals, Bruce gave a demonstration of full-contact sparring. At that time people didn't really know what to make of it. But less than ten years later, full-contact karate started in this country.

Bruce Lee was really concerned with the real-world application of martial arts. He even went back to Hong Kong in 1965 and sat on a panel with various Chinese martial art instructors and told them—point blank—that there was too much "myth, legend, and tradition in the Chinese arts." Bruce believed that all of the talk of "internal power" and superhuman *"chi"* was actually hurting the martial arts. He commented that, now that he had been in the West, martial arts students were more interested in the scientific approach to the martial arts. While Bruce respected the traditions from which the Chinese arts came, he thought that they had served their purpose in the eras that created them, but now it was time to move into the twentieth century.

So this expanded training led to the creation of jeet kune do. What were

the styles that Bruce had studied in Hong Kong?

When Bruce was in Hong Kong in the 1950s his only formal martial arts training was in the art of wing chun. And his only instructor, truthfully, was an elderly gentleman named Yip Man. Bruce practiced wing chun diligently, probably six hours a day for a period extending from the age of thirteen to the age of eighteen.

When Bruce found out he was going to return to America, he decided that he wanted to introduce different elements of gung-fu to America, so he learned some of the fundamentals of other Chinese styles. He would teach cha-cha dancing to other martial art instructors in exchange for their sharing with him some of the fundamentals of, say, hung-gar, fu jow, crane, jeet kune, t'ai chi ch'uan, eagle claw, pa-kua, choy lay fut, monkey, hsing-I, and southern praying mantis gung-fu. Bruce wanted to show Americans what Chinese gung-fu was all about. Bruce said once that you could never learn all of the Chinese gung-fu arts that there are in one lifetime. There are simply too many of them. But he did want to introduce them to America, and he did want to broaden his own understanding of the Chinese arts.

Now Bruce Lee's martial arts went through several stages of development. Would you outline those stages for us?

When Bruce came to America, he was immediately impressed with the caliber of Western boxing. He had been exposed to that a little bit in Hong Kong, having actually won a "boxing championship" while still in high school. But he came to America with a sound grounding in street fighting, wing chun gung-fu, and at least a passing familiarity with a few additional Chinese styles.

However, once Bruce was in the United States he realized that he couldn't teach pure wing chun for a number of reasons—primarily respect for Yip Man's wishes. But he could teach, or share, gung-fu, which is sort of a generic overview of the Chinese martial arts. So he taught what he called "nonclassical gung-fu," and as he taught it, he was also being exposed to other non-Chinese arts like judo and jujutsu. And he began to think that wing chun, while good, nevertheless had limitations.

Bruce began to research particularly the realm of fencing, where he was very taken with the idea of the stop-hit. He found that to be a revelation because in a lot of martial arts blocking and hitting was a two-step process: block and *then* hit. Whereas with the stop-hit, you could accomplish both things in one motion. In 1965, Bruce wrote a letter to his student James Lee, this was after he went back to Hong Kong for his father's funeral, saying that he was working on his "own system" and that it was chiefly "a combination of wing chun, fencing, and Western boxing."

By 1967, Bruce had opened his school in Los Angeles, and was teaching the "Jun Fan method."

Did the Jun Fan method have a set curriculum, and how did it differ from nonclassical gung-fu?

Yes, it did have a set curriculum. And there were also set curriculums in his Seattle and Oakland schools, too.

Shortly after the Los Angeles school opened, Bruce realized that just calling what he practiced "nonclassical gung-fu" was inadequate and inaccurate. What he had developed was now distinct enough that Bruce felt he should give it a distinct name. So he looked at the most distinguishing attribute of his system at that time—the idea of "interception." This was not a system of "block-and-hit" but one of fluid motion: stop-hit, stop-kick, time-thrust, etc. So, it was the "stopping fist way" and by "fist," as you know, in Chinese the word *"kune"* also means "boxing." So, it was the "stopping boxing way" or the "stop hitting way." Bruce then went to a friend of his who was a linguist at UCLA to check on the correct phonetic spelling for the name of his "style," which henceforth became known as "jeet kune do" or "the way of the intercepting fist."

Since jeet kune do came after the Jun Fan method, was there another change in curriculum or emphasis?

Well, not really. What was taught remained essentially the same, only the name changed. So while the system, *per se,* remained unchanged, in July of 1967 the name officially changed to jeet kune do—according to his day-timer for 1967, anyway.

That was the defining attribute: stop-hitting, interception. And Bruce defined jeet kune do as a "purely offensive art, one hundred percent offensive." In fact, Bruce said that blocking was the absolute last resort in his style; you wanted to hit your opponent before he hit you, or before he even thought about hitting you. That was jeet kune during in the Summer of 1967.

It wasn't that long afterward, perhaps just prior to when Bruce reinjured his back in 1970, when he was reading more and more Krishnamurti, Bruce realized that any "way" or "system" or "method" is, by definition, limiting because it is simply "this," and thus "not that." He realized that in combat, as in the spiritual matters Krishnamurti spoke of, you cannot have what Bruce called "an effective segment of a totality," and words are always poor symbols for what they represent. For example, if I say over there "is a beautiful table," there are probably a hundred different types of beautiful tables, so that doesn't really describe the table for you in any precise way. And in fighting—and you know how vast that topic is—Bruce initially said that his way was "the stopping fist way," which means that it is not a blocking way or anything that was **not** an intercepting way. And that is limiting. Bruce believed that it didn't matter how effective a method was, any method, by definition, is a restrictive way of doing things.

I suppose this is also the time that he was known to repeatedly say in response to his system's name: "It is just a name; don't fuss over it."

The important thing was to simply "stop the enemy at the gate"; to shut him down; to adapt to what was happening. And that's when a lot of his writings and teachings started to shift to what he called "the art of expressing the human body." How can you "as a human being" react properly to what is unfolding in front of you? You can't do it through a method. Even if the method is good.

Bruce decided that truth in martial art is a "pathless path." And this doesn't mean that you have to study a hundred different arts, as that would just simply be following a hundred other "paths." The idea is to erode all barriers that exist in any path or method or style so that you are not restricted, so that you can do whatever needs to be done in any situation. In order to do that, you need to have body awareness and self-awareness. You have to know, for example, that if someone picks a fight with you, you can punch nonstop for fifteen minutes; you have to know that if you go to the ground, for example, you can fight your way back to your feet; you have to know that if you clamp a headlock on a guy, you will be able to choke him out; you have to know that you have a kick so powerful that you can drive a guy back fifteen feet; and you also have to know that you can enter the mind-set of "no-mindedness" or *"wu-hsin,"* where you do not have any set thoughts or a game plan or a set method, but your mind is free to respond reflexively to the situation as it unfolds before you. However, Bruce did not expect the student to simply begin in this "stage of artlessness" level; the student—even in his "backyard sessions," which were continued long after he closed his schools—was expected to develop proficiency in the fundamental techniques and principles that had been tried and tested with great results through his school curriculum.

Without a general game plan or idea of how to react or respond to an opponent, how did Bruce prepare his students for such an encounter? After all, the minute he taught someone how to block a punch he was setting a precedent that would affect a mode of action.

First of all, it would not be accurate to say that Bruce's students were "without a general game plan" or a knowledge of "how to respond to an opponent." This is what his "three stages of cultivation," "root" or fundamental teachings–such as the on-guard position, lead punch, shin/knee stopkick—to name but a few—were designed to impart. This, in addition to full-contact sparring sessions—which no other art with the exception of the grappling arts were into at the time—gave Bruce's students not only an "idea of how to respond to an opponent," but sharpened their tools expressly for that purpose. Also, Bruce had his students do their own homework, just as he did. Bruce didn't just show them a technique and say, "There you go!" He expected them to work on it, digest it until it was second nature to them. Probably anyone who has been in a real fight, if you ask afterward what happened, they have a tough time telling you—because a fight is almost a reflexive thing. The limbs move of their own and all you know is what you feel, whether it's rage or fear. At least for the people who are not trained fighters, that is what it is—an "emotional reaction."

In martial art, Bruce wanted to cultivate that emotional reaction, but have the limbs move correctly. He did that through dedicated training and practice in laying down neuromuscular pathways. And then you have "the three stages of cultivation": the "stage of ignorance," where you know nothing about fighting but you have that honest passion and emotion in what you do; the "stage-of-the-art," where you learn the fundamentals of efficient human movement or martial art, but your movements are very mechanical as you are learning things that may be very awkward or different to what you are accustomed to. And if you continue with your training and effectively lay down those neuromuscular pathways, you can enter what Bruce called the "stage of artlessness." This means that when you do enter a fight you will react with the same purity and emotional intensity you had in the first stage, but the limbs will move in a correct manner. This will improve your chances of success in a real encounter.

The problem is that a lot of people now misinterpret what Bruce was doing and think he was just being eclectic—taking "the best" of this and that. But what is "the best"? What does that mean? The "best" is a fixed ideal; something static—combat, on the other hand, is never fixed or static, but always unpredictable and dynamic.

I guess as an example of the public's, and even some of his students', misinterpretation of what Bruce was doing is found in a letter you once read to me that Bruce had written to Jerry Poteet, in response to a request from Jerry to mix jeet kune do with Ed Parker's kenpo. When was the letter written and what was the genesis of it?

I think the letter was written in about 1970 or 1971. I guess Jerry had said to Bruce that he wanted to share some of Bruce's teachings with the kenpo students, by way of mixing in some awareness drills from JKD into kenpo. And Bruce wrote that he shouldn't do this because: X is jeet kune do. Y is the style you will represent. To represent and teach Y one should drill its members according to the preaching of Y. This is the same with anyone who is qualified and has been approved to represent X. To justify by interfusing X and Y is basically the denying of Y—but still calling it Y. A man, as you put it, is one who is able to stick to the road he has chosen. A garden of roses will yield roses, and a garden of violets will yield violets. (pg.50, *Jeet Kune Do: Bruce Lee's commentaries on the Martial Way,* Charles E. Tuttle Company) In other words, to mix jeet kune do and kenpo and still call it kenpo is to deny kenpo. It is no longer kenpo because you have changed the nature of kenpo." And Bruce's whole idea wasn't to create a melting pot of different styles, his idea was to do away with styles completely. The thing is that it is *you*, the individual, which you have to deal with. You have got to find out about *you, your* reactions, *your* prejudices, *your* abilities, and *your* limitations. Styles separate humans and erect barriers to growth, understanding and self-expression, so let's erode those barriers and share in a process of continuing growth.

Is that what Bruce meant by his now-famous phrase: "Absorb what is useful."?

Right, and it's also what Bruce meant by his statement "using no way as way." Bruce was telling people to research the cause of their own ignorance with emphasis on "cause" or "root." By ignorance, Bruce wasn't implying that people were idiots, but that they needed to try to develop the necessary sensitivity to become aware of those things they were presently unaware of. To find out where you, for example, might be lacking and what can be done, if anything, to help you improve in those areas so that your chances are better for success, not only in combat but in life. In simply going from studying one style to another to another, all you're doing is going from cage to cage to cage in terms of voluntarily placing limitations on yourself. Maybe some people can do it without getting trapped. That's good for those rare few, but I don't know that that is the most efficient way of doing things.

Isn't researching your own ignorance, then, realizing that you are ignorant in grappling, for example, and going out and studying judo?

No. An organized style is *not* the answer, You don't acquire freedom by entering a cage. I think what Bruce would ask is: "What is the *essence* of grappling?" It is not important to study judo from A to Z and then study wrestling from A to Z, but rather to discover what is the essence of efficient ground fighting. What is the commonality of effective human movement for fighting on the ground?

Like Bruce said, "If you understand the root you understand all of its blossoming." Underlying all forms of human combat runs the denominator of our humanity. Human beings are not tigers, they are not monkeys, or praying mantises, so if you try and base your fighting methods on another animal's fighting attributes—rather than on the human animal's—you are headed for disappointment. It's just not in our genetic make-up to do that. Things will work better for you if you fight as a human being, since you are a human being. Like Bruce said, "You have two hands and two feet, and the most important thing is how to make good use of yourself. That's it."

So how did Bruce relate to his students the method of relating to themselves while teaching his class?

That aspect of martial art Bruce taught mainly through private instruction. In fact, realizing that such "teaching" could not be accomplished on a mass scale was one of the reasons why Bruce decided to close his schools. He continued to teach people privately, sharing with them what he believed and cautioning them to use their own minds in an independent fashion. He said, "Create immediately an atmosphere of freedom so that you can live and find out for yourselves what is true, so that you are able to face the world with the ability to understand it, not just conform to it. One can tell for oneself whether the water is warm or cold. In the same way, a man must convince himself about these experiences, only when they are real" and "all I can offer is an experience but never a conclusion, so even what I have said needs to be thoroughly examined by you." In other words, Even what I have taught, you have to question it. I am like a signpost to help you, these are the things I have found to be true; try them out. The important thing is to not take what I say on blind faith just because I said so. Understand it yourself, really research it for yourself. Try to find out and understand for yourself what is the most efficient movement in combat for human beings—don't simply follow the "way" of someone else. And don't just go with what comes easy for you; that's another popular misconception of jeet kune do, resulting in people—again—dealing with only one dimension or "segment" of the "totality" of combat.

I agree. It is often frustrating to listen to and read things a lot of JKD people say in terms of "rejecting what is useless." They often reject what they cannot immediately do, regardless of its actual usefulness. And besides, without earnestly training on something for an extended period and studying it from various perspectives, how can one say that X is useless and Y is useful?

But there is a difference between seeking and studying the "essence" of a thing and "studying it from various perspectives." You could end up stuying something from everyone else's perspective but your own! Moreover, feeling compelled to look at opinions and perspectives may prevent you from ever touching the heart of the matter. Question, probe, reason—seek out the truth of the issue for yourself—but also be aware of your own prejudices and fancies that may obstruct your vision of the reality you seek. It's not about simply falling into the habit of doing something that happens to come easy to you. It's about learning how to really grow in all areas by applying yourself diligently to your total growth and development—physically, mentally, and spiritually. That was the idea. I've heard some "authorities" and instructors claim, for example, that if you are a big guy you ought to go to grappling because that is a close-range art and will play to your strength. And while you probably would do well in it, the problem lies in getting hung up on that and making it *"the* way" for you because you are restricting yourself and you may find that you have more potential than you think you do.

In fact, Bruce told Daniel Lee, another student of his, in a phone conversation that Dan recorded, that was why Bruce closed his schools of jeet kune do. It was simply "too easy for a member to come in a take the schedule as the truth and the agenda as the way." The idea is that the individual must do the work. Sugar Ray Leonard, for example, could show you one of the greatest left jabs in boxing, but if you're not going to go home and practice it thousands and thousands of times—which is what is required to culti-vate it—what use is it? It never becomes part of you, you never experience the truth of it.

So Bruce came to the realization that he should not have schools at this time, as the students could be limited too much in adhering to a fixed schedule?

Yes, Bruce wanted to protect the students from his own influ-ence—as all great teachers do.

Well how else, then, unless they are self-motivated—we know most people are not—would his students go out and become great fighters?

I think you've answered your own question because great fight-ers *are* self-motivated. Bruce simply gave his students the "tools"—how they developed them was up to them. Not everyone who trained with Bruce wanted to be a "great fighter." Kareem Abdul-Jabbar wanted to be a better basketball player; Steve McQueen wanted to be a better actor; James Coburn wanted to learn more about transcendence and about himself; Stirling Siliphant wanted to become a better writer; others simply wanted to get into better shape. The emphasis at Bruce's school was not "I'll make you a great fighter," because a lot of that is attitude. Bruce even said that it is very "difficult to teach someone their own attitude. His idea was to make his students more aware human beings. And the only way you can do that is by pointing them in the direction of self-knowledge, and that is what Bruce tried to do.

If you could become a "great fighter" or a more enlightened human being simply by learning a few techniques from an instruc-tor, then there would be far more "great fighters" than there are. In fact, were this possible, then every martial art student would be their instructor's equal. Bruce once commented on this false belief. He said, "Often times people come up to an instructor and say 'What is the truth' and 'Hand it over to me'." As if you could. And Bruce would say, for example, if you went to an instructor of, say, Japanese karate, the instructor would give you the Japanese way of doing it; if you went to a gung-fu school, the guy would give you the Chinese way of doing it. But, as Bruce concluded, unless there are human beings with "three arms and four legs," there can't be a "different" way of doing martial arts.

The idea was to use martial art as a vehicle of self-knowledge in order to become a better human being; to not get caught up in anything that would limit or restrict your growth as a human being in all areas that entails. This includes the physical realm, which has many categories as we already discussed, and the mental realm, since it is your brain that drives the muscles that execute your martial arts techniques. And the more intelligent you are, the better your ability to recognize combative options when they present themselves. Your awareness increases, which, again, has to do with self-knowledge. And on a spiritual or metaphysical level, the two previous categories merge to provide you with an understanding of the relationship you have with all that *"is."*

And that was really Bruce's emphasis in teaching, and later in his career, I think the movie screen became his classroom. Look at the lessons that he began to teach through his films—not his first two films as much, because he didn't have as much creative control.

You see this overtly in such TV appearances as "Longstreet."

Yes. "Longstreet" is loaded with lines like: "I cannot teach you, only help you to explore yourself, nothing more." And Longstreet says: "Well you weren't born knowing how to take apart three men in a matter of seconds." And Bruce replies: "True—but I found the cause of my ignorance." And that's what jeet kune do is all about. It is a tough thing to grasp, and definitely not something for the casual enthusiast. It requires a great deal of time—in Bruce's case, a lifetime—of compassion and commitment to realize its higher aspects. If you look at Bruce's later writings, he wrote an essay called "The Ultimate Source of Jeet Kune Do," in which there are no martial art techniques at all. It's all philosophical insights on morality, life, death, and reality—it deals with a higher purpose than simply punching and kicking.

Additionally, Bruce wrote a letter to a fellow named "John" in 1972, which said, "With all the training thrown to nowhere, and the self vanishing nowhere, the art of jeet kune do attains its perfection." So these are Bruce's words on the ultimate nature of his art.

When Bruce wrote in philosophy scenes for films such as *Enter the Dragon,* he specifically talks about the "art of fighting without fighting," and "I don't hit, it hits all by itself," and "a good martial artist must take responsibility for himself and accept the consequences of his own doing." These are philosophical statements.

In *The Way of the Dragon,* where he fought Chuck Norris in the Roman Coliseum, the lesson Bruce was teaching was about adaptation, the need for martial artists to be able to adapt in a fight and not have a one-dimensional approach. And, in the same film, when Bruce is speaking to his friend in the alleyway, his friend says, "I don't like karate—it's foreign," Bruce reprimands his friend and says that he has the completely wrong attitude, because it had created a barrier for himself. The whole idea behind jeet kune do is to dissolve barriers, not only of style, but of race and nationality. And that was the lesson taught through that scene. Look at yourself not as a member of a style or race but as a human being. And not only in the realm of efficient human movement; ie., in the realm of hand-to-hand combat, but also more importantly, in matters of mental and spiritual growth.

So what has come out of all of this in the past ten years or so, since there has been so much written about jeet kune do, are three specific movements. There is the "original" jeet kune do approach headed by people like Gary Dill; the jeet kune do "concepts" approach, headed by people like Dan Inosanto; and the so-called jeet kune do "matrix" approach, headed by people like Jerry Beasley. Why do you think there are so many variations of what Bruce was doing when in fact he was very specific about his thoughts and feelings?

Really, the only person qualified to comment authoritatively on this is Bruce Lee. And since Bruce is no longer with us, all we can do is look to what he said about it via the printed or recorded word. I can only tell you what Bruce said in regard to his art. To my way of thinking, his is the only word that counts when speaking about jeet kune do, and what does or does not constitute its proper comprehension. All anyone else can do is—assuming that they actually spent time training with Bruce Lee; and two of the three people you just mentioned did not, by the way—provide some context or anecdotal material that may serve to better bring home the meaning of Bruce's words on the subject.

The way I see it is that the two major battle lines drawn or demarcated are between what is called the "concepts" method and the "original" method. But if you take either of these extreme approaches and follow them through to their logical conclusion, they end up saying the same thing. These camps seem to be at cross-purposes for the most part.

If you look at his writings, Bruce Lee never used the word "concept," that was his assistant instructor Dan Inosanto's phrasing. In fact, Bruce was vehemently opposed to the term "concept"—particularly with regard to combat—because a "concept" is an intellectual abstraction, something you do not have the luxury of indulging in combat. Remember Bruce's instruction to the young student in *Enter the Dragon*: "Don't *think*—feel!" For the sake of the illustration, however, let's assume that the term "principles" is what Dan means by his use of the word "concepts." And let's not take anything away from Dan, a good martial artist in his own right, but a principle or "concept" is either valid or invalid. If, for example, you are talking about the principle of progressive overload as it applies to increasing one's muscular strength, well, that's valid. It works. So, if you apply Bruce's method of strength training—which made use of the principle of progressive overload—you are employing an effective principle, or "concept," if you will, but inasmuch as it was part of Bruce's training techniques, if you use it then you are still dealing with his "original" materials. And when it comes to martial art techniques, the same applies: a technique is either valid or invalid; effective or ineffective; ornamental or functional. If you only accept the valid, effective, and functional in martial art, I think you will ultimately be left with the same "original" martial techniques that Bruce Lee came up with.

I agree, but that doesn't change the situation as it exists today. You still have the original guys who are grasping fastly to the "original" curriculum, which in Bruce's mind became limited, and the concepts guys who are attempting to go beyond Bruce Lee.

Well, first of all, and despite the egos of martial artists generally, no one has "gone beyond" Bruce Lee in terms of physical combative skill which is why he remains the gold standard today in terms of martial art. Secondly, the problem with saying an "original approach," is that, to borrow one of Bruce's similies, it is looking at the "finger," and not the moon it's pointing at. That is to say, if you just look at the techniques as *the truth,* and the techniques are true, and valid—but they are not true *because* Bruce used them. Rather, Bruce used them **because** they are true—and that, if you see it, is the only reason why you should want to incorporate them into your training. That's the problem. A lot of people say that "this is what Bruce did—and for that reason alone—it must be truth." That's when dogma creeps in.

But it is truth inasmuch as Bruce found it to be valid.

Right. And if you can find out *"why"* the principles and techniques that Bruce recommended are valid as a result of your own independent judgment, then you've got it. But if you just look at the curriculum and say "that is what Bruce did and it's good enough for me!" and leave it at that, then you are becoming dogmatic. You are then only looking at the finger instead of what it is pointing at.

The "concepts" camp, conversely, say, depending on to whom you speak, that the techniques that Bruce Lee taught are largely outdated now—what the "finger is pointing at" is irrelevant, in other words—and they recommend that you start from scratch for yourself. And this is just as erroneous. I think of it as comparable to learning physics from Albert Einstein; the guy was obviously onto something and it could only benefit you to take a look at what he did and then experiment with it. And like Bruce said, "Even what I have said needs to be thoroughly examined by you." Examine—not try it once and see if you can pick it up.

But you look at the concepts guys, for example, and you see people studying silat and arnis and shooto and stuff that Bruce wasn't doing and to try and develop themselves in the so-called fighting ranges of kicking, punching, trapping, and grappling. However, it looks nothing

like what Bruce Lee was doing. But not that it has to either.

Well, the reason it is different and doesn't look like what Bruce was doing is because those are separate "styles"—and Bruce was opposed to the idea of "styles" of any kind.

Yes, but they are going by this concept of "Absorb what is useful and reject what is useless," and I think they are taking that to mean absorb what is useful to me, and reject what I can't do. And my retort to that is how do you know the technique is useless if you have not spent sufficient time practicing it and attempting to understand it?

Exactly. Bruce Lee himself spent hundreds of hours practicing his techniques, until they were fully integrated with his very being.

So, on the one hand, they are discarding things that are useful just because they can't immediately make them effective. On the other hand, they are grabbing arts to fill combat ranges rather than to develop an efficient system.

Well, the only "ranges" I ever saw Bruce writing about are three: "long," "medium," and "close."

Right, because you can certainly kick in trapping range and punch in grappling range.

Yeah, and from my perspective, there is only one range: and that is the range you happen to be in at the moment. The rest are unimportant, because that is the one range you ought to be able to operate in. For example, if I am in "kicking range" and I kick at you and you trap my leg, what "range" are we in?

I don't tend to get off on the peripheral issues like "concepts people say this" and "original people say that." It doesn't interest me, and more importantly it's not what Bruce was about. These are peripheral issues to Bruce's own words on the matter—and, again, his is the final word on the matter of his art. The "original versus concepts," or "matrix versus that," are not worth the brain cells required to comprehend them all. In the end, you either get it or you don't. You either understand what Bruce said and see the truth that he was pointing at—or you don't. And Bruce said, "Jeet kune do is not something you can be a member of; either you get it or you don't. And that is that." So if someone says, "Well Dan Inosanto is doing it this way," I say, "Good for him, but what about you? Do *you* see the truth that Bruce Lee was pointing at?" People have to realize that Dan Inosanto is not Bruce Lee—nor, for that matter, is anybody else. My only beef is when somebody claims falsehoods in Bruce's name—like "Bruce Lee said you should formally study many different styles," when Bruce was vehemently anti-style. They've missed the whole point of Bruce's art and philosophy.

But don't you think that they are all correct in a way? If they are all following the concept of identifying and overcoming their own ignorance, then in fact they are correct.

Yes, *if* in fact they are identifying and overcoming the cause or root of their own ignorance. The problem exists if you are just stockpiling techniques, and many people are doing this. They figure that they are being open-minded by going and checking out all these different arts. But that is all you are doing: checking out arts. That is a completely different animal than saying I am looking for the efficient root or essence underlying all efficient human combative movement.

Now, for example, a fellow like Ted Wong, whom I know and have briefly studied with, and Taky Kimura, Bruce's close friend, assistant instructor, and highest-ranking student, both of these gentlemen do what Bruce taught them, but they also both *understand* what it is they are doing. They are not doing it solely because Bruce told them to. Ted and Taky understand the efficiency and validity of the techniques and philosophy that Bruce advocated. Ted, for example, has really gotten into and examined the mechanics and the principles underlying efficient mobility, footwork, and the on-guard position. He also has done his own experimenting and research on issues such as: how do you use mobility effectively against a grappler. Ted just gets it.

I am not knowledgeable enough about every other practitioner of jeet kune to vouch for their degree of competency in the art, and I wouldn't attempt to. But I do know that for someone like Ted Wong, who has been pigeonholed as simply an "original JKD"

guy, that label simply does not apply. He is just a guy who *gets it;*
he understands what Bruce was saying because he spent hundreds
of hours with Bruce in private lessons and has done his own thinking and research. And he really didn't have a cultural and martial
bias when he started studying with Bruce. He didn't go there with
a previous martial arts base; he went there *tabula rasa* and Bruce
explained to him the importance of searching for the fundamental
principles of combat and of not doing something simply because a
tradition demands it. Always ask "why?" Those are the areas that
JKD, for want of a better term, says are to be developed by the
individual. You have got to ask those personal questions. You have
really got to discover the cause of your *own* ignorance. And that
does not simply mean that you adopt someone else's ignorance or
"Way" and say now you have discovered the cause of your ignorance because it is apples and oranges; that is *his* ignorance and/or
solution to his ignorance—his "Way"—not yours.

**Let's talk about the formation of the Jun Fan Jeet Kune Do Nucleus.
Wasn't there originally a JKD Society?**

There was a "JKD Society," but that was certainly before I came
on the scene. I don't know much about that, other than it was an
attempt to bring people together who were practitioners of the art.
As Bruce himself prognosticated, "you cannot organize truth."
Oftentimes, when you get a bunch of people in a room, you end
up with a committee, not truth. And that's a tough thing to guard
against—and every group has that, to some extent.

With the formation of the Jun Fan Jeet Kune Do Nucleus, we
are very sensitive to this. We are experiencing growing pains and
trying to counter some of the problems that happen when you
have an organized group. One thing that I think is helpful with us
is that we do not have any leaders, *per se;* every one has an equal
say. This checks against against dogma and is perfectly in keeping
with the viewpoint that we are primarily an educational body
interested in trying to understand Bruce Lee, what he taught, and
to present a full picture of this as best we can to the public, emphasizing what Bruce Lee believed in and what he found important
enough to teach. We believe that everyone holds a piece of the puz-

zle and that no one piece is bigger or "more important" than any other piece, because without even one piece you are left with an incomplete puzzle.

What we want to do is to encourage anyone who had any kind of contact with Bruce to share their knowledge and contribute it to our database so we can try and flesh out this picture of Bruce Lee, his art and philosophy. But we want accurate information, not faulty recollections, not things that some people *think* Bruce said. It has got to be the real data, otherwise we just end up all over the board. So, we basically have restricted ourselves to an oral tradition that is verifiable, and Bruce's written body of work, and any audio and video material that can help as an adjunct to this.

How is the JFJKD Nucleus spreading around the word? Are you hosting seminars, making training videos, conducting lecture series?

At the moment, we are just doing annual seminars. The first one was in San Francisco, one was in Torrance, and this year's will be in Seattle. What we are hoping to do is to really expand that and, because it does involve a lot of people doing research on their own, we hope we can broaden our archives so that people can come and visit and spend time researching the various areas of Bruce Lee's teachings that they find interesting and important to their own lives. We have just established the "Bruce Lee Educational Foundation" (bruceleefoundation.com) which I believe will prove tremendously useful in this regard.

Some people feel that Bruce was just about martial arts, simply fighting. And if that is the case, then Stirling Siliphant should not have gotten anything out of JKD, nor should James Coburn or Steve McQueen, nor ninety percent of Bruce's students. Jeet kune do is ultimately about personal growth—not just fighting.

In truth, if fighting was the only touchstone as to the effectiveness of jeet kune do, then Joe Lewis, Mike Stone, Chuck Norris, Bob Bremer and Daniel Lee are probably the best fighters, qua fighters, that Bruce Lee ever taught. But fighting, to me, is but a segment of the totality of jeet kune do. Fighting is certainly part of it but it is not the whole thing by any means. And people who get hung up on that are again looking at a "finger" of a different sort.

Speaking of Joe Lewis, who was one of my idols in the martial arts, I find it interesting that for years he promoted the Joe Lewis Karate System, and now he has jumped on the JKD bandwagon, with articles, books, and videos on the subject.

Well, Joe Lewis did know and train with Bruce Lee. And there is a chance he learned something, I suppose. But I think that if you really get the point of JKD you don't need to get up on a grandstand, as one of Joe's students recently wrote in a magazine article, and say things like "Lewis was Bruce's best student." Certainly Bruce *never* said Joe Lewis was his "best student." Again, the whole thing is do you get it or not? And if you do get it, then you don't need to thump your chest. And you're no better—or worse—than any other student who "gets it."

Getting back to the philosophy of jeet kune do, tell me about the class you will be teaching.

The course will be held at a private school here in Idaho, and we are hoping it will serve as a template for other academic institutions. We feel that, particularly with what is going on with East and West as we speak, and the way the business world is operating, it behooves people in North America to understand the culture they are going to be dealing with. And Bruce Lee certainly does represent a perfect bridge between the two cultures and the first step toward establishing a global philosophy, as opposed to a partisan philosophy.

So, that is what I'm working on right now. It is set to be a twelve-lecture course with Q & A sessions afterward. There will also be reading assignments and essays. The course deals solely with Bruce Lee's philosophy—not how to throw a punch.

Was that course the impetus for your book, *The Warrior Within*, or *vice versa?*

Well, *The Warrior Within* was written several years before the course came about. And the impetus for the book resulted from the realization that it was Bruce Lee's mind that set him apart from every other martial artist of his generation, and that's what made his martial art unique. But Bruce Lee has so much more to offer a person than simply a more effecient way to dominate an opponent in unarmed combat.

As Bruce said in 1971, "You just don't go around on the streets these days kicking and punching people or else you get shot!" In other words, violence is wrong, and if you go around using sort of the equivalent of a "pistols at dawn" mentality, you are going to get killed. Bruce's words reveal that a human being's greatest weapon is his mind—not his fists.

The martial arts must serve another purpose, then.

Right. Brandon Lee said that, too. And that is what separates the true martial artist from the street fighter. The true martial artist doesn't go around looking for fights whereas the street fighter does. A martial artist avoids fights because he understands the brutality and violence that it involves.

Where do you see the jeet kune do movement headed?

It is hard to say. Some are quick to say that "real jeet kune do died when Bruce Lee died." Others say that they have "evolved Bruce Lee's art and have taken it into a lot of new directions." Again, the thing is, in the final analysis, it is about an awareness of reality or truth. This you cannot "evolve." And to say that it "died" is equally false and nonsensical because truth always outendures those who observe and comment on it. It isn't the property of any one person—no matter how impressive his pedigree.

So jeet kune do, as a philosophy, is like Taoism. How one can say the truth, or the Tao, can evolve?

Right. It simply "is." And you either experience it—or you don't. "The point is to utilize the art as a means to advance in the study of the Way" as Bruce Lee said.

So while jeet kune do will remain, do you see the practitioners of the art evolving to meet it or better understand it?

I think there is hope for those who avail themselves of Bruce's "signposts" or writings. But this is a difficult path and it requires a lot of research and an on-going process of self-knowledge. There are too many martial artists who simply want to be told what to do—"second-hand artists," as Bruce called them. But if you read his writings, it becomes very clear what Bruce was saying. It is not about building barriers, it's not about building your "own styles," or going from style to style. It is about removing the whole notion of "style" and trying to become a fully developed human being.

In fact, in *Jeet Kune Do: Bruce Lee's Commentaries on the Martial Way,* Bruce writes: "Self-actualization is the important thing. And my personal message to people is that I hope they will go toward self-actualization rather than self-image actualization. I hope that they will search within themselves for honest self-expression."

In other words, find out the "whys" of everything. Experience it, explore it, research it, discover it. The key is to understand it yourself, not just repeat what Bruce did or ape his movements because that, in the final analysis, avails you nothing. You are merely able to impersonate somebody. But if you can integrate that with your being and feel it and understand it, you will *get it.* If you merely copy someone, you don't have it. Conversely, if you go wandering off without Bruce's signposts, you can spend years heading down blind alleys. The good news is that you do not need to do that. Bruce has set out the signposts for you.

There is no need to get sidetracked on issues such as what anyone else says or thinks about jeet kune do and Bruce Lee. The question is "What do *you* think?" If you want to explore Bruce's philosophy of jeet kune do, read what Bruce wrote and follow his signposts to discover the cause of your own ignorance.

Until recently, however, many of these signposts have not been readily available. However, with the combined help of you, the Bruce Lee estate, and Tuttle Publishing, people can read volumes of Bruce's own words and thoughts in the Bruce Lee Library. How did you get involved in this project?

Well, this project came about as a result of an article I originally wrote about Bruce's training methods in *Muscle and Fitness* magazine. While growing up in Canada, I was shocked that there was such little material about how Bruce trained. He must have done something more than just study martial arts. He didn't have a naturally strong physique, so how did he build himself up? But, as is typically the case with a magazine article, there are reams of material you cannot include as a result of space limitations. So I said to Adrian Marshall, the Bruce Lee estate attorney, "there is so much material that didn't make it into the article that we're not giving people the full picture. "Perhaps I should write a book."

Adrian spoke to Linda, who thought it was a great idea. And then Linda invited me to come to Idaho to work on the project, which I did. I hadn't been off the plane three minutes when she handed me three volumes of Bruce's writings, and said, "this would be a good place to start."

Now I didn't know really what to expect. I had interviewed a lot of people who studied with and who knew Bruce Lee for my article, and I thought that was just about as much information as I was going to get. I thought most of his writings had already appeared in *The Tao of Jeet Kune Do*. So I was stunned to find boxes and boxes of Bruce's writings, over six thousand pages, in fact, not to mention his library of 2500 books, most of which had annotations in the margins reflecting his thoughts on various issues that had never been seen by anyone except Bruce Lee on the day he made them.

I ended up taking two trips back to Idaho. The first time I returned with sixty pounds of photocopied material. Linda had rented a copier for me. And the second time I came back with about twenty-five or thirty pounds of photocopies. Over a period of four years I was able to transcribe all of these writings and tried to arrange them into three volumes. Then Linda, Adrian, and I met with some people from Tuttle Publishing who looked at the three volumes and said the size of each individual volume was too large to publish. They asked me if I would be willing to break them down into twelve volumes, wherein I could really focus on different aspects of Bruce's life, art, and career. And that's what we did.

The uniqueness of this series is that it is all Bruce's own words—so people now no longer have to rely on former friends' and students' faulty memories, or pay huge fees for heavily "interpreted" presentations of Bruce's art and philosophy. Whenever they want to visit with Bruce—experience his wisdom and teachings firsthand—they can find him within the pages of his books.

PART THREE

MARTIAL ARTS
AS SPORT

HAYWARD NISHIOKA
The History and Evolution of Judo

Hayward Nishioka has been involved in judo since 1952, and currently holds a seventh dan in the sport, as well as masters degrees in both physical education and administrative education. Nishioka sits on several judo committees: with the United States Judo International he is on committees for promotions, coaches, and referees, and is chairman of the judo research committee; with the United States Judo Federation he is chairman of the teachers institute committee. In addition to his judo practice, Nishioka also holds a black belt in Shotokan karate and was a former athletic director and chairman of the physical education department at Los Angeles City College. Nishioka is a full professor at LACC, where he currently is an instructor and teaches physical education and health full time.

We are all familiar with what Dr. Jigaro Kano did with judo, but we are less familiar with his exposure to the martial arts that led to his creating judo. Could you share some insight into that?

Well, probably someone else could give you a better history of Dr. Kano's goings on before he got into judo. But apparently what he did was to get into jujutsu. Apparently, there were two or three different types of jujutsu that he had studied. Isshin Shinyo-ryu and Kito-ryu are two of the ones that he had practiced. In fact, one of them was taught to Dr. Kano by the father of Fukuda Sensei, who is here in the United States. That is how he kind of got started. She, Keiko Fukuda Sensei, in turn came to learn judo from Dr. Kano.

Jigaro Kano got started in Kobe, Japan. Because he was not a very big person or in very good health, as a young boy he studied jujutsu. It also afforded him an avenue of getting a sense of control over his environment.

Eventually, Dr. Kano became an English teacher. His ability in English afforded him opportunities to expand into international relations and eventually he became an astute politician and was also the first president of the Japanese Normal School. He was also the founder and first president of the Japanese Amateur Athletic Union. Dr. Kano's ability as a statesman led to his becoming the first Asian representative to the Olympics.

What year did Dr. Kano become the first Asian representative to the Olympics?

I think it was around 1908 or 1909. I don't know whether he was in the games or in the meeting in preparation for it. I am not sure what.

What do you think Dr. Kano's impetus was for moving away from the jujutsu that he had learned and developing judo?

I think the primary thing he had in mind was that he wanted to have something left over from the feudal days of Japan that would lend itself to building the character of anyone who would take part in judo. There was a cultural link, I think, at the beginning. Later, because of his ability to speak English, and because of his contacts, he was able to come into contact with many educators, not only in Great Britain and the U.S., but also throughout the world.

How often did he come to the United States, and how was his art received?

He came, I think, about two or three times to the United States. The people here received judo fairly well, but in the beginning they thought of it as a curiosity rather than something that would be a physical culture, or something that would help in the development of human beings.

Dr. Kano did meet with one person that I think greatly influenced him, although not very much is written about it. That was John Dewey, our American educator. John Dewey, if you had studied him, was a pragmatist. I think because of John Dewey and his ideas that there were microcosms in various activities and that those activities, when expanded, could lead to a better human being, a better person. That's part of the format that Jigaro Kano took and incorporated into judo.

I had heard that it was Dewey's ideas were the influence behind Kano's three maxims of judo.

It's a possibility that Dr. Kano was influenced by Dewey when devising his three maxims. The first maxim is "self-perfection." This means that you should always try to better yourself in every way. The second maxim is "mutual welfare and benefit." Competition breeds excellence. It takes two to compete. The third maxim was one of the ways of getting there. And that was that of "maximum efficiency with minimum effort." What that means is that you don't do the least amount, but that you do the least amount necessary to do the most amount of work. So you want to be as economical as possible.

I think you will find that these three precepts or maxims are within the education system of today. Most certainly John Dewey was a proponent of that. And I think there are letters to show that while John Dewey was here in the United States, he and Kano had sent letters back and forth. Those three ideas are found within any civilized society that tries to raise the level of the citizens of their country.

Sometimes, though, I think this concept becomes a conflict because how can you have self-perfection when in certain instances you have to better another person or beat another person? But yet I think competition breeds excellence, and that would be one answer. The other answer Dr. Kano had presented was that if there is a choice to be made, if you expand that idea of self-perfection versus mutual welfare and benefit, that you would probably find yourself to be more selfish in nature. Yet, if you expand that idea to a greater degree; let's say that the United States wants to cooperate with another country. Well, if you can't cooperate, what do you do? You revert back to being a U.S. citizen, and you do the best for the U.S. If you can do something beyond that point that would contribute to both societies, then you would most certainly do that.

Was such a pragmatic philosophical base common in Japanese martial arts at that time, or did this set Dr. Kano apart from the mainstream?

No. Dr. Kano's three maxims made judo a unique activity because it now had a philosophy rather than just movement. And Kano felt that there were two kinds of judo: small judo and large judo. Small judo would be just the activity itself. But if you could use the concepts that you found within judo and apply them to your everyday life, than that would be termed as large judo. Large judo is using judo as a microcosm, using judo as a stepping stone or place where you can learn valuable lessons. For example, if you were attempting to accomplish a goal such as perfecting a throw through hard work, that in the trying there is this promise of something at the end. For many of us in judo, I think it is probably a gold medal or trophy or some type of reward. Likewise, in society the same kind of concept applies: if you work hard you'll get somewhere.

It seems that large judo, as it were, crosses over to many Martial Arts Talk in that they are character-building activities.

The other thing that I think Dr. Kano did not foresee, that I think probably today is most prevalent, is the idea that judo is an activity that takes up time; time in which, whereas it is a positive activity, it takes up the time of a growing child who needs that kind of influence to better himself and stay out of trouble. If a child is in the dojo, he is not out in the streets. As one of my friends who is a world champion, she said that judo is probably the "physics of drug control." Her name is Ann Marie Roussy.

That's an interesting idea. How so?

When I asked her what she meant by that, she said: "Well, matter cannot be in two places at one time. So if your child is in the dojo, he or she can't be out on the street." So, those kinds of concepts are important in the development of a person, and most certainly Dr. Kano's idea of judo is that while being challenging, while being a sport, while being an activity that people can enjoy and feel some pride and ability to overcome other people, and do it in a nice way, that he provided that avenue as well as the philosophy. He provided all kinds of things. And judo is an activity that once most people get into it, it becomes a positive, lifelong addiction.

At this time, was there a noticeable difference in curricula of jujutsu and judo, or was Dr. Kano teaching jujutsu but calling it judo?

Judo was actually founded in 1882. Now before that time, I think around 1880, Japan didn't have a formalized public education system. And I don't think that if they did they had physical education as a curriculum. What Dr. Kano did was that he instilled judo as part of the curriculum at a later date. At that time, however, his idea while he was at university—and he was about twenty-two years old when he founded judo—was probably what judo would be like if he got it into the police system as a method of control and a method of physical culture, as a method of making people strong. There was then this big tournament in which they had many of the jujutsu schools as entrants and judo prevailed over the top schools of the time that were competing at the Imperial Police Station. They were competing, in a sense, to see who would get the contract to teach the police department. Judo won out.

Do you think there was one outstanding factor that led to judo's ability

to stand out?

I think probably the one big factor in helping judo to win out was the idea of *randori*. It is a little bit different in *randori*, which is like sparring, as opposed to *kata*, which is what most of the jujutsu school were—*kata* based. So judo has this free-flowing energy, whereas everybody else had to kind of rely on their *kata* which didn't quite prepare them for the unexpected movements of people that were really trying to get at them.

Was *randori* something that Dr. Kano initiated, or was this type of free-flow training already occurring in Japanese arts at that time?

I really don't know if it was or not. I do think that the big factor was the use of *randori* in judo.

I have read in various places that there was a shift in judo at some point that lead Dr. Kano to then refer to it as "modern judo." However, judo in and of itself is a modern or contemporary Japanese martial way and sport.

I am not quite sure about that. I think at different eras there have been different shifts in judo; great shifts where things happened. Probably the big thing that Dr. Kano did was that he placed a big emphasis on *ukemi*. *Ukemi* is the art of falling, which enables practitioners of judo to fall without getting hurt. Whereas in some jujutsu schools, you learned how to fall just as a result of working out in that art. But Dr. Kano made an art and science out of falling. The other thing was this *randori* business where he had free sparring. Dr. Kano was an eclectic, so he kind of selected for judo all of the things that could be easily and quickly executed. So he just selected what he thought were the best techniques from every school; the safest ones that he possibly could find without compromising the strength of the art.

You couldn't do *randori* in the original format where there was training called *atemi-waza*, or hitting techniques. Kano had those techniques, in the form of kata, but he didn't go into the boxing aspect of them. But he did have these *atemi-waza* type techniques which may have been taken from different jujutsu schools that relied on punching and hitting, and in some instances kicking.

However, it may have been influenced by Gichin Funakoshi, whom he was also well aquainted with. So those were included. In the end, Dr. Kano emphasized the throwing arts more than the grappling arts or boxing.

Aren't the *atemi-waza* taught as *kata* in judo?
I don't think that there is a *kata* right now.

Really? While I was observing judo classes at the Kodokan in Suidobashi, Tokyo last year, I saw some elderly *sensei* there practicing defenses against a gun attack. They performed the same routine over and over in a *kata*-like fashion.
Oh yes, they have guns and knife defenses. That is goshinho, forms of self-defense.

So Dr. Kano didn't do away with *kata*. As is also evidenced by the fact that he created the essential "seven *kata* of judo."
Yes, but what he did have that was different was *randori*. That gave him quite an advantage. *Kata*, however, was used to preserve certain concepts and ideas and is still practiced today.

At that time, judo mainly emphasized throwing and not grappling. What caused the art to shift, once again, into incorporating or emphasizing grappling techniques?
In the earlier phases of competition judo, not too much was done in the area of matwork. I think it is only now that the European *judoka* is in the picture that matwork has become an important part of judo. That's mainly because Japanese *judoka* were not doing matwork. If you practice something that the Japanese are not doing, you are going to be better than them and possibly win in tournaments. Also, the rules that apply are more subjective in throws than grappling, that are determined by time or submission.

It is commonly believed that what we know of today as a colored-belt ranking structure in the martial arts was in fact developed and instituted

by Dr. Kano. When and why did he develop such a system of rewards?

I don't really know the date that he started using a belt system. You know, I had thought that judo was the originator of that, but I don't think it was. I now think that there were other arts that had ranking available, but most certainly judo is the one that made it famous. It had this black belt, which was to exemplify excellence. And I don't know exactly how the evolution of it came about. In thinking of it, it was probably that there was somebody working out with a white belt and over time, and not washing it, it started to turn brown. And after a while it got black and dirty. So, maybe they decided that it was a pretty good idea, let's make a progression of colored belts from white to brown to black to show that black was the darkest color after having practiced for a long period of time. Although, that's just conjecture and not historical in nature.

At what point did Dr. Kano begin using the various *dan* levels for the black belt?

I am not really sure when, but I think he had that right from the beginning. Kendo had a *dan* level as well but did not use a belt to denote its rank. As far as changing colors of belts goes, that is something that Dr. Kano may have invented. The main three belts, because he was dealing with adults and not with children, were the white, brown, and black belts. Kendo would give *dans* by just naming a level. *Dan* means level in Japanese, so *shodan* means first level, and *nidan* means second level, and so on. I think he may have taken that concept from kendo.

The Kodokan building in Tokyo is quite large and impressive. When did Dr. Kano found the Kodokan, and why did he feel he needed such a large place?

Dr. Kano founded the Kodokan actually in 1882. Its origination was in a Buddhist temple, actually. It started out with, I think, something like nine *tatami* mats; it was a nine *tatami* area. And having lived in Tokyo, Mark, you know how small that is. When I was living in Tokyo, I had a six *tatami* room and it was barely big enough to get air in there!

I didn't know that. When did it move to its current location?

I think it had about four or five different moves. Sometime after World War II, the one that became the more famous one that everybody knew about, was at Suidobashi. That one was probably a couple of years after the war was ended, because the Japanese government was prohibited from the practice of any martial arts at that time. Right after that, the next biggest one was the Kodokan where it stands now. Except that now they rent out the bottom floor to a bank. They have some kind of a deal where the bank pays for part of it and the Kodokan pays for part of it. Of course land being what it is in Tokyo, they made a trade off and I think they did very well.

It is a well-known fact that American President Theodore Roosevelt practiced judo. Was he a student of Jigaro Kano?

No. He may have seen Jigaro Kano, he may have met Jigaro Kano, but I think the person that really went there to teach Roosevelt was Yoshiaki Yamashita. This was about 1906 or 1907.

How and when did you begin your journey in judo?

My first introduction to judo was somewhere around 1952. That was with my stepfather, Dan Oka, who said to me that he was going to take me somewhere. I went into this temple, which is now the Japanese-American Museum in Los Angeles. Although they are now building a new location for the museum, the place where it currently stands used to be a Buddhist church called Nishihongangi. At that temple they had a judo tournament going on. I didn't know exactly what it was at the time, but he explained to me that he had practiced it before when he was young. And we saw these people going down the isle. It was very impressive and it kind of stuck in my mind that I would like to try something like that. In fact, when we got home I kind of challenged him; he promptly showed me the floor. I was just a kid, so he was throwing me all over the hardwood floor, on which I kind of landed my heels several times.

I took to that because, of course, I was living in East Los Angeles at that time. You need some kind of physical ability if you live in East LA. My stepfather started teaching me. I started to get better and better and just took a liking to judo.

You started judo in 1952 with your stepfather. When did you first begin serious training at an established dojo?

Actually, my first official dojo I went to wasn't until 1953. It was Sen Shin Dojo, which is still around but not very strong now. This is in East Los Angeles.

When did Jigaro Kano pass away?

1939. He was returning to Japan from the States and looking forward to having the Olympics in Japan. I think he was a little heartbroken because of things that were going on in Japan at the time.

What kind of things are you referring to? Internal disputes within judo or political turmoil?

Well, as you know, Japan had at that time decided to sign a pact with Germany, rather than the United States. They also had some problems in Southeast Asia. As you know, Japan is an island nation. They don't have any natural resources, so they were trying to expand and use the resources of the neighboring countries, like Manchuria, which they called Manchukuo, which they kind of annexed in a sense. They were also into parts of Korea and parts of Indo-China. Those areas had strategic material in them that the United States really didn't want any other countries to have. I think Roosevelt probably put the stop on natural resources from the United States that were going over to Japan, such as iron—mostly junk iron and salvaged iron—and also a lot of the oil. Japan knew that it only had about a year or two of reserve of fuel oil so they relied heavily on the United States for that. So, if they decided to go to war they had to have other resources and so they started to expand into other parts of Asia.

What was the effect of all of this on judo, if any?

Well, this aggravated the situation for Dr. Kano, who was kind of trying to make judo a worldwide sport, hoping that it would be in the 1940 Olympics. However, it did not happen.

Judo is now a well-known and popular Olympic sport. In what years did judo become a demonstration sport and an official Olympic game, respectively?

The first time was in 1964 in Japan. Once any sport is accepted, it stays out the following Olympics and goes in on the following games after that. So they have kind of a waiting period of about eight years before they are a full-blown sport.

The late Donn F. Draeger was the first Westerner to achieve the rank of fifth dan in judo. I had heard that he was as a sort of liaison for foreigners coming to Japan to train at the Kodokan.

Well, he wasn't actually a liaison, but it was certainly a good thing that he was there. He would help out with people wanting to know what it was they needed to do. I had a lot of respect for him, and he most certainly helped me out considerably.

He was responsible for writing quite a number of books on judo.

Yes, and he also introduced weight training to Mr. Inokuma, first of all. He received some acclaim from having taught Mr. Inokuma weight training. Mr. Inokuma credits Donn Draeger as having helped him to have the strength that most other judo players may not have had. No one else was really weight training at that time.

Has weight training become an accepted part of judo training today?

It has become an accepted idea now. I think there are other things that go on besides weight training. They have some other types of activities as well now, though weight training does play a part.

It is understood that once a cultural artefact, such as judo, is introduced into another country or culture it often changes to meet the demands of that culture or environment. How has judo developed differently in Japan, Europe, and the United States?

Japan's model has always been that of technique. They believe that it is the technique that is going to save the day. American judo has pretty much followed the Japanese model. But we have people within the United States now that are capable of following not only the Japanese model of techniques but the European model of gamesmanship. Therein lies the difference. Europeans rely more on gamesmanship, although they do have the ability to have techniques, they do place an emphasis on a little bit more strength, they practice a little bit more as far as specificity of movements and physical conditioning, which also includes running. Whereas Japan primarily has been geared toward having the person just work out, which, in their eyes, is going to be good enough.

What do you mean exactly when you are referring to the European gamesmanship model?

The Europeans, they are thinking in terms of gamesmanship. They train scientifically by dividing up the minutes, and there are four minutes in every match. So they divide up the minutes and count the number of attacks that they execute during each minute, how to take a different grip or release a grip so that the Japanese can't get hold of them, or to get them where they are least expecting it, which would be on the mat. They use the rules to their advantage. Those kinds of things are what make European judo a lot different than Japanese judo.

You mean that after all this time the United States hasn't been able to develop its own model? Why do you think there has been such a resistance to do so and to remain with the Japanese model?

Yes, the United States has not developed its own model. But that is mainly because the people that are here were taught by the Japanese. You talk to some of the old timers here and ask them what rank are they, and they invariantly like to say, "I'm a Kodokan fifth *dan.*" They like to insert the word Kodokan in there. Whereas now every country has the ability to elevate and utilize their own rank system by international charter.

What are some of the better judo associations in the United States?

Well, I think probably there are only three that are here in the United States. The first one is United States Judo Incorporated (USJI), which is the parent organization. They have the contract to get into international competition and represent the United States. So any team that goes abroad has to check with United States Judo Incorporated, whose head offices are at the Olympic Training Center in Colorado Springs, Colorado.

The next organization is the traditional organization, which is called United States Judo Federation (USJF), which is the one I am aligned with. The USJF has these clusters of judo organizations called Yudansha-kai. They function within a specific locality. For example, Nunka Yudansha-kai is located in the Los Angeles basin; Hokka would be in the San Francisco area; and so on. They are all over the place.

The United States Judo Association (USJA) is the newest judo organization in the United States. They function on a club basis. They have their national office in Colorado Springs, everything else revolves around the clubs. So the club has a direct access to the central office, whereas the USJF has this Yudansha-kai system where they have a local organization that serves all the local members, and they pay into the national organization.

The USJI has four levels of membership. The first one is called A membership, which is comprised of the two judo organizations, the USJF and the USJA. The B membership is composed of the state organizations, and each state that applies and has a charter and registers with the state can get membership within the B category. Although the structure of the state organizations have equal footing and votes as the USJF and USJA when we meet biannually. They also have other types of memberships like honorary members who get inducted, and also C class members which include the YMCA, Boys Club, the Marines, and so on.

The first generation instructors received their rank from the Kodokan, do they have to filter the rank they give their students through one of the U.S. organizations, or can they go directly through the Kodokan?

They have to go through the Kodokan Committee, which is controlled by Mr. Yonezuka in New Jersey. All applications go through him and they apply to the Kodokan for acceptance. But this is very expensive, so most of the people in the United States are now going toward the U.S. certification, which is being awarded through the three organizations I mentioned.

Are the basic requirements for rank promotion the same in the United States and Japan?

They were different up until this past meeting and now they decided that they are going to be the same. However, implementation is different than an agreement. The idea is there and I think that over a period of time they will evolve into one promotion system.

Do the judo schools here in the United States teach the judo *kata*, the *atemi-waza*, and the like, or do they focus on the competitive sport aspect of the art?

I think there are certain requirements depending on the organization. For the United States Judo Federation, they require the ability to do *nagano kata* and *kata meno kata* to proceed beyond the *nidan* level. Although it doesn't always follow that everybody knows them.

What are some of the developments in international judo competition?

There are a lot of developments in international competitions. I think that what the United States needs to do is to study a little bit more of the European model, probably devise a system that can be truly called the American model. We haven't done that yet. We haven't figured out quite what this new judo is like. Everything is in constant change and the changes are in small increments. Often they are so small that people don't see the difference, and everybody thinks that judo is the same. They also think that judo is not as strong as it was in the old days. In actuality, however, I think it is actually stronger than it used to be.

Well, you know how people tend to dwell in nostalgia and think that things were always better in the "old days."

Well, I don't think that holds true for judo.

How did such notable American judo instructors such as Gene LeBelle and Willy Kahill get their start in the art?

Gene is a good friend of mine and was one of my instructors. He learned basically here in Southern California and was going to Hollywood Dojo, which still exists today, although not in the same location. Willy Kahill did his judo in Northern California and he's one of the big names in judo. He was one of the Olympic coaches and did very well.

How about Mike Swain, our multi-time judo Olympian?

Mike Swain was a five-time Olympian and one of the best competitors that the U.S. has produced. He was the second world champion that the United States produced. The first was Ann Marie Burns; Ann Marie Roussey is her name now. Mike was just a very capable person. Right now he sells a lot of judo mats and equipment and is trying to get judo on a different level, as a professional sport. He is doing a marvelous job bringing judo to the front and presenting it to the public; something that was sorely needed. And traditionalists sometimes criticize the avenue that he is taking because it kind of veers away from what we consider to be normal judo, but if you consider the rules we have today and make a comparison to what judo was in the forties to what it is at the close of the nineties, they are two different things. The activity has really changed a lot. So who are traditionalists to criticize? At least he's popularizing judo.

BILL WALLACE
The History of Martial Sports in America

Bill Wallace retired as the undefeated PKA middleweight karate champion in June of 1980. His record included twenty consecutive wins, eleven by knockout. Prior to entering full-contact karate competition in 1974, Wallace was rated three times by Black Belt *magazine as the top fighter in the country, and had won virtually every major tournament title. Among his successes were winning the U.S. Championships three times, the USKA Grand Nationals three times, and the Top Ten Nationals twice.*

For several years, Wallace taught judo, wrestling, and weight training at Memphis State University, the institution from which he earned his masters degree. In addition to his two books on martial art stretching and kicking, and his series of instructional videotapes, Wallace has authored a college text-book on karate and kinesiology.

150

**Since your competitive career basically began as martial arts competi-
tion in the United States was developing, why don't we use that time
period as a starting point. When did you begin your competitive martial
arts career?**

I started competing in 1966, in San Bernardino, California.

**I remember reading an article of yours, and this is going way back,
where you mentioned how you and a buddy of yours used to drive from
Point A to Point B and drop in on as many karate schools as you could
find for impromptu sparring.**

It was probably with my best friend I ever had in karate, Glen
Keedey. He's from Anderson, Indiana. It was when I was going to
school at Ball State University in 1967. I met Glen that Christmas
season and we just hit it off because I was going to school in
Muncie, Indiana, which is about fifteen miles from Anderson. And
Glen had just opened up a dojo and we just started going over
there and training with each other. He was a very, very good competitor. He wasn't real fast or strong, but he was really, really
sneaky. We had an absolute ball together.

**So what were the first major tournaments in the United States that you
competed in?**

The first major tournament that I fought in was the USKA
International. It was sponsored by the United States Karate
Association. But the very first tournament I fought in was the
Mid-East Grand Nationals, held in Lexington, Kentucky in 1968.
Victor Moore was there, Glen Keedey was there, I was there, Artie
Simmons was there. These are guys who were really good and well-
known back in the sixties. And, luckily, I won the grand championship. It was the first really big tournament I fought in and it was
really nice because I had only fought out on the West Coast before
that. It was a good tournament. The fighting was different, they
had allowed groin kicks and light face contact.

Weren't the tournaments of that time using no-contact rules?

No, no. Noncontact tournaments started around 1971. Pat
Johnson kind of tried to initiate that kind of tournament. These

tournaments were light-contact, meaning that if you didn't knock your opponent out and if you didn't cause blood, you got the point.

This is what you were training for in the sixties?

Yes. In the Sixties, contact was not a problem as lawsuits weren't a rampage. But light contact to the face, which meant a touch—as long as you didn't hit the guy hard, or cause blood or swelling, you got the point. And the body, most of us at the time threw our techniques there as hard as we could. We did this simply because we knew that if we only touched our opponent's body, at the same time he could go over the top and strike us. So we threw pretty hard to the body just so it made a nice noise. It would make a thump that the judges could hear and you would score.

At this time, and even in many light-contact tournaments today, the premise for scoring a point is based on the one-shot, one-kill idea.

Yes. See that still, even to this day, is supposed to be the rule. You know, a killing or maiming technique pulled short of actual contact is supposed to be the rule. It is often not any more, as I see people getting points for flipping their hand at a guy with no focus or power or intent.

These tournaments are certainly not very realistic.

Yes, I think it sucks. The thing of it is, back when we were fighting in the sixties—and this is just our ideas in the sixties—it had to be a hard shot and not a glancing shot to score a point. If a kick slipped off your opponent, there was no point awarded. If a punch slipped off, it was not a point. At that time, we didn't call a backfist to the body a point. You didn't call ridgehands to the body a point. But if you delivered and made contact with a good, solid, hard shot, it was called a point.

What were some of the martial arts styles that were found competing at that time?

Mostly Shotokan, Goju-ryu, Shorin-ryu. You know, Japanese and Okinawan styles. There was some kung-fu. Well, not really kung-fu so much as in the sixties; Al Dacascos was competing and doing a style called kajukenbo. You also had the kempo system because of Ed Parker out here in California. At that time, in the mid-sixties, there was not too much taekwondo as it was just starting to become popular.

What style is your martial arts background in?
Shorin-ryu. Joe Lewis and I are in the same system.

That's interesting because your fighting styles are so completely different. Did the two of you train together in Okinawa?
No. He was there a year-and-a-half before I was. I was stationed in the Air Force there in 1966 and 1967.

Where in Okinawa and under whom did you study karate?
Kadena Air Base in Naha. I studied under Eizo Shimabuku.

You have become famous for your three kicks. When you were competing in the sixties, were you using the entire arsenal of Shorin-ryu techniques?
No. You see, I hurt my knee before that in judo. I started martial arts training in 1963 when I joined the service. Since I was a wrestler before that, and the Air Force didn't have a wrestling team, I joined their judo team. I did very good against the judo instructor because every time he came in for a throw I would just pick him up and throw him down and start to wrestle him.

And then I hurt my right knee really bad in 1966 during judo practice. So that took care of my judo career. So I started karate. That's when I started kicking with my left leg and fighting left side forward.

In that karate is an art that relies on mobility and balance stability, didn't you find your injured knee to be a major obstacle?
No, it wasn't. Ironically enough, because I was in a cast all the way from my ankle to my hip, when I started karate training I couldn't kick with the right leg at all. So when the instructors had the students do 15,000 kicks with their right leg and then 15,000

kicks with their left leg, since I was injured they just kept me left side forward. So I threw 30,000 kicks with my left leg when everyone else only did 15,000 on each leg. That kind of helped me develop power and stamina in my left leg.

You are also quite well known for your flexibility. In fact, you have written a book on stretching and kicking, and you teach seminars all over the world on flexibility training. Were you naturally flexible, or is that something that you developed over the years?

Well, I was always fairly flexible. A little bit because as a wrestler I was a leg wrestler, a scissors man. I had pretty good control with my legs, but I didn't really have that much flexibility. I mean, I could kick to the head without a problem. But as I started to fight and develop my training, I just worked more with the flexibility. Shorin-ryu, and the Okinawan systems in general, doesn't have a kick above the stomach. All their kicks are aimed at the stomach and below. Hands are high and feet are low.

You said that your Shorin-ryu teacher was Shimabuku Sensei, but I thought that he was the founder of Isshin-ryu.

No, Tatsuo Shimabuku is Isshin-ryu; Eizo Shimabuku is Shorin-ryu.

Oh, okay. When you returned to the United States from Okinawa and started competing in the point martial arts tournaments, what were some of the other big ones? Wasn't Ed Parker's tournament also going on?

I never fought in Ed Parker's Long Beach Internationals. I watched it in 1967, but I never did compete in it. The USKA Nationals, the U.S. Championships in Dallas, Texas were the two main and largest tournaments I fought in during the sixties. And of course the Mid-East Nationals, which they only had that one year.

When kicking-based styles like taekwondo and tangsoodo and people like Chuck Norris came on the scene, how did that affect what everyone was doing at the time?

It affected the hard fighters because as they came in on an opponent to try and punch him, they were countered with a spinning back kick. They scored with those kicks at the time because they were fast and none of us had seen them before. Also, you had the guys who were really good punchers who could get inside on the kickers and hit them in a straight line when they were launching their circular kicks. So, along with the kickers you had guys like Tony Tulleners who could step inside real fast and counter the kickers.

Like everything, human beings are good at adapting, so we learned to develop and throw the reverse punch. And other guys learned to counter and work with the spinning back kick and throw it themselves.

What we see as a result of these early mixed martial arts tournaments is Americans diverting from their learned karate traditions and developing their own styles.

Oh, yeah. That's one hundred percent correct. Even in Nishiyama's karate system and his All American Karate Federation, they use high roundhouse kicks to the head now, front leg kicking techniques, backfists, spinning kicks. He was even featured on the cover of *Black Belt* magazine, which is something he never allowed before.

I find it interesting that while the practitioners of this time were busy revolutionizing their fighting techniques, they were still holding fast to forms practice.

Yes, and forms competition at that time still wasn't as good as the fighting aspect. They were into forms, but only the traditional forms. At the tournaments, forms competition was basically divided into three categories: Korean forms, Japanese forms, and Chinese forms. There were no open forms or musical forms divisions at that time. And there was no wushu.

What do you think about these new musical forms and the modern wushu forms?

Well, you know, it looks good because there is a lot of gymnastics. All I know is that a lot of times in some of them there is very little striking.

Actually, there are very little real martial arts techniques being performed in these types of forms.

I agree. You have gymnasts and acrobats, moving all over the place. But you know, it's pretty to watch. I don't know about the effectiveness of it because I was a fighter and don't know much about their format. I mean, I had to do the traditional forms for my ranking and so forth, but that's all. But they serve their purpose because, well, have you been to tournaments lately?

No, not really. I go to a few here and there, but generally only stay for an hour or so. To be honest, I get bored since I rarely see true fighting techniques.

The last event of the tournaments used to be the grand championship fighting. Now the last event is the grand championship forms. The entire focus has changed. Because of martial arts in films and on television, a lot of people think that if they win a grand championship they will automatically become an international movie star. I've talked with a lot of people who say their main purpose in entering tournaments is so somebody will see them and maybe decide to make them the next Jackie Chan or Chuck Norris or Bruce Lee.

When you developed your three lead-leg kicks, why did you choose roundhouse, side, and hook kicks? Couldn't you have as easily developed a front kick or ax kick?

No, I had no choice. You see, my right knee at the time, and still to this day, is injured to where I can't extend it. If I do extend it, there is a very good chance that it will come out of joint. This means that I also can't push off of my right leg. So, if I am standing left side back and I throw a front kick and I drive forward, that means I have to push off with the right leg. This is something that I can't do. So as long as I stood left side forward, I could bring my left leg up and do either a side kick, roundhouse kick, or hook kick— and all from the same chamber position, since I don't have to pivot.

I remember reading an article on you in *Sports Illustrated* around fifteen years ago that featured your kicks. I thought it was great that they fea-

tured a karate guy in the magazine. I remember thinking at the time that here is a guy who only has three kicks and is an undefeated champion, while there are people with a million techniques who can't seem to pull it all together.

Yes, but those three kicks work for me really, really well.

Exactly. And also if you look at Joe Lewis, who only has a side kick, back-fist, and reverse punch, and he also became a champion.

Right. He really worked and mastered those techniques. Joe could cut you in half with his side kick.

You guys are proof positive of the saying that a few techniques mastered are better than a thousand half learned.

Yeah, and that's why there are so many techniques in the martial arts. Each individual is different and has to find out what works best for them. I mean, the reason I don't throw a reverse punch is simply because I can't pivot on my right leg to face my opponent.

So why was it that when you entered full-contact kickboxing you were able to throw hooks? I recall you TKO'd Joe Corley with a hook to the body during one of your comeback fights in the eighties.

Well, that was my old fun thing.

Moving on now to the shift from point tournaments to full-contact, didn't you and Joe Lewis and Jeff Smith become the first champions of kickbox-ing in your respective weight divisions?

Well, you see, that fight you are talking about wasn't really the first one. The first full-contact competition in the United States was in 1968, when they had a tournament down in San Antonio, Texas. It was not no-holds-barred, but it was hard contact.

Similar to the Sabaki Challenge?

Yeah. I think Jim Harrison, Victor Moore, Fred Wren, Joe Lewis, Ed Daniels, and Skipper Mullins were all in the tourna-ment. These were all hard guys, and that was basically the first full-contact tournament—although they didn't bill it as such.

So we're talking here about hard-contact karate without pads?

Yes, this was before pads. Then the first legitimate or official full-contact tournament was held in Los Angeles in 1970. Joe Lewis did a fight with Greg Baines, who he knocked out in the second round. The actual full-contact tournaments and the association started in 1974.

Was that the Professional Karate Association or PKA?

Yes, right.

Unlike what we have come to know as kickboxing, at that time you guys were wearing those little safe-t chop gloves and not boxing gloves.

Well, the first three events I fought in 1974, 1975, and early 1976, we wore karate safe-t pads. Today, the safe-t kicks are still worn. After June of 1976 they changed it to boxing gloves.

Was that because you were doing more head punching?

No. They switched to boxing gloves because the safe-t punch pads kept coming off.

You know, at first we did everything we could do to keep full-contact karate from looking like boxing. That is why we initially fought on a platform rather than in a ring. That's why the referee wore a karate gi. At the time, we tried to do a lot of kicking and to wear the *gi* pants and black belts. Then all of a sudden, for some silly reason, the PKA decided to make it look like boxing. They then put us in boxing gloves and into a ring.

Is that when they stopped calling it "full-contact karate" and coined the term "kickboxing"?

Yes, I think so.

Apparently this completely altered the sport. What we see today are boxers who learn a few kicks and become kickboxing champions. After all, all they have to do is throw a minimum of eight kicks per round and then box.

Right. And they can be front kicks, too. See, that's what basically happened in 1975. 1974 was good because it was all karate

people. But then in 1975 and 1976 some not-so-great boxers realized that they could make it in kickboxing. So what happened was
that they learned a front kick, side kick, and roundhouse kick so
they could flick a couple kicks out there, but they still had the jabs,
the hooks, the right hand, and the endurance. Whereas with karate
people, the first thing we are taught is how to control our techniques. Now all of a sudden, we had to learn how to hit hard and
take a hard shot. All a boxer had to do was learn a few simple
kicks. The boxer was quick to realize that the kicks were aimed at
the same spots as boxing punches, and so they didn't have to
change their defensive strategy or hand position or anything. It was
quite easy for them.

**What was the impetus behind your decision to one day leave point
karate and begin full-contact?**

Mike Anderson and Joe Lewis decided in 1974 that they were
going to try this. They then got some money people behind it. Joe
and Mike called me up in April of 1974 and said they had picked
me for their team. And I said, great, where are we going to fight?
And they said Germany and that we were going to fight full-contact. I said, what? And they said we were going to fight full-contact
in Germany and try to knock each other out. I told them to go to
hell. I said point karate is fun and I don't want it to be hard. I told
them I didn't want to do it. As a point fighter, I was known to
score a point and get the hell out of there. So, I didn't want to play
the game of machismo, and all that. I also didn't think it would
catch on at first. But they talked me into it and we went over to
Germany and then came back. We had the fights on September
14, 1974. We put full-contact karate on the map.

How many years did you fight in the full-contact arena?

Six years. I retired in June of 1980.

And you retired undefeated?

Yeah, I got lucky.

I think skill had something to do with it. Who was your toughest opponent?

Every one of them. It's like with boxers, you have to train for every fight. If you don't train the correct way for every fight you are going to have a lot of trouble. Everybody that I fought had the ability to knock you out, so I had to train accordingly. I never thought one opponent was going to be easier than another. If someone hits you in the right spot and at the right time you are going to go down. Luckily for me, I was always feeling good in the ring.

I used to watch you fight and wondered how it was that you were fighting full-contact and always, without missing a beat, had a big smile on your face.

Well, yeah, but that was because I was feeling good and was having a good time. I mean, I knew several guys that because the fights were being broadcast on television, even though they had the flu or a cold, still fought. Ernie Hart from St. Louis, Missouri was one of those guys. He fought Bobby Ryan and had the flu and was in bed for the whole day one time, but because the fight was television he got up at night and fought his fight. He couldn't cancel the fight, so he lost the title.

During the eighties, kickboxing seemed to have picked up steam. It was televised frequently and gyms opened up and the magazines covered it. So why do you think its popularity waned?

Yeah, it was big there in the eighties for a while. I think what happened is that we found out it was easier to punch for five or ten rounds than it was to kick. And all those jump flying kicks were discarded.

I mean, look at the movies and you'll see martial artists jumping and flying and kicking through the air. In martial arts fight scenes who cares about the punching? All you see is a guy jump up and do a spinning back kick and knock a guy out. Van Damme's movies are a perfect example of this. The audience then talks about that amazing kick. So the fans of these films decide to go to a kickboxing match to see the competitors kill each other like in the movies. They're disappointed first when they see boxing and only a few kicks. But the worst thing about it is that you hear the corner man yelling to his fighter that after three more kicks he can just punch his opponent.

So think about it. If I am a boxing fan watching this, why wouldn't I just go and watch boxing to see better punchers? If I am a karate fan watching this I get the impression that if this is what is happening, boxing must be more effective.

The athletes we had fighting, granted they were good fighters, but they didn't do what the fans wanted them to do. People watch people do things that they themselves can't do. You watch basketball because you can see this guy who is 6'9" dunk the ball, where you at 5'7" can't even touch the net. Why do people like to watch gymnastics? To see the double somersault over the bars that they can't do. The same goes for ice-skating where they televise the freestyle and not the figure skating part. But anybody can throw a punch and what the fans came out to see in kickboxing—the spinning and jumping kicks—wasn't happening anymore.

Another thing is that we didn't have any heroes in kickboxing. It's kind of ironic and I don't want it to sound like false humility, but I have been retired from fighting for eighteen years and I am still considered the best kicker. Something has kind of got to be wrong with that.

Right. Everyone still talks about you, Joe Lewis, Benny Urquidez, Paul Vizzio, and Don Wilson. I don't think I could personally name five of the leading kickboxers today. When I was young I used to think that when I grew up I wanted to be Benny one week, Don the next. But now, as you said, unlike Tyson and De La Jolla in boxing, there are no heroes in kickboxing.

Right. You see, all of the guys you just mentioned, our roots were in martial arts. But after we retired, a lot of the new guys would go right out and learn how to box and how to kick and put it together themselves. Today's kickboxers have little real martial arts background.

This really came into focus with me in 1988 when I moved out to Chicago to work at the Degerberg Academy.

Okay, I know Fred Degerberg; we go way back.

At his academy, aside from straight martial arts, they train amateur kick-boxers. But what I saw was boxing oriented guys learning to throw and combine a few kicks. It was no longer full-contact martial arts, but boxing with kicks. It was kind of a let down for me, in a way.

Right. That's what people were doing all over in the sport. And you wonder why nobody wants to watch it anymore. There are no heroes. The only guy out there fighting now that I even know is Rick Roufus, and he throws maybe four or five kicks high. He works a lot of leg kicks, though. Now don't misunderstand me, low kicks are very powerful, very devastating. But I don't think Americans like them. They look like cheap shots. I mean, a three-year-old can kick you in the leg and you can't block it.

We saw a shift into using leg kicks in American kickboxing with the emergence of the World Kickboxing Association or WKA.

The WKA was the first to allow the leg kicks. That's just one of those things where, while they are very effective, you've got to point your line. I mean, how come I can kick you in the back of the leg? See, the whole purpose of kicks to the legs is to be so devastating as to knock your opponent off his feet or to injure his legs so bad that he can't kick you with them.

It's like when Jack Dempsey used to punch his opponent's arms so hard that they could barely lift them to fight or defend themselves.

Exactly. That's what Rocky Marciano used to do, too. He'd hit your arms so hard that you couldn't hold them up, then he'd knock you out. To kick me in my legs you have to come around with it, you can't come straight in. Well hold it, if you are trying to hurt my legs, why can't I take your knees out with a side kick? So, you can kick to the legs, but only in certain ways? They could never get their rules straight.

Other kickboxing styles that use leg kicks also didn't make it big here in the United States, like muay Thai or savate. I even competed in the first two North American savate championships, but the turnout and quality

of fighters was low.

And it looked like kickboxing. I like the savate uniforms.

The main problem was, I thought, that there wasn't enough trained savate competitors in North America to have championships. In essence, a bunch of karate, taekwondo, and kickboxing practitioners were given seminars in savate before the events. So, it was a savate competition that did not much resemble savate. When you see the savate competitors in France and Spain, they look awesome. I mean, people like Richard Silla are legends over there. Being a kicker yourself, what is your opinion of the savate kicks?

The kicks are a little different. The thing is, in savate they do work the side kick to the knee. Evidently they never seem to have any injuries with them. They also wear kicking shoes, so you don't have to worry about breaking your toes. As much as you don't think they do, savate people punch a lot, too. To the untrained eye savate looks the same as American kickboxing. So if there is a lack of interest in one form, there is a lack in the other.

What I find interesting about savate, at least as it is practiced in Europe, is that your points are awarded not only on your ability to connect solidly with your opponent, but in maintaining proper techniques in the delivery of the blows. They have managed to keep the art alive in the sport. This seems to be reminiscent of what you said about the early days of karate tournaments where if the kick slipped off, you didn't get the point.

Yes, the art form has not degenerated in savate yet. This is good because they are protecting it. The art is still French.

Muay Thai is another full-contact art that although it is becoming more popular in the United States, just can't seem to make it on a large scale. Why do you think that is?

The reason is that most sanctioning bodies or boxing commissions in the different states say very simply that if you are going to compete in a combative sport all striking weapons must be padded. In Thai boxing, you have the use of knee and elbow strikes and they don't even pad their feet. It is hard for Thai boxing to get sanctioning, and without the pads it is viewed by the sanctioning bodies as nothing more than a street fight.

What I find interesting about Thai boxers is that they hold their hands up very high, often above their head, exposing their midsections.

Thai boxers are known for taking a lot of punishment. They don't mind getting hit in the body and they take some really good shots there. One thing I noticed, too, is their smell during training. They cover their bodies in liniment, which I think deadens their nerves. If you look at their knees, they've got those three little holes all over them all of the time from orthoscopic surgery.

They take so much punishment that the average competitive life span of a Thai boxer is three to five years.

Exactly. After retirement they become the catcher. The catcher is the guy who stands there holding the pads and "catch" the technique thrown at him by the fighter in training. The fighter doesn't tell the catcher what he is going to throw, he's just got to catch it.

Even though Thai boxers are known to be really tough, American kickboxers like Benny Urquidez went over there and beat them. How do you figure that happened?

No, from what I was told, Benny didn't win. I mean, Benny went over there and fought these little, lightweight Thai boxers, and those little guys are mean. I can only tell you what I heard. I heard Benny went over there and fought them, but he didn't do well. He then brought some of those fighters over here. But the real Thai boxers don't come here. They stay in Thailand because they don't speak English or can't get a visa. And they are bad little dudes. Don Wilson also went over there to fight one of those Thai boxers and lost. He got kicked in the back and almost broke his back. I mean, to get kicked in the back by a round kick and almost have your back broken, and you've got to step back and admire the power of the kicks of those fighters.

We have seen an evolution in martial sports in the United States thus far in our discussion from light contact to no contact to full-contact karate

and kickboxing to the emergence of savate and Thai boxing. But we also had a resurgence of full-contact karate with the Sabaki Challenge, developed by the Seidokan karate group, an offshoot of Mas Oyama's Kyokushinkai.

The Kyokushinkai fighting has been from day one. That is how they fight. They started the Sabaki Challenge in Denver, I forget when, but I have some very good friends in Kyokushinkai in Australia and on the East Coast and that's the way they've always fought and trained. What is funny about their rules is that I can hit you anywhere with my foot and I can hit you anywhere with my hand, except the head! Now, I can kick you in the head as hard as I want, but I can't punch you there? It's just funny.

I guess punches come too fast to block and can therefore create more injury. I don't know, but I have always felt these rules to be skewed.

They even say it's too easy to hit someone with a punch, and where is the sport in that. Well, go ask a professional boxer how easy it is for him to hit his opponent in the face. It ain't easy! Look at how many punches are thrown in a boxing match that never land.

I guess it's almost a throwback to the original days of sport martial arts in this country. Competitors of your generation started out with contact rules similar to the Kyokushinkai group, later padded their hands, and ended up with kickboxing—a degenerate form of full-contact karate, as it was originally conceived.

That's exactly right.

I think one reason so-called full-contact martial arts or kickboxing never really made it big is that it debunked the myth of the one-shot kill. After all, competitors are getting hit dozens of times in the course of a bout and not being carried out of the ring.

Well, I don't know about that. The whole idea was to count points as killing or maiming blows. And certainly a lot of people in these tournaments have been knocked out with one blow.

You see, point tournaments are very arbitrary. I mean, is that backfist to the face a devastating or killing technique? Well, the first time I ever threw a backfist in a kickboxing match, I just started laughing. This guy came charging at me and I threw this backfist, and I had a glove on, and it didn't even slow him down. That's why boxing has a jab, because a jab coming straight out can stop an oncoming opponent.

In reality, though, with or without a glove on, there is no power in a backfist.

Not at all.

I think the use of the backfist is one of the biggest myths in the martial arts.

I agree, but it is a good weapon if you have a bare knuckle. With exposed knuckles, you have the back two knuckles making contact on the fleshy part of the face, which can tear skin or break a nose. You have penetration with a backfist, whereas a boxing jab is a concussion-type punch. So that's the difference in the punches. Pads against no pads.

And now you have the kicking techniques. And to make a high kick effective you have to have a certain amount of flexibility to reach that. You have to have a certain amount of speed and torque to generate that power. The problem with the kickboxers is, you know, they didn't want to go to all that trouble of working that flexibility, so they would just go ahead and throw the kick. But of they couldn't reach, or if they had to lean into it, they lost all of their power.

Nowadays, we have more interesting full-contact events from Japan like K-1, Shooto, and Pride. Unlike American kickboxing, these events seem to be generating interest and enthusiasm from the crowds.

Oh, yes. The thing of it there is, they have the money behind them and they are building heroes. Have you seen the K-1 advertising? I mean, they are really building their fighters into larger-than-life heroes. And when Rick Roufus won the last month, he became an instant star!

As traditional martial arts tournaments have evolved into full-contact events, we then saw the emergence of such no-holds-barred competitions as the Ultimate Fighting Championships. Of course, you were a ringside commentator at the very first UFC.

As I said earlier, I was a wrestler in high school and college. I understood right off the bat then when you pit a stand-up fighter against a ground fighter in competition, one hundred percent of the time the ground fighter will win. The main reason is that the stand-up fighter has no power on his back.

If you look at the fight where Mike Tyson fought Frank Bruno, these guys were just bumping each other and fell down three or four times during the match. In essence, all the ground fighter does is wait for that clinch to happen in the fight. Name one boxing match where there were no clinches. Name one kickboxing round where there was no clinch. You can't.

The other reason the ground fighter will defeat the stand-up fighter in these no-holds-barred events is that the floors are padded so much that he doesn't care if his opponent falls on him during a take-down. Also, one of the main problems at the first UFC was that they used a crash pad, which is about five or six inches thick, on the floor so the stand-up fighter could not step forward and punch or step forward and kick because of unstable grounding. It would be like if you stood on your bed and tried to throw a kick: very difficult.

What is your opinion of the whole no-holds-barred mixed-martial-arts movement.

I think they have become pretty good now for the simple reason that the stand-up fighters are learning to defend against the ground stuff, and the ground fighters are starting to do some kicking and punching. Now it is becoming, as much as I hate to say this, to a point where you are finding out what does and does not work. Remember in the old days when all of these forms came around and there were these techniques in them that you did but had no clue what they were for? I did all of the Shorin-ryu forms and on half the moves I had to guess what they might be for. You're catching a leg, you're catching a hand. Hold it! Your catching a hand? Give me a break!

The same delusion of what types of techniques work and don't are so rampant in the martial arts world. Just a glance at the aikido practitioners shows they have no clue about the real power and timing behind a legitimate punch. They think they can snatch an in-coming hand out of mid-air and execute a wrist lock and throw a guy. I'd like to see one of them grab Sugar Ray Leonard's jab and throw him.

Oh, yeah! In aikido, you have to touch me to make a technique work. In jujutsu the same holds true. That's why in this Ultimate Fighting all these wrestlers are doing really good now. They know how to do a double-leg takedown. You know, and the same thing, too, is you have these karate people who say that when the grappler drops down to do a leg takedown, they will just elbow them in the back.

But the no-holds-barred events have not shown this to happen.

Yeah. The leg takedowns come in too fast and unexpected and the stand-up fighters end up on their butt. What I do now at seminars is to put these misconceptions to the test. I tell a participant that I am going to drop down and just grab his legs. Somebody on the side is going to count to three, and on three I tell him to punch me or elbow me as hard as he can in the back of the head. They all say okay, but I tell them it will never happen. So someone counts, and on three I just jerk his legs out from under him and the guy lands dead on his butt. They always try to come up with an excuse as to why and I cut them off. I tell them times up and they are on their butt and now what are they going to do? They have no idea because they have no idea of the purposes of ground fighting. The very first martial art was grappling.

It's the most primal.

That's right. If I don't like you, I'm just going to throw you over the cliff.

Aside from your seminars, you helped spread martial sports through a series of videos.

Yeah. I did some videos for Joe Jennings of Panther Productions. They were very successful and popular, I guess.

**I thought one of the videos you made was quite interesting, almost inge-
nious. The one where you sparred the camera.**

It was great, but in the beginning I thought it was absolutely
stupid. I didn't want to do it, but Joe Jennings talked me into it.
He told me to spar the camera and tell the watcher what to throw
and then I was to defend against the technique. In the end, it was
really neat and kind of fun to do.

**You have been involved with sport martial arts in the United States from
the beginning. You have seen tournament styles come and go and fighters come and go. With all that has transpired over the past forty years,
where do you see martial sports headed?**

It is always evolving and it will always evolve. We have our little
peaks and valleys, and right now it is kind of down a little. Karate
tournaments and the like are low on participant and spectator support all over the country. I think one of the reasons is that there is
not a karate movie out there right now for kids. Jackie Chan's *Rush
Hour* was okay, but it's not really a karate movie but an action film
with fight scenes. We need a strong martial arts movie out there,
which has not been done in a long while. Also, there are so many
other things to do like soccer and baseball and video games competing for the time of children and teens. This keeps them out of
martial arts. I am confident that martial arts lessons and also martial arts competitions will have another resurgence.

**With the introduction over time of various systems into the tournament
scenes, the once traditional participants were forced to adapt and add to
their styles to stay ahead of the game. And now with the full-contact
mixed martial arts events, there is more cross-training than ever. In the
end, it has been the evolution of martial sports that has evolved a truly
American martial art heritage, vastly different than its Asian counterparts.**

Exactly, but the problem with the martial arts is that once we
Americanize it and call it American this or that, it loses something.
Why did you start martial arts, Mark?

Well, basically, I was getting picked on in school and wanted to learn

how to send the bullies flying with one strike.

Right. But think about it, if you really wanted to just learn how to fight and defend yourself you would have gone to the local YMCA and taken up boxing. But no, you wanted to go to a martial arts school to learn some mystical way where you didn't have to work very hard and could still use a devastating technique to dispel your opponent. You didn't want to learn how to throw a jab, but a jump spinning kick. You didn't want to learn how to wrestle someone, but how to throw him. You wanted something really mystical and really Oriental.

So people go into a martial arts school and see all of this Oriental terminology and paraphernalia and think it is neat. But now when you go into an "American martial arts" school you find basic techniques like three kicks, two punches, a heavy bag, and some mats. You no longer find the makiwara striking board but focus mitts. Now all the fog surrounding martial arts is gone. People are dissatisfied with this. And if you have an Oriental instructor, well, it just makes it all look good since he is short and his punches and kicks don't travel very far so they look fast. And even though he may not be any good, he sure looks like he is. All of a sudden that is going by the wayside and we are getting out of the fog and have discovered what techniques work and what techniques don't work. Ironically, this is part of what is killing the martial arts.

The mysticism is gone. As I brought up earlier, people see these no-holds-barred tournaments and have discovered that their deadly reverse punch is just not as effective as they were told it was.

You see, at one time, techniques like the reverse punch did work. The reverse punch, backfist, sidekick did work hundreds of years ago. It worked then because the people were kind of frail. Look at the Oriental people of that time: they only ate fish and vegetables and didn't lift weights and have strength trainers. So at the time, that one punch could do the job. But if you take an American now that is 6'3" and two hundred and fifteen pounds, your reverse punch is just going to bounce off. On the same token, you can't say that boxing is a good self-defense either because how many boxers will punch you without gloves on.

None. More than that, though, boxing doesn't teach self-defense skills.

That's right. Boxers aren't trained to defend against being tackled or kicked. Granted, even the jujutsu stuff with the chokes and the armbars, hey, sometime or other you are going to go down on the floor. Those techniques are good on the mat or on a carpet, but not on the concrete or stairs. If you try a double-leg takedown in the street you will tear your knees apart. And if the guy knows how to counter it with a cross-face, as most high school wrestlers do, you won't like having your face slammed down on the hard, dirty street.

So, they're all good. All martial arts are good, it's the person doing them and the situation that determines their true effectiveness. See, people don't say that too much, but it is the situation that often determines whether a technique will work or not. If you are in a phone booth or wearing tight jeans, let me see you try and use a high kick.

This leads us into another broad misconception that has evolved out of the earlier ones. In the past, people believed in the one-shot kill. Time has shown this to not happen—at least not frequently enough to make headlines. Now that we have these no-holds-barred events, the myth has returned: people again assume that because their techniques work in these tournament settings that they are the ultimate in fighting or self-defense. Again, and what is quite evident, is that no martial sport is truly suited for street fighting or actual self-defense.

Yeah, right. The jujutsu guys claim that since they are grapplers they can beat anyone anytime since most fights end upon the ground. Well, that's simply not true. Most fights don't end up on the ground, but consist of maybe one or two shots. Number one, if I am going to get in a fight with you and I know you're tough, you're not going to know when I hit you. I'm going to walk up to you and start talking to you and hit you when you don't see it coming.

If you look at the Brazilian jiu-jitsu competitors, they are taking an awful lot of shots from their opponents on the way in. They don't seem to have developed strong defensive, entry skills. If Mike Tyson or a strong street fighter hit them once, I'm sure they would go down.

Oh, yeah. This is also true for muay Thai boxers. They take an awful lot of shots to the body in the early rounds. Each round is a little more action packed then the previous, but it isn't until the last round that they go full out. The fighters pace themselves because they want to save their bodies and endurance to be able to finish out the fight.

Now with the Ultimate Fighting tournaments, there is no time limit. Who is going to let you roll around the floor for a half-hour in a real fight? Nobody. I have a friend who will pull you off me or who will stomp on you and kick you while you're on top of me. Or I may have something in my pocket that is gong to stick you pretty hard and make you get off. You know, why would you want to get that close to me in a real fight, not knowing what I have in my pocket?

Most street fights that I have experience with were multiple people on one. Grappling or ground fighting techniques simply aren't suited to such situations.

That's exactly right. And if you look at the rules of the UFC, why is it that you can break my arm, but I can't jam my finger in your eye to make you let go? The competitors in these events should be or make themselves aware that what they are training for and engaging in is a rough competition with rules and not street fighting. The arts and the techniques used must be looked at in those terms. Again, it's the situation and the individual that makes the techniques work. It is not and has never been a matter of style.

PART FOUR

MARTIAL ARTS
AND ENTERTAINMENT

ANDRE MORGAN
The Martial Arts Film Genre

Andre Morgan has been involved in the martial arts film business since its infancy. After graduating from the university, Morgan relocated to Hong Kong in 1972 and joined the Golden Harvest film studio, where he began his career as an office boy, translating subtitles from Chinese into English, and as translator on the set of Bruce Lee's Return of the Dragon.

A one-time share holder, Morgan sold out his interest in Golden Harvest in 1984 and went into business with Dixon Poon of D&B Films in Hong Kong and with Al Ruddy to form the Ruddy Morgan Agency in Beverley Hills, California. With partner Al Ruddy, Morgan has developed and produced such television series as "Walker: Texas Ranger," starring Chuck Norris, and "Martial Law," starring Sammo Hung.

Andre, you have been involved with the careers of so many top martial arts action stars, from Bruce Lee to Michael Yeoh. Could you give us a bit of a chronological history to the martial arts film genre?

Well, the martial arts films have a long history in China. Are you familiar with a Cantonese folk-hero named Wong Fei-hung?

Sure. Absolutely.

Those Wong Fei-hung movies are the outgrowth of folklore, magazines, and books. First the Cantonese film industry and subsequently Shaw Brothers then later Golden Harvest made and remade Wong Fei-hung movies over the past forty years. I look at the Wong Fei-hung movies and the stories of the Shaolin monks as the genesis of the martial arts films in Hong Kong.

The first company that was actually built on martial arts films was Golden Harvest, which started in 1970–1971. One of the actors they signed to a multi-picture contract was Jimmy Wang Yu. Jimmy Wang Yu at the time was the reigning action star of the Mandarin films. He had created the *One Armed Swordsman* classics and the *One Armed Boxer* classics. One of the first successful martial arts films that Golden Harvest produced was *Zatoichi and the One Armed Boxer.*

Zatoichi and the One Armed Boxer was the first major co-production for Golden Harvest. That film was shot in Japan.

So, how did the film originally end? I mean, the Japanese audience would want Zatoichi to win and the Chinese audience would want the One Armed Boxer to win?

They shot two endings to the movie. They shot a Japanese ending in which Zatoichi triumphed, and they shot a Hong Kong ending in which Wang Yu triumphed. And the film was very successful and certainly the bright starting point for Golden Harvest as a film company.

At the same time that Golden Harvest was looking to develop new talent is when Bruce Lee enters the picture.

When "The Green Hornet" went off the air Bruce was pretty disappointed. So, he went on a PR tour to promote "The Green Hornet," which was going to be on television in Hong Kong. That is where Raymond Chow and a couple of his producers saw Bruce doing this demonstration on TV and they contacted him to see if he would be interested in doing movies for Golden Harvest. That was in 1971.

One of Golden Harvest's senior producers at the time was a woman named Lan Leong Wah, who was married to Lo Wei, a prominent director at the time. His specialty was action films. Lan Leong Wah came to the United States and signed Bruce Lee to a two picture contract. The first was the film shot in Thailand called *The Big Boss.*

If I am not mistaken, wasn't that film was called *Fists of Fury* here in the United States?

The film ultimately became *Fists of Fury* in America. On the same lines, *Fists of Fury* became *The Chinese Connection* in America, and *Way of the Dragon* became *Return of the Dragon* in America. I am going to stick with the Hong Kong titles to keep confusion down.

So Bruce was set to this two-picture deal with Golden Harvest. Lo Wei and Bruce Lee and another young actor that had been signed to a multi-picture contract to Golden Harvest, Tien Chun, went off to Thailand to shoot the film. After seeing the dailies for the first couple of weeks, Golden Harvest made a decision, if you look at the film carefully you'll see the parts are equal in the beginning but that ultimately one of them has to die in order for there to be a third act in this movie. And the decision was made to kill Tien Chun and to keep Bruce Lee alive. And that was the beginning of the Bruce Lee style of martial arts fighting choreographed in Hong Kong films.

Certainly that film had a tremendous impact on the market as most of the martial arts films that followed had more realistic fight sequences in them.

I use *The Big Boss* as the jumping off point. If you look at a Bruce Lee martial arts fight in *The Big Boss,* where Bruce is not totally in control of the choreography, it is a transitional film from the traditional Chinese-style martial arts film, with a lot of leaping and flying through the air—rather unrealistic kinds of things—to the style that Bruce evolved into by the time we get two movies down to *Return of the Dragon,* where the fights are much more realistic and totally in the style of Bruce Lee.

Now what happened was that as soon as *The Big Boss* was finished, Golden Harvest knew that they had a big hit on their hands and they rushed *Fists of Fury* into production with an even bigger budget than originally planned. That film was actually shot in the studios in Hong Kong. By the time that film was finished, *The Big Boss* had opened and broken all box office records in Hong Kong and it was starting to clean up around Southeast Asia. Bruce Lee had gained a celebrity status and was clearly the young rising star that threatened Wang Yu's position of preeminence. It was quite a *coup* for Golden Harvest at that stage to have the reigning champion with Wang Yu and the rising star with Bruce Lee. When *Fists of Fury* was completed and went into release, it broke the box office record that had been established by *The Big Boss* only five months earlier. Bruce Lee was launched and on his way to becoming a major international star, although at that point in time, late 1971 to early 1972, we are talking about Bruce Lee being a star in the Chinese communities in Southeast Asia.

The traditional market for Chinese martial arts movies, up until 1975 and the end of the Vietnam war, was Hong Kong, Taiwan, Singapore, Malaysia, Thailand, Indonesia, the Philippines, and Indo-China (Vietnam, Laos, Cambodia), and also Korea. Bruce Lee's films also represented the first successful marketing of a Chinese picture into Japan. But that was to come later even though *Zatoichi and the One Armed Boxer* was released in Japan (it was released because it was a co-production and not as a Chinese picture). Do you see the distinction, as opposed to a Chinese doing martial arts and being in a situation where people were coming to see him because he was Bruce Lee, a movie star?

Yes, and add to that the fact that in Japan Zatoichi defeated Wang Yu.

So that brings us up into the late Spring of 1972, where you really start seeing the emergence of what I would call phase two of the martial arts films. As Bruce Lee's popularity took off in

Southeast Asia, Hong Kong producers dropped making sword fight movies and gangster movies to jump on the bandwagon of making more martial arts movies. And so you get a real blossoming of Chinese martial arts pictures—*Five Fingers of Death* and all of the movies that Shaw Brothers was turning out.

Meanwhile, Bruce had decided that he was going to direct himself in his next movie so that he could control both the story and the fight scenes. As happy as he was with *Fists of Fury* he still felt that it wasn't exactly the way he would do the fights if it was up to him. That next film was *Return of the Dragon*. Now at the time it was being shot it was actually called *Enter the Dragon*.

I thought that it was originally called *Way of the Dragon*.

Yes, but it actually had three titles. The reason it got three titles is that by the time Bruce had finished editing the movie and it was going into release in Hong Kong, we were already in pre-production on the Warner brothers co-production. And the title of the film was originally called *Blood and Steel*. But everybody knew *Blood and Steel* wasn't a very good title, but they fell in love with the title *Enter the Dragon*. And so it was decided that we would re-title—in English, anyway—the movie that Bruce had shot in the coliseum in Rome with Chuck Norris—which is Norris' entry into the world of martial arts films—and is also the first film I actually worked on personally. It was the summer of 1972. They thought that the title was a good international title, so then we changed the title of the Rome movie to *Way of the Dragon*. When it was released around Southeast Asia it was called *Way of the Dragon*, but the release in America was held up to be after the release of the Warners co-production now called *Enter the Dragon*. Therefore, *Way of the Dragon* became *Return of the Dragon*, as it was released after *Enter the Dragon*.

So you have to look at the *Return of the Dragon* film as being the first quintessential Bruce Lee martial arts film. If you look at the fights in the film between Bruce and Bob Wall and between Bruce and Chuck Norris, you will see quintessential Bruce Lee choreography. It is very different than you would see in a Wang Yu film, for example.

What was your role in *Return of the Dragon?*

I had actually just joined Golden Harvest, so I worked as a translator on the set. I was one of four people inside Golden Harvest that was bilingual. I had gone to Hong Kong in June of 1972 on a one-year contract to work as an office boy or whatever and study Chinese. Little did I know that it would be a turning point in my life.

How interesting. You studied Chinese at the university and went to Hong Kong to strengthen your language skills and went on to become a leading figure behind the martial arts film genre.

My major at the University of Kansas was Oriental languages and literature in Chinese, and then I also had a major in Asian history, and I had a major in Asian studies. So, at the time I was training to be what was called a "China watcher," back before ping-pong diplomacy; the height of the Vietnam War. So when I decided I was going to Hong Kong, I was really going because I wanted to become more fluent in reading and writing Chinese. I thought the trade off would be that while I wouldn't get to use my Mandarin very much, my reading and writing would improve significantly and I could learn another dialect of spoken Chinese language—Cantonese.

Little did I know that my first job would be translating subtitles from Chinese into English and my second job would be acting as translator on the set of *Way of the Dragon* and meeting Bob Wall and Chuck Norris and Bruce Lee. And out of that I became friends with Bruce; sort of a camaraderie formed between us. Golden Harvest in those days was a very small company, we had very small offices in downtown Kowloon. We took over the studio in the summer of 1972.

Willie Chan, Jackie Chan's manager in those days, was working for a company called Cathay Films. He was the studio manager for them. Golden Harvest made a deal with Cathay, and we took over the film studio. I signed the receipt of delivery for Golden Harvest and Willie signed in behalf of Cathay. We took over the studios in August of 1972.

What were some of the films that came out of the new studio at that time?

I was working on a film then called *HapKiDo,* which I guess was retitled in the U.S. as *Lady Kung-Fu,* starring Angela Mao, Sammo Hung, Yuen Biao, and a whole team of young martial arts choreographers who were just getting started in the film business. So I went from *Return of the Dragon* onto *HapKiDo.* I worked on *HapKiDo* from the end of July through the end of August.

At that time, Bruce and Raymond Chow came back to the States to negotiate a joint venture between Golden Harvest and Warner Brothers studios. The project was *Blood and Steel* which became *Enter the Dragon.* Raymond actually called from Los Angeles and said to me: "You are going to be producing a film, we signed a co-production with Warner Brothers and I am sending you a script and I want you to do a budget and a schedule. Bruce and I will be back in a week and we have to go to work on this movie right away." And so lo and behold, four days later by air freight, a script called *Blood and Steel* arrived. I read it and went to work getting a budget done. But how to find a local crew that could speak enough English to work with an American director, an American producer, and American stars. They were trying to shoot the first co-production in Hong Kong.

When Raymond and Bruce came back, while that was the number one priority, Bruce decided to go ahead and begin his next project, *Game of Death.* And so I went to work on *Game of Death* while I was preparing *Blood and Steel.*

How is it that in a very short time you were able to go from being an office boy to making budgets and schedules for Bruce Lee's films?

Like every other producer: opportunism with a great deal of bravado and bullshit.

The truth was that Golden Harvest was a small studio where everybody had to do a lot of different jobs. So, the great thing about working at Golden Harvest in the early seventies is that it was the greatest training ground that any young man could have in the film industry. One day you're working in distribution and negotiating to sell a picture to South America, the next day you're writing subtitles, and in the evening you're out having dinner with Chuck Norris talking about whether or not he has a career in films. So you have an awful lot of exposure and experience very early on and in fairness to Raymond Chow and Leonard Ho, they were of the old school where their attitude was that there was nothing that beat experience. And the only way to get experience was to go out and do it.

My deal with Raymond Chow was that I would come to work for Golden Harvest on a Chinese salary, not an expatriate salary, and if I paid my way to Hong Kong he would give me that salary and give me a return ticket at the end of twelve months back to America. So I was working and living as a Chinese in Hong Kong, as opposed to the life of luxury as an expatriate. With hindsight, though, I wouldn't have wanted it to have been any different, it was a great time, and those were cultural times in the world. It was the height of the Vietnam War but at the same time it was the end of the colonial era in Hong Kong and the beginning of the Chinese era, and Golden Harvest was right there in the middle of the maelstrom. We were making films that were very different than the films that had ever been made before in Hong Kong. It was a fun time.

So, to answer your question, it was perfectly logical in only the Golden Harvest way of doing things. They thought they were doing a co-production and the only other person who spoke English in the company were Raymond Chow, his secretary, and Bruce Lee. Clearly I was the low person on the totem pole, so obviously I had to go be the producer. I can't be the boss.

Opportunity is a funny thing, and often life changing. I can imagine that you had a lot of exposure to various jobs at Golden Harvest, but how did you learn the ropes of producing to be able to pull this off in such a short time?

Another one of my mentors in Hong Kong was a Chinese film director named King Hu. King started the Chinese swordfight movies and had had the first Chinese film to ever win the Palm D'or award at Cannes. King had sort of taken me under his wing in Hong Kong. I went to see him and told him that Raymond had called me and that I have to produce this film. I asked King what a producer does. He looked at me and said that if I was smart I would hire a good production manager. I asked him where I could get one of those. He told me he would lend me one of his.

And literally that night I went to dinner with the guy I hired to be the production manager on the film. And he and I did the first budget and schedule for the film. Much to the consternation of Golden Harvest, because they didn't like my assistant since he was a freelance worker, I talked Raymond into keeping him on the film and he stayed right through to the end of the shooting of *Enter the Dragon.*

You must have done a good job since Bruce kept you on for Game of Death.

Bruce and Raymond returned, and while I was preparing the budgets and waiting for Fred Weintraub to come to Hong Kong, we went to work on *Game of Death.* Since I was already working with Bruce on *Enter the Dragon,* it was perfectly logical that I should also go to work on *Game of Death.*

There were a lot of things that Bruce would talk about that were beyond the frame of reference of the people in the company in Hong Kong; they hadn't lived in America and didn't know what he was talking about. At least having grown up in this country, or at least partially in this country, we had a similar frame of reference when it came to films. When Bruce talked about this film or that film, or this TV series or that TV series, I knew what he was talking about. Most of those shows, like "How the West Was Won," had not played in Hong Kong.

Remember, in those days in Hong Kong there was Redifussion, that broadcast very boring British programming, and TV-B was the commercial station. It was a mixture of English programming and locally generated programming. There wasn't very much from American Programming on the air. The release of foreign films was not day and date. Most foreign films lagged because there was no such thing as piracy in those days, there were no video cassettes, DVDs, or anything else. You played a film in the theater so you didn't have to worry about whether it played the same day in

America as it played in Hong Kong. They saved the old prints of films after they were released in England or America and they shipped those prints out to Hong Kong and just reused them with subtitles. It was a very different film industry than today.

So Bruce and I became friends and worked on Game of Death. Bruce was hiring people to be in his films that were not necessarily from the traditional film industry of Hong Kong; like Danny Inosanto came over to do a scene in Game of Death. Danny is Filipino from America. He doesn't speak Cantonese; he speaks English. Chuck Norris, Bob Wall, and Kareem Abdul Jabar all came over. I spent ten days hanging out in Hong Kong with Kareem Abdul Jabar. It was an interesting time. So we shot all of the fight scenes with Bruce and all of the different martial artists in the tower set right there at Golden Studios.

I was working on the set as a line producer. I was getting the experience that was going to help get me through *Enter the Dragon*. At the same time that we were shooting *Game of Death,* we were preparing *Enter the Dragon. The Big Boss* and *Fists of Fury* were sold oversees and being prepared for release throughout Europe, South America, and we were even in discussions in Japan. I had to oversee the dubbing of these movies in Hong Kong into English. Everyone was working very long days, sort of making up the rules as we went along.

Sammo Hung has become one of the world's top action stars. Weren't you responsible for giving Sammo his first break by putting him in the opening scenes of *Enter the Dragon*?

Yes. Sammo and I hung out together as young bachelors in Hong Kong. When we were shooting *Enter the Dragon,* that scene at the beginning was actually a scene that Bruce came up with and expanded on, because it was his introduction in the film. It was actually the last scene we shot in the film after Bob, Fred Weintraub, Paul Heller, and John Saxon had left for the States. That scene was shot with Bruce Lee directing. And Bruce wanted to have a young, good martial artist that he could work with so that he would have a chance to explain some of his theories of the martial arts. And if you see the new box set version of the film, they restored *Enter the Dragon* to its original long version. (Actually, it's not that much longer, but it does include the whole scene at the beginning of the movie, where Bruce talks to Sammo and the other young guy that he fights with.) So, what Bruce was looking for was somebody that was not only a martial artist, but somebody who was also an acrobat, they came up with the idea of getting Sammo to be in the film. I had to make a deal with him that was supposed to only be one day's work, which became three day's work. That was the only film Sammo ever did with Bruce Lee.

Jackie Chan also worked on the film as one of the insane people locked up in the basement of Mr. Han's fortress.

Yes, but he was just a stunt boy in those days.

Sammo would have only been twenty years old when we made that film. So, using Sammo to do that scene was not only a good shot for Sammo, but more importantly, it added another dimension to the film. Instead of having phony acrobatics, like in the earlier Bruce Lee films, these were the real thing. When people flew through the air, you could see they were really doing it. I look at Bruce Lee as being the delineation point between the early martial arts films and the Bruce Lee generation martial arts films.

By the time we had finished shooting *Enter the Dragon* in early March of 1973, *The Big Boss* and *Fists of Fury* had already begun showing in Europe and America and were doing terrific business. The Bruce Lee phenomena had started. Obviously at the one end people were really excited that the films were being well received. Even in America they were released through a company called National General Pictures, which was later bought by Warner Brothers. The fact that the movies caught on sort of cleared up a big question that had been hanging over everybody's head. The American public was willing to accept Chinese-style martial arts films; especially Bruce Lee-style Chinese martial arts films.

When was the first martial arts scene shot for an American film or television episode?

When I grew up, the only martial arts we ever saw was Tom Laughlin in *Billy Jack* and David Carradine in "Kung Fu." To see the Bruce Lee-style of martial arts was revolutionary, and what happened as soon as the Bruce Lee films were released, Shaw Brothers swamped the market with all of their knock-offs. That is where you get *Five Fingers of Death, Intercepting Fist, Enter the Tiger,* and all of the other bullshit titles that came out. So there was this abundance of bad Chinese martial arts films that followed on the heels of *The Big Boss* and *Fists of Fury.*

Weren't you also working on Jhoon Rhee's *When Tae Kwon Do Strikes* around that time?

I went off to Korea with Sammo Hung, Angela Mao, Yuen Biao, and a director named Hwang Fung to make a film starring one of Bruce Lee's friends, a taekwondo teacher named Jhoon Rhee. It was called *When Tae Kwon Do Strikes,* which I produced in Korea. The movie was specifically designed as a vehicle for Jhoon Rhee and he brought with him one of his students. We put them plus Mao Ying and Sammo into this film as a way of showing a whole other kind of martial art. Taekwondo is a very different kind of art than wing chun or other Chinese styles. I stayed in Korea in March, April, and early May of 1973 doing that film. I have an acting part in that film; my first time in front of a camera.

I finished that film and went back to Hong Kong to work with Bruce, who had done his looping on *Enter the Dragon,* and gone back to the States to have a physical. We were going back to work on *Game of Death* to try and get it finished before he left for the PR tour for the opening of *Enter the Dragon.* I was waiting for Bruce when he got back from Los Angeles, where the doctors at UCLA told him he had a body of an eighteen year old. So much for doctors.

Bruce Lee died right after that, didn't he?

I was working with Bruce and George Lazenby, who had just starred as James Bond in *On Her Majesty's Secret Service.* George was in Hong Kong and we had contacted him about co-starring with Bruce in *Game of Death.* The day that Bruce died, George and Bruce had spent the morning in my office going through ideas on how to incorporate George into the movie. We were all going to have dinner that night to sort of consummate George's involvement in the film. However, as they say, other things were to intervene.

Bruce passed away and Raymond Chow asked me to bring Linda and the children back and to make the funeral arrangements in Seattle.

Two days after the funeral service in Hong Kong we flew to Seattle. When Linda, Brandon, Shannon, and Linda's best friend in Hong Kong, Rebu Hui (who is married to Hong Kong singer and actor Sam Hui), she agreed to come along to help look after the kids while we were going through the funeral services in Seattle. We actually used the tickets that Warner Brothers had sent to Hong Kong for Linda and Bruce to come back for Bruce to be on "The Tonight Show" for the opening of *Enter the Dragon*. We flew to Seattle and made all the necessary arrangements and everybody was there from Hollywood: Steve McQueen, Jimmy Coburn, Teddy Ashley. It was quite an impressive funeral service in Seattle.

I left Linda and the kids in Seattle and I came down to Los Angeles. I had a Chinese cameraman with me named Charlie Lo, who had shot the behind-the-scenes footage on *The Making of Enter the Dragon,* and I brought him to LA to do the interviews with Americans who had known Bruce Lee, that went into the documentary movie *Bruce Lee the Man and the Legend.* All of that footage was actually shot in the two weeks immediately after Bruce's death.

I then met Lo Wei in Los Angeles and got him set up to shoot a movie in San Francisco starring another Chinese martial artist by the name of Shang Kwan Ling Fung. She was a female swordfighting martial arts expert that had been a child star and come back to Hong Kong. We had signed her to a two-picture deal. Then Lo Wei had decided to put her in the movie with Sam Hui. I met them here in California and took them around in San Francisco and Los Angeles. Then I went back to Hong Kong to work on *Bruce Lee the Man and the Legend.*

This was the summer of 1973. To me, that was the watershed summer. With Bruce Lee's passing you get the end of one period of martial arts movies. Bruce had redefined what a martial arts movie needed to have in it in order to be successful.

In what ways?

Well, if you look at what happened, Golden Harvest did not turn out any martial arts movies until 1974 because we were trying to figure out what direction to go in. You know, with Angela Mao, with Wang Yu, with Sam Hui, Cheng Pei Pei, Shang Kwan Ling Fung, and all of that generation of stars.

Didn't John Woo get his start around this time with Golden Harvest?

John Woo had signed a contract at Golden Harvest in 1972 as a young director. He was apprenticing at Golden Harvest, making whatever movies Golden Harvest assigned to him. He was also studying how we made co-productions, with the goal of getting to Hollywood. So, many, many years and movies later here we all are on this side of the Pacific.

The summer of 1974 is the middle period of martial arts movies where everybody was trying to do martial arts movies with very real action. Very authentic action as opposed to the Wong Fei-hung kind of flying-through-the-sky action. The martial arts craze was now in full swing around the world—anything to do with Bruce Lee and his movies. For Golden Harvest it was a very difficult period because it was a question of what direction to go in. We were sitting with an unfinished Bruce Lee film called *Game of Death,* which everybody was clamoring for us to finish.

So in what direction did you decide to go?

We tried a lot of different formulas. By the summer of 1974, *Enter the Dragon* had been a phenomenal success. It was bigger, box office wise, than all of the other Bruce Lee movies combined—outside of Asia. In Asia, *Enter the Dragon* was the second smallest grossing Bruce Lee film of all, second only to *The Big Boss.*

The reason was the style, the photography, and the editing of the fights are quite different in style to those in Bruce's other films. The cutting patterns are much more choppy; there are much more inserts. There is less stress on seeing all of the actions in one master shot. That is one of the primary differences in taste between Eastern audiences and Western audiences in their likes and dislikes for martial arts films.

Golden Harvest was trying different formulas of combining Eastern and Western sensibilities because clearly the market was beyond Southeast Asia. The money involved was so much greater. That's when you get the period of a lot of movies that attempt to cross over, such as *Stoner.*

Stoner was a direct outgrowth of the original deal with George Lazenby to do *Game of Death.* Now Bruce was gone, we didn't know when we were going to finish *Game of Death,* but we had a relationship with George Lazenby. We took Hwang Fung and Sammo Hung and Yuen Biao, and off to Australia we went. This is the first time a Chinese crew had ever shot in Australia. There wasn't much of an Australian film industry in those days. We shot the film on location and then back to Hong Kong to shoot in Hong Kong and finish the film there.

How did a film like Stoner do in the United States? Did it even receive a theatrical release?

I really don't know. Golden Harvest was producing over twenty movies a year. On a bad year we did eighteen movies; on a good year we did twenty-eight movies.

So we tried *Stoner* as one example. We did another film with Lazenby in Hong Kong with two American actresses in it. I can't remember the titles of all of these movies. The plot, though, was around an attempted assassination of Princess Margaret. It was a big action piece directed by a Taiwanese director named Ting Shan Hsi. I took Sammo and Mao Ying and made the first Chinese film ever shot in Nepal. Actually, the first film to ever shoot in Nepal was called *The Himalayans.* We were in Katmandu on and off for five months.

It certainly sounds like you had a great deal to do with the emergence, spread, and acceptance of the martial arts film genre around the world.

We had taken the first Chinese film crews to Australia and India. We had done the first Japanese and Korean co-productions. We had sent film crews to Thailand, Indonesia, Los Angeles, and San Francisco. We were reshaping how Chinese films were seen within the Chinese marketplace and at the same time starting to introduce Chinese films and Chinese film directors to the rest of the world.

We had moderate success. But what was interesting is that I believe it laid the groundwork for this generation of young directors and actors.

If you look at the way cinema works, it's sort of like a tide that ebbs and flows. Everybody is influenced by everything that went before them. For John Woo to be influenced by Sam Peckinpah is perfectly logical. In turn, Quentin Tarantino is influenced by Ringo Lam and John Woo. So it goes from generation to generation, it passes back and forth and around the world.

If you think about it, not many new genres get created in the world of film. But martial arts became a new genre, even in the West. We didn't know it at the time, but that is what happened. Those early movies became the inspiration to future generations of filmmakers.

When I meet young directors like Stanley Tong or Peter Chan, they can tell me exactly where they were when they heard that Bruce Lee had died. They can tell me the first time they saw *Enter the Dragon* and *Fists of Fury*. It had such an enormous impact on that generation of Hong Kong filmmakers.

Ashai Shimbun from Japan is doing an end of the millennium piece on the 200 most influential people of the century, and they have picked Bruce Lee as one of the 200. From an Asian perspective they are right because of his impact, culturally, in terms of the first male hero, leading man, Asian star to break the racial barriers of the world and to be a role model to future generations of actors, young filmmakers, and just guys in the street. I don't think that we in the West have totally come to terms with Bruce Lee's impact on that part of the world that represents over thirty percent of the world's population.

So what was Wang Yu up to at this time? I am sure Bruce Lee's death opened a new venue for him to recapture his limelight.

Wang Yu was by default back to being the number one star in Asia—but only by Bruce Lee's death. Golden Harvest, in their search to find a new international star, decided to put their hopes on Wang Yu and Angela Mao. We were trying to find a way of bringing them to the States. Wang Yu had done a film in Japan called *Yellow Faced Tiger* and he and I went to do the first Hong Kong–Australia co-production, called *The Man from Hong Kong.* This Australian director by the name of Brian Trenchard Smith had come up with the idea of using hang gliders. The film opens with a hang gliding sequence under the Sydney Harbor Bridge and a hang gliding sequence across the Hong Kong Harbor.

Golden Harvest made a real push to make Wang Yu the new international star. We made a deal with a music group in England called Hot Chocolate for a title song called "Sky High." The record became number one for sixteen weeks in Europe. We made more money off the record than we made off the movie. We sold the movie to Fox in America, but they didn't do a very good job of marketing it. Wang Yu did not capture the American public.

Did the American film industry jump on the wagon and begin to follow suit at this time?

What's interesting to me is that nobody in America at that point in time was doing anything to seriously try and mimic what was happening in Hong Kong, except in the Black films. If you look at Weintraub's and Heller's career after *Enter the Dragon,* they did a couple of Blaxploitation movies with Jim Kelly. And the Shaw Brothers tried to do a couple of Blaxploitation movies with Warner Bros., *Cleopatra Jones* movies. Nobody found a successful way to really do martial arts in a Western movie on anywhere near the level it was done in *Enter the Dragon.*

What was interesting was that the martial arts thing was starting to run out of steam in Asia and the rest of the world. There was nobody to replace Bruce Lee. And so if you look at what happened in the film industry in Hong Kong, it sort of starts to trail off in 1977.

Jackie Chan was certainly able to recapture the imagination of Asian filmgoers. How did he suddenly come onto the scene?

Things were slow until Jackie Chan came along in a film called *The Drunken Master,* under contract to director Lo Wei. Jackie captured the imagination of the movie-going public. Not trying to out "Bruce Lee" Bruce Lee, but by creating his own style. I think that the essence of martial arts films is that when people try and mimic what has gone before they are doomed to fail. When they follow their own instinct and their own voice—if they have talent—they can achieve greatness. That is exactly what Bruce Lee had done once he had created his own style. Not just jeet kune do, but his own style of martial arts film. And here comes Jackie Chan. He stays as far away from Bruce Lee and Bruce Lee's style of fighting as he can in order not to draw comparisons. But his movies are delightfully funny, they're warm, they're charming. Jackie has a magic to him, he has a charisma, and he's an amazing acrobat.

Sammo Hung was able to build a successful career at this time also. In fact, he and Jackie worked together quite a bit in various kung-fu comedies.

Right. By that point in time, 1978–1979, Sammo Hung had come into his own as a director in Hong Kong. He had gone from being a martial arts choreographer and co-star to being a leading man and an important director. So you look at 1979–1980 as being the beginning of the Jackie Chan era, the beginning of the era of comedy kung-fu. And the two largest proponents are Sammo Hung and Jackie Chan, both of whom were working with Golden Harvest. Golden Harvest was by then on its way to being the dominant film company in the Chinese-speaking world. As Shaw Brothers was winding down and focusing more on television, Golden Harvest was the dominant force. Sammo's movies are exciting and energetic, full of acrobats and comedy. And Jackie's movies center around Jackie and set pieces of Jackie's acrobatics. Those two guys set the new high water mark for what martial arts movies needed to be in Hong Kong.

By 1981, we were trying to find a way to bring them to the international marketplace. We had been successful in marketing Jackie into Japan where Golden Harvest had an ongoing relationship with Towa-Towa, who distributed most of the Golden Harvest movies. We worked together to build up Jackie to be a star in Japan.

Sammo left Golden Harvest. He went out on his own because

he could make more money freelancing as a director than he could at Golden Harvest. Jackie stayed under long term contract with Golden Harvest. And the *quid pro quo* for that was that we also had to find international vehicles to put him in. That's why I put Jackie in *Cannonball Run.*

Didn't your becoming a partner at Golden Harvest at this time have an effect on much of what was to come, including Jackie's first U.S. films?

In 1976, I became the first non-Chinese partner. We created a group of companies called Golden Communications.

We put Jackie in the original *Cannonball Run* as a way to introduce him to the American public without forcing him to carry a whole movie. And then we designed a film called *The Battle Creek Brawl,* which was released in the U.S. as *The Big Brawl,* to be Jackie's first American film. There was one problem, which presupposed that Jackie was going to learn English. Jackie was delayed on his film that he was finishing for Golden Harvest, so he didn't get over here in time to study English before we had to shoot the film, and so they had to go and re-write the film on location to take into account the fact that Jackie didn't speak more than twenty-five words of English.

We also realized that when the movie was released in America, that America was preconditioned to Bruce Lee in martial arts, they weren't ready and they didn't have enough knowledge of martial arts to be able to enjoy the comedy of martial arts. There wasn't the depth of knowledge or cultural experience yet in America, enough aficionados of skill in martial arts to appreciate what it was that Jackie did. And even though they subsequently tried a couple more English-language pictures with Jackie, they fared no better.

Films like *The Protector?*

Yes. *The Protector* was actually the last film I was developing at Golden Harvest before I left. I sold out my interest in 1984 and came back to the United States. Well, I thought I was coming back to the United States, then I went into business with a man who had just formed D&B Films in Hong Kong. D stood for Dixon Poon and B stood for Hung Kam Bo, otherwise known as Sammo

Hung. He had set up this joint venture with Sammo to make movies and I was introduced to him, and he was ambitious about trying to break into the international film industry and he was signing up actors on long-term contracts.

Of the actors you signed at this time, who went on to become major stars?

One of the first actors D&B signed was a young beauty queen from Malaysia named Michelle Yeoh, who Dixon would go on to marry. That was in 1985. Sammo Hung and D&B decided to go head-to-head with Golden Harvest in making action movies and martial arts movies and making big, expensive movies. So not only did Dickson have Michael Yeoh under contract, he signed a multi-picture deal with Cynthia Rothrock. He took a young director named Corey Yuen and asked him to make Michelle and Cynthia into the next generation of martial arts stars in Hong Kong.

Really? I thought you had formed a partnership with Al Ruddy in Los Angeles at this time. In fact, wasn't Brandon Lee working as an office boy for you in Los Angeles?

Yes. I was in business with Al Ruddy in LA and with Dixon Poon in Hong Kong. Brandon had dropped out of Emerson College and had decided that he was going to become an actor. We gave him a job as an office boy for six months so he could get to meet people and get to know Hollywood. We introduced him to Jan McCormick, who became his manager, and Mike Simpson, who became his agent (we didn't have a management company in those days). Dixon heard that Brandon was working with us in Los Angeles and asked if Brandon would be interested in making movies in Hong Kong. I negotiated a two-picture deal for Brandon with D&B Films in Hong Kong.

One of the young martial arts choreographers who had been training Michelle Yeoh was assigned to train Brandon was Stanley Tong.

Do you consider this period now as a third or fourth phase of martial arts films?

No, I look at it as still being part of phase three because they were still redefining what female action could do at the same time that Jackie and Sammo were pushing the male comedy. So what you've got was the dichotomy between male comedy action and female hard action.

This is interesting because Michelle was far more successful than Angela Mao had ever been. Dixon was intent on making Michelle an international star so we set up a fan club for her in Tokyo. The long and short of it was that it was time for the women to play catch-up with the men. These martial arts movies were starting to run out of steam in the mid-eighties, 1986–1987. With the exception of Jackie, Sammo, and Michelle, martial arts movies were not making money in Asia. They were not being exported in any significant numbers to the Western world for anything other than video and television release.

But the hard-core action films of John Woo came into public favor.

Yes. And what was very interesting, though, was John Woo as a director had come into his own. He left Golden Harvest and teamed up with a young actor who wasn't a martial artist named Chow Yun-Fat to start making hard-core, reality-based action pictures. And from John and Tsui Hark you get the Ringo Lam's and the Ronnie Yu's of this world. There's a straight evolution here.

You have to look at that in the context of the run up to 1997, and more importantly to Tiananmen, because Hong Kong was in a golden age. People were making money hand over fist.

How did this event affect the careers of people such as Jackie Chan and Stanley Tong?

Jackie's movies were no longer as successful as they had been and his career also started to go into a bit of a tailspin.

Stanley Tong made a very low budget movie in Irian Jaya called *Stone Age Warriors* that has outrageous fun tongue-and-cheek action. It was made for next to nothing. It so impressed Leonard Ho, Raymond Chow's partner in Hong Kong, that he told Jackie that instead of Jackie directing he would pay Jackie the same salary but wanted to hire Stanley Tong to do *Supercop: Police Story III*.

***Supercop* is one of my all-time favorite Jackie Chan films.**

It is the first time that Jackie is with a co-star, Michelle Yeoh. Stanley redefines the Jackie Chan persona, ever so slightly. But Jackie goes from being the little boy into being the slightly inept, but quite smart superhero. That begins the period of collaboration between Stanley and Jackie. The three highest grossing Chinese movies of Jackie Chan were with Stanley: *Supercop, Rumble in the Bronx,* and *First Strike.* That launches Stanley Tong's career.

Why do you think that is?

Because Stanley represents that next generation of truly international filmmakers. John Woo is a Chinese filmmaker from Hong Kong who has brought his style to America. Stanley, on the other hand, is part of that next generation of international filmmakers that grew up watching not only Bruce Lee but "Charlie's Angels" and James Bond. If you ask Stanley his favorite movie, he'll tell you it's *The Sound of Music.* Stanley Tong and Peter Chan are the first true international generation of Hong Kong filmmakers. They are the generation that can cross over into Hollywood.

If people are now interested in reality-based action, how do you explain the popular reemergence of the swordsman and supernatural films, like *A Chinese Ghost Story* and *The Bride with White Hair,* in all of this?

Sammo was actually the one who reinvented the fighting ghost stories and zombie movies and brought them into the popular lexicon in the eighties. But those are not martial arts films. That is another discussion altogether.

But even Jet Li's films have a great deal of supernatural and superhuman qualities to them, such as when he is flying through the air and so on. Don't you see this as a throwback to the first phase of martial arts films?

Yes, but Jet Li movies come out of Wong Fei-hung. So they are really redoing Jet Li as Wong Fei-hung, and an integral part of retelling those stories is being able to fly through the air.

Now, what has never worked is the Shaolin Temple stuff in America with flying monks, or Wong Fei-hung. If you look at Jet Li, he is the most popular martial arts star in Asia, except for Jackie

Chan. But, he is a very straightforward martial artist and he's very good. He is probably the best martial artist to make films. Whether his acting skills will allow him to break into the American market, I guess we'll find out when *Lethal Weapon IV* opens.

Where do you see Chinese action films going in their next generation?

Well, that I am not really sure about. You see, what has happened with directors such as John Woo, Tsui Hark, Ringo Lam, and Sammo Hung all working here in the United Stated, martial arts has become just another tool within the action genre. The martial arts get designed into a film. You know Corey Yuen just finished doing the choreography on *Lethal Weapon IV* for Jet Li. That's great. We are also doing "Martial Law," starring Sammo Hung, as a TV series now for CBS. My partner Al Ruddy and I created another show called "Walker: Texas Ranger," and sold it in 1990 to CBS.

You mention the new martial arts television shows, but I suspect that there was an interesting parallel in the martial arts film industry here in the United States. I mean, before Van Damme and Seagal came along, Chuck Norris was synonymous with martial arts films.

Chuck Norris, under Canon, became the primary practitioner of martial arts films in America. In the late seventies and early eighties right through to the end of the eighties when Canon films went out of business, Chuck was the premiere guy. Below him you had the Michael Dudikoffs and the Christopher Lamberts. Jean-Claude Van Damme was the European answer and Steven Seagal was the American answer. But if you look at these two guys, you can't really compare their martial arts skills on camera to the Sammo Hungs and the Jackie Chans. They may be good martial artists, don't misunderstand me, but there is a difference between cinemagraphic martial arts and martial arts as practiced day in and day out.

So where do you see yourself going with all of this?

Actually, we are involved in a lot of different things. I look at my life as being a bridge between East and West for the last twenty years. I went to Hong Kong in 1972 and it is now 1998 and I am still back and forth. The fun side for me is to see many of my colleagues and old friends from Hong Kong now succeeding on their own terms here in America. I believe that Sammo Hung, for one, is destined for big things in America. I think "Martial Law" will be a terrific platform for Sammo, but I believe that Sammo will have a great future in this country as an actor and as a director.

At the same time, there is this whole generation, the Stanley Tongs and the Peter Chans that I am working with. I am having a ball with these guys because it is international cinema. We speak in a lexicon that is part Hong Kong cinema and part American cinema. Stanley and I want to do some big multinational action pictures together, things that have not been seen and not been done before. We have those in development. At the same time, my partner Al Ruddy and I are executive producing a new TV series for NBC called "Murder Incorporated," which tells the story of the Mafia in America.

We have our finger in two worlds, which to me is the fun part of it. I think that the film industry is about to write a new chapter and I think there will be a new chapter in television at the same time. I hope that "Martial Law" will be as much of a watershed for action on television in America as *Enter the Dragon* was for martial arts in film.

We have some other ideas like a TV series to be filmed in the Philippines called "Code Red." We brought in a couple of new partners to help develop that and I'm hoping that we will convince the networks to allow us to use a couple of young directors from Hong Kong to give it a whole new style. And I think that is part of the ongoing dialogue; that tide effect I keep talking about.

Now that "Martial Law" has been picked up for twenty-two episodes, will you be working on your adaptation of *Charlie Chan* for Sammo Hung?

That's on hold for now as we have to get "Martial Law" up and running on its own. However, we are looking to do a film with Sammo Hung during his hiatus in March and if it's *Charlie Chan,* so much the better. Look, it's exciting that we are even able to be having this kind of conversation, Mark, about an actor that four months ago in America was not known outside of the aficionados of Chinese martial arts films. That's kind of cool.

MARK DACASCOS
A Career in Martial Art Films and Television

Mark Dacascos was born in Hawaii to internationally renowned martial arts master Al Dacascos, the founder of won hop kuen do, and has become one of Hollywood's most exciting leading young men and one of the martial arts' shining stars. After starring in several television shows, including "General Hospital" and "Tales from the Crypt," Mark was discovered on the streets of San Francisco by director Wayne Wang, who cast him to act opposite Joan Chen in the film Dim-Sum. *Since then, Mark has starred opposite the likes of Edward James Olmos and Maria Canchito Alanzo in a dozen films. He currently stars in the highly popular television action series "The Crow: Stairway to Heaven."*

Mark, you have had a successful career as both a martial arts tournament competitor and as an actor. When did you first begin studying martial arts?

My dad tells me that when I was four years old I started kicking people in the shins during his classes.

Was your first instructor your father, or did you also study with your mother?

Primarily my father. When I was in my early teens my mother started teaching me a lot. My mom was also a student of my father. Now, I do have two moms. I have my birth mother, Moriko, who was also a martial artist, and then Malia, who is the one who raised me.

The style that your father teaches and you practice is won hop kuen do. Is this style the same as kajukenbo, or an offshoot style?

It is not the same as kajukenbo. It is an offshoot, but is completely its own entity. It has more of a Chinese and Filipino influence than kajukenbo.

Who were your father's main instructors?

There was the founder of kajukenbo, Professor Adrian Emperado, of course, as well as Professor Cid Asuncion. My father had also spent some time with Sifus Bok Sam Kong, Paul Eng, and Wong Jak Man. He has actually never stopped learning from teachers, even to this day. The whole time that he has been teaching martial arts he has also been studying from someone. He has been studying escrima for the past couple of decades with quite a few different teachers. He's always, always learning. In fact, my dad told me that he believes that a teacher should never stop being a student.

So how was it training at such a young age with such a serious martial artist for an instructor and parent?

It was strict. It was hard. It was fun. All of those things. And although my father and mother taught the same style, they taught it differently. With my father, we'd go to class, salute, and Bam! we would start fighting. Immediately. No warm-up. And it kind of made sense but it was hard. I would say, Pop, you know, I don't understand this. We are going to pull muscles with no warm-up. So, what's the deal? And he would reply, "Well, do you have any time to warm-up on the street?" So I never asked him that question again.

With my mom's class, on the other hand, we'd go to class, salute, and run—immediately start jogging for fifteen minutes. Then we would do a fifteen minute horse stance, fifteen more minutes of other exercises, then drill techniques like the side kick on the air shield. Her training program was very simple, very hard, and very practical. Needless to say, when it came time for the tournaments we had unbelievable conditioning. And we'd win on side kicks, or whatever we were practicing at that time. She also taught a Friday night fight class at like six o'clock or seven o'clock. And when you finished that class you pretty much needed the weekend to recover.

But my close friend, Emmanual Bettencourt, and I liked to train six to seven days a week. We trained on Saturday and sometimes even Sunday on our own. We would just work out and train and fight. You see, the thing is, he is from West Africa and I am originally from Hawaii. But our common language at the time was German. So you would see this African kid and this Hawaiian boy speaking German in Germany. We were foreigners and our only little sanctuary was the kung-fu school. He was working for Lufstansa airlines and I was still in school. As soon as we finished our stuff for the day we would head over to the kung-fu school. In the school we has saunas, a pool table, ping-pong table, foos ball, in addition to our boxing room and our kung-fu room. So we would go there and spend the whole evening training, playing games, shooting the breeze. That was our whole life. Six hours a day in that kung-fu school. And that was every day for seven or eight years.

So what brought you to Germany?

My mother and father had done a world martial arts tour with Bill Wallace, Linda Lee, and other famous American martial arts personalities. And while they were performing in Berlin, a German businessman offered my father a deal to be the first kung-fu teacher to teach commercially in Germany. So he agreed and they set up shop. You see, the thing in Europe is that the martial arts schools are amazing in that they usually have full on bars, saunas, weight rooms. I was there from ages of ten to eighteen.

I can only assume that you attended school while in Germany. Did you speak German before relocating there?

Oh, no. I spoke pigeon English before I went there. I learned German by attending school. I went to a German school called Volksschule, meaning The People's School, for about a year and a half. I was in and out of different regular classes and also in classes for foreigners. That was where foreigners really worked on their German. Later I was bumped up to a gymnasium, which is like a prep school for university. I went to gymnasium for about a year and a half. Then at about the age of seventeen I left for Taipei, Taiwan. There I trained with a northern Shaolin teacher named Muo Hui Shen. I stayed there for six months.

What was training like with Muo Sifu? I have also lived and trained in Asia and know that sometimes, especially with Chinese masters, it is very difficult for foreigners to actually learn anything of value. I mean, they are generally allowed to attend class, especially when the class is held outdoors, but often they get no serious training.

We trained in the park from Monday through Friday and in the school on Saturday. We practiced shuai chiao on Saturday as the mats were in the school. Classes went from seven o'clock until around eleven o'clock. And for me being a foreigner and also being new at the school, the first two weeks I spent the entire class doing a horse stance!

Four hours in a horse stance! Talk about discipline.

All I did was a horse stance while watching everybody else practicing. But Muo Sifu later told me that that was how he could tell if I was really serious about taking his class and whether or not I was strong enough to work out with his class. I loved it. I mean, afterward. But during that time I was seventeen years old and doing a horse stance all day kind of annoyed me. But then that stubbornness kicked in where I would tell myself, You know, I am going to show this guy what I'm made of. I can do it. Now of course I didn't do a four hour horse stance. I would do it for a few minutes and stand up. Then go back down again. This went on for four hours. And that was acceptable as long as I stayed down longer than I was up.

So after six months of hard-core training did you return to Germany or go back to Hawaii?

I went back to Germany to help my father out with teaching. A few months later I returned to Hawaii.

Weren't you an active tournament competitor at this time?

Yes, but actually I entered my first tournament when I was around seven years old. I competed in fighting. Then I won the Long Beach Internationals when I was nine—pee wee division. After that I was fighting almost every weekend up until the age of eighteen. I fought and competed in forms all over Europe. I retired from competition when I was eighteen.

You retired but decided to fight again a few years after that?

Yes. But, interestingly, I have never taken first place since I left the circuit at age 18. I think that I didn't place first at my last four tournaments because, in my mind, I hadn't trained hard enough to deserve it. So, I took second. It's so funny. I had this tournament in Germany and hadn't trained for it in years. But because of the big training deposit I made when I was young I was able to make a savings withdrawal. I made it to the finals, where we had two "sudden deaths." At the very last point, I was telling myself in my mind—while fighting—that I had jet lag, I did not lose face, and I did okay. And that urge for wanting to be first was not there anymore because I didn't feel that I deserved it. And before I could finish the sentence in my mind, Boom! I got hit!

Well, that's good. You seem to have a very realistic outlook on life and a strong sense of self. Paradoxically, that is rare in this field.

Thank you. That's the great thing about being a student. There is always someone out there who can kick your butt. When you look at your teacher, and if he is older and humble, you see there is no reason for you to be conceited.

So at the age of eighteen you retired from tournament competition and returned to Hawaii. Did you have a plan about your future martial arts directions?

No. I returned to Hawaii and was trying to figure out what I wanted to do. I knew I wanted to go back to school but I had absolutely no money. My mother and father were separated at this time and my father was still living in Germany.

Now I was living way up in Kalihi Valley. I had to wake up at four o'clock in the morning to take the bus down to Honolulu so I could take a job as a busboy. After work I would go to the park and practice gymnastics and martial arts. I was trying to figure out what I wanted to do. I hadn't lived in Hawaii for over a decade, so it was good to be back with my family and play in the water. But I knew that I had better do something serious with my life. So, I stayed there for about eight months, just working as a busboy in two different restaurants and getting myself together.

I heard that your mother, Malia, was one of the originators of the aerobic martial arts craze, and that it was about this time that you began teaching martial arts aerobics for her?

Yes. I then moved to San Francisco where I started teaching aerobic defense, which I learned from my mother, Malia. This was in the early Eighties. While I was in San Francisco, I would work out every now and then at Anthony Chan's wushu school. Although I only took about a half-dozen classes, it was fun and a good contrast to the more traditional northern Shaolin I learned in Taipei and my father's art.

We taught there for about three or four months, then her school in Los Angeles opened. But since we went to LA a little early the school wasn't quite open yet, so I took a job as a bouncer. I was the skinniest, smallest bouncer you've ever seen. This was on Hollywood and Vine at a place called The Palace.

Then my mom's school opened so I started teaching for her. I think mom was incredibly innovative. She taught martial arts techniques to music. My dad was also doing techniques to music a couple of decades ago. He would play drums or Earth, Wind, and Fire tapes during class.

Your acting career seems to be going quite well. Did this begin with your role as Conan the Barbarian at the Universal Studios Theme Park?

Actually, no. Prior to doing Conan I had acted opposite Joan Chen in a Chinese film called *Dim-Sum*. It was a film about five women that director Wayne Wang ended up cutting into a film about three women. Unfortunately, my scenes didn't make the final cut. I also acted in various theatrical productions, like "West Side Story," and appeared on several television shows, such as "Tales from the Crypt," "General Hospital," and "The Flash."

I did Conan the Barbarian for about five years, from 1986 until 1991. I quit a few months prior to filming *Only the Strong*. When I did *American Samurai,* which was the year before *Only the Strong,* I only took a three month leave of absence and went back to work. Conan the Barbarian was a great job because I got to play young Conan and a warrior. So I was in the whole show playing two different characters. It was good in that doing the same show year after year takes a lot of discipline. As an actor you have to constantly find different things to motivate you and keep it fresh. I mean, during the summer time I would sometimes do seven or eight shows a day. And on a few occasions, when someone else asked me to pick up their shift, I would do ten shows a day.

***American Samurai* was the first film on which you worked. You were able to land the role of the lead villain. I heard an interesting story about your audition for the role, where you injured yourself with James Lew's sword. So, what's the scoop?**

That's a funny story because in the audition I was using a sword I borrowed from James. It was a Chinese sword, but I wasn't used to it. In *American Samurai* I was to use a Japanese sword. So I played around with the Japanese sword backstage a little bit. I have to say that I am quite the novice when it comes to using Japanese swords.

Well, you must have done okay since you got the role.

I honestly just faked the use of the Japanese sword during the audition. And they had told me that whoever got the part would have a crash course in kendo and iaido for four weeks prior to shooting. I told them that if I did the film I did not want to disrespect Japanese martial arts or make a fool of myself. So, I told them that I would show them what I could do with the sword but with the understanding that if I got the part they would arrange for proper lessons.

So in the audition I played with the Japanese sword. When I picked up the Chinese broadsword—which I have been using for years—it felt really comfortable. But James' sword was a bit thinner and lighter than the one I am used to. Anyway, I thought this would be great because I would be able to move faster. So there I was, really moving this thing around. Then in the very end I did the cat stance technique where you place your hand on the back of the blade and slide your foot forward, thrust, and pose. Well, I did that, and faster than usual because of the thinner blade, and it sliced my wrist and cut through my tendon. But I didn't know how bad I was injured yet because the adrenaline was pumping. All I knew was that I had cut myself. At the end everyone was staring at my hand so I thought, Wow I must have done really well. Then I saw that my hand was all bloody.

That must have been traumatic. I mean, being in the middle of an audition and cutting yourself.

Yes, it was, and I wasn't done with the audition yet. Then they wanted me to do the physical stuff again so someone else could come down and watch. They asked me if I was okay, and I said yes, but asked for a bandage or tape to close the wound. They brought me some cotton and I taped my hand up. I still didn't know how bad it was yet. After that, like a crazy, motivated guy, I go into my back hand springs on this bad wrist.

So I did the audition and reading and it went really well. Then I left and got into my car and just let out this incredible scream! I faked it the whole time but just died in the car. I drove myself to the hospital. As it turns out, I had cut halfway through my tendon. So it took sixteen stitches; half of them on the inside to hold the tendon together, and the other half to stitch the skin together. When I got home I called my manager and told her I was hurt but that I felt the audition went well. She said that yes, I had gotten the part.

American Samurai **went straight to video while your next film, *Only the Strong*, had a theatrical release.**

Yes. I was fortunate to get the chance to audition for Sheldon Lettich, the director of *Only the Strong,* a twentieth Century Fox film.

In *Only the Strong* film, you play a guy skilled in capoeira. I have always been fascinated with capoeira. Does your interest in the art go way back or did you just learn some moves for the film?

I have actually known about capoeira for a good fourteen or fifteen years now, and have always been interested in the art. Two good friends of mine, Emmanual Bettencourt and Earl White, both studied the art with Sifu Bill Owens who, in addition to being one of my father's students, studies capoeira with Maestre Bira Almeida. About three months before I even knew about the audition for *Only the Strong,* Earl talked me into visiting a capoeira class given by Amen Santo. I loved it and enrolled in classes.

It is funny how things turn out. A few months later I auditioned for and landed the lead role in a film that highlighted capoeira.

In retrospect, how do you compare the roles in your first films? In one you played a villain and in the other a hero. Do you see a philosophical connection between the roles, as far as what both characters are trying to achieve?

Absolutely! You see in Kinjiro's mind he was not a bad guy or doing bad things. He was just trying to uphold tradition. And everything came from his father and his art and his respect thereof. Sure he was a little jealous and stepped overboard, but the character had a lot of passion and I could relate to that. While it was not the best film, it was one of my favorite characters.

I see a connection with your character in *Only the Strong* because he was upholding the tradition of capoeira when he fought the evil *capoeirista*, and upholding the tradition of his former high school by giving back to the kids and fighting to keep drugs out.

And in the kids he sees himself a few years ago. I can connect with both roles because I love my father and I love martial arts. I try to uphold my martial arts and family tradition. Both characters hit home.

A string of decent roles soon followed where you got to work with some well-known actors.

Yes, I did a movie called *Roosters*. It was smaller role but I got to play opposite Edward James Olmos, Maria Conchita Alonzo, and other fine actors. It was a film about family values. Then I did *Double Dragon,* with Alyssa Milano, Robert Patrick, Julie Nixon, and others. There were huge special effects in that film.

I recently saw one of your newer films, *Drive*, on HBO. The fight choreography was reminiscent of the recent Hong Kong action films. Was that the look you were trying for?

Yes! My three all time favorite fight film stars are Bruce Lee, Jackie Chan, and Jet Li. The only time I got to do fight scenes like theirs was in *Drive*, where I act opposite Kadeem Hardison. I loved doing the film. I loved working with choreographer Koichi Sakamoto and I think director Steve Wang is brilliant. That is the first film in which I feel I was really able to cut loose with martial arts.

In the scene in *Drive* before the final fight, you are singing and dancing in the nightclub. Has that type of entertainment profession ever been appealing to you? Is it a road you may take in the future?

No, although my whole family has always had musical talent. My grandfather on my father's side was an orchestra leader in Hawaii. All of my aunts and uncles either dance, play an instrument, or both. My father plays the ukulele, the guitar, sings, and also had his own band at one time. My biological mother, Moriko, was also a singer. I suppose it is in my blood, but I have never considered myself a singer or dancer.

Steve Wang decided to develop the scene in *Drive* where I sing and dance. Actually there are two versions of the film, a producer's cut and a director's cut. The producer's cut I do not like. They keep the action and laughs but there is no back story. You don't know why the characters are doing any of the things they do in the film. And he took out a few key dramatic scenes. The director's cut has all of those things in it as well as a different soundtrack.

You also got a chance to play the lead character in the movie version of

the *Crying Freeman* comic book series. I think the character is a great one to play, but I didn't see the film in this country. Why?

Crying Freeman was actually made before *Drive* but hasn't yet been released in the United States. In October it will be four years since I made the film. I am not sure why, since the film has done really well overseas. I know that at one time they had two or three offers on the table to bring *Crying Freeman* to the States, but the producer declined.

So what are your all-time favorite films?

Without a doubt, *Braveheart, Roman Holiday,* and *Apocolypse Now* are my favorite films of all time. But of the films I've worked on, *Drive, Crying Freeman,* and *Boogie Boy* are my favorites.

Boogie Boy. Now there's an interesting name. What is the film about?

I did *Boogie Boy* last year, and acted opposite Emily Lloyd, Jaimz Woolvett, who played the kid in *Unforgiven*, Frederick Forest from *Apocalypse Now,* Tracy Lords, and rock star Joan Jett. It's a story about a guy who spent most of his time in jail, gets out, and wants to be a drummer, but needs to shed his old skin in order to make a new life for himself.

This sounds like one of the straight-ahead acting films you have been aiming for. Do your fans have any action scenes to look forward to?

There is one brief fight in the middle and one at the end where James Lew and I just have a straight out brawl. Although it is not an action movie, it feels like one because the pace of the film is very fast. It is very much like an art house film and is currently making the festival circuit.

So after all these years of not knowing what your next film will be and where your career is headed, you are finally getting your just desserts. You play the lead role in the hot new television series "The Crow," based on the popular comic book series and the feature films.

Thank you. I am excited and honored to play the role that the late Brandon Lee brought to us on the big screen. I have been taking guitar lessons, singing lessons, acting lessons, and working on

my martial arts. I do everything on the show. My wife and I relocated to Vancouver, where we will be for the next nine months
while I film twenty-two episodes. The show will air in October.

Do you have a big movie deal signed as a follow-up to "The
Crow," or will you be shooting the series for an additional season?

No, I am leaving my options open. We'll see how it goes. My
manager and I agree that unless the project is really spectacular we
are going to stay free. After nine months of work you want to take
a break and it's not worth sacrificing family time for mediocrity.
So, well see how the series turns out and take it one step at a time.

JAMES LEW
Martial Arts Stunts and
Action Choreography

James Lew is no stranger to the martial arts, having begun his television career as a stuntman in 1972 on the TV series "Kung Fu." He is perhaps best known in the martial arts world as a former tournament forms champion, author of the book The Art of Stretching and Kicking, *and as the former owner of Dragon Master Supply Company. Since then, Lew has become one of Hollywood's leading stuntmen and action choreographers, having worked on such films as* Big Trouble in Little China, Rambo III, Escape from New York, Lethal Weapon IV, *and* Rush Hour. *He is currently working as the stunt coordinator on the TV series "The Crow: Stairway to Heaven."*

You have now become one of the most recognizable faces in the martial arts film industry. You have done stunts and acted in so many films and television shows and commercials. What was the first project you worked on?

The first thing I did was the "Kung Fu" TV series with David Carradine in 1972. I worked as a stunt double doing a lot of the martial arts action stuff. But I was just a grunt at that time.

How did you get the job? I am sure with this being the first martial arts television show that there were hundreds of people vying for the same few openings.

There was a call for actors and martial artists to work on the show. So, I just went down to Warner Bros. to audition and they chose me to work on the series as a stuntman.

How has stunt fighting changed since the "Kung Fu" series aired?

It's more realistic now than before. Before, people didn't really know what to do, or how to do it. There was no real craft. Nowadays, the viewers want realistic action and fight sequences. So, we have to choreograph stunts and fight sequences that look like something a person could and would actually do.

You have doubled for so many people from so many martial arts styles. What is your martial arts background?

It was in several different things. I studied taekwondo in high school. I also studied kung-fu with Douglas Wong in the Sil Lum five animal style. I also studied pak mei, the white eyebrow style. White eyebrow is actually my favorite style. It is like a combination of wing chun and jumping kicks. In high school I was also a member of the martial arts club. It was headed by this guy who was in the Green Berets. He taught a mixture of Green Beret combat techniques and a choy li fut kung-fu adaptation.

You were also one of the first national tournament forms champions in the United States. Did you compete before or after the "Kung Fu" television series?

Right after the series. What happened was that we had all gotten a lot of money from working on the show and we didn't know what to do with it. So we decided to open up a kung-fu school. Then, through that, we decided that the best way to promote the school would be through tournaments. We competed in sparring and in forms. Our team was so strong that we would place first, second, and third all of the time. It got to the point where the promoters asked us not to compete anymore but to give demonstrations instead.

Didn't you also write your book, *The Art of Stretching and Kicking*, around this time?

Yes, I wrote my book right during that time because I was also working with Curtis Wong on *Inside Kung-Fu* magazine. Curtis decided to begin the magazine because we had gotten into designing and making kung-fu uniforms and we had the school. So he felt the best way to sell the uniforms to a large population and to promote the school was to start a magazine and to advertise. So, my function was to run the Mantis Supply company.

It's funny to see the old issues of *Inside Kung-Fu* because there are lots of photographs of you holding kicking shields for people and being "beaten up" by all of the people demonstrating their art in the magazine.

Yeah, I got in front of the camera to model for the equipment. We wanted to do it cheap.

When did you start your own Dragon Master supply company?

I was doing Mantis Supply company, but at that time I was engaged and was going to get married. I decided that I better go and handle things on my own to make a better living. So I started Dragon Master in the early eighties.

Were you also doing tournaments or stunt work at this time also?

No. I didn't do too much of that at this time. Actually, at that time there wasn't much work available for Asians in Hollywood. It was real sporadic. The only things being made were about Vietnam, and I am a bit too large to double for a Vietnamese.

So I concentrated on Dragon Master and elected not to do too much stunt work in order to be a little more stable. Then my marriage started falling apart and I asked myself why I was sacrificing myself sitting at home doing the mail order supply company when what I really wanted to do was be in the movie business. So I started to look at my career and life and decided to get rid of Dragon Master and put my efforts into film work. Actually, at the time I did *Big Trouble in Little China,* which starred Kurt Russell.

Big Trouble in Little China was your big break into films, then?

Yeah, it got me into a business where I knew I belonged. This was in 1984 and I did all of the choreography for the film. I also stunt doubled for about half of the cast. There was a joke on the set where when I walked on everyone would say "What are you going to do today? What hat are you wearing today?"

Anyway, I wanted to both get out of a bad marriage and get into a film career. So, I started my full-time job in Hollywood. I really came to the realization at that time that if I was going to do anything well, I would have to put more than one hundred percent into it.

You know, when the film came out I was working for Asian World of Martial Arts. It seemed that everyone who came in was talking about how cool the movie was. The film has definitely come into its own as a cult film, but why do you think it wasn't a large box office success?

Well, I don't know if it was a combination of marketing or studio politics at that time. You see, that was the time that Barry Dillard took over Fox and there was this power play because *Big Trouble* wasn't his project. The project he was pushing when he came in was *Aliens.* So, he wanted to stuff *Big Trouble* so he could get *Aliens* into theaters and make that his big show.

Although after *Big Trouble* I had some idle time, I did a bunch of small projects here and there. I was working more as a stuntman. Actually, I didn't really know if I wanted to only be a stunt coordinator at the time. I love being in front of the camera more.

There is a lot of responsibility and headache being a stunt and fight coordinator and so I just found more pleasure being out there doing it.

So what happened with you and *Rambo III*? Weren't you originally associated with that project as Sylvester Stallone's trainer?

Actually, Stallone had tracked me down because he saw my work on *Big Trouble*. However, my time with Stallone was short lived. I was supposed to train him and choreograph the fight scene at the beginning of the film where Sly fights the Thai boxer. However, things didn't quite work out.

Why? What happened?

Well, I was showing him this simple reverse shuffle. To do the technique you have to be kind of light on your feet; he was heavy on his feet. He felt a bit embarrassed that he was having trouble doing it. I was trying to do things fairly simple for him, but he took it personally and let me go. Anyway, I got my revenge when I did the *Rambo* spoof in *Hot Shots Part Deux* with Charles Sheen.

So what did you do between *Big Trouble* and *Rambo III*?

To be honest, there were so many small projects that they all seem to blur together.

When did you do that beer commercial with Joe Piscopo? I thought it was hilarious, but I don't recall it running very long.

I think that was right around that time, too. It was a part of that whole series of spoofs that Joe did on different people. In this commercial he was spoofing Bruce Lee. Apparently there are a few Asian watch groups that protested and said that the commercial was bigoted against Asians. That actually caused enough flack for them to not push that commercial too much. I think it comes down to those people being jealous that they were not in the commercial and making money for being Asian. I guarantee that if they had the opportunity to be in the commercial and make some money, they would have done it and not said a word.

Do you think that groups like this were in part responsible for the short run of *Big Trouble* in theaters?

Oh yes, absolutely. The same group complained that we were type-casting Asians as bad guys and gang members in the film. But in the film the Asian parts are completely balanced. Although the star of the film is American, the co-star, who also plays a good guy, is Chinese. But, it came down to people being jealous about work—or lack of it. That is the real inside scoop.

You also did the stunts in *Boogie Boy*, which stars Mark Dacascos and Edward James Olmos? I believe you and Mark had a pretty dynamic fight scene at the end of that film.

Yes, that is one of the more recent films I worked on. The bulk of my work happened over the last ten years. This is when I did *Hot Shots, The Perfect Weapon, Best of the Best, Time Cop,* and so on. But I worked on these films in different capacities as stuntman, stunt coordinator, and actor.

You also had a part in *Escape from LA*.

Yes, but I don't understand why the film was so poorly produced when they had the money to put into it. *Escape from New York* was a much better film. In *Escape from LA* they cut out all of the great action scenes we had done. In fact, we did two weeks worth of shooting on the finale where there is the helicopter scene. We had long fights and all kinds of stuff, but none of that was in the final picture. Also, when I got shot off of the helicopter they don't show me falling all the way to the ground. I spun, flipped, and rolled on my way down and slammed myself to the ground. But they took too tight of a shot and only got me falling off of the helicopter.

That's one of the frustrating parts of the film industry. You do all of this acting or stuntwork, and most of it ends up on the floor of the editing room. This leads to my new quest to become a director.

You have recently been working with some pretty big names in the business, including Jackie Chan, Jet Li, Mel Gibson, and another project with Mark Dacascos.

I did stunt work on Jackie Chan's new American film *Rush Hour*. I also have a pretty good part in *Lethal Weapon IV* where I fight Mel Gibson and Jet Li. I also just finished fight coordinating the first few episodes of "The Crow" television series starring Mark Dacascos. If things go my way, I may actually get my directing debut on that show. I will then be the first martial arts guy to go from stunt work into directing.

You have also been busy lately doing a bunch of television commercials.

Yes, I do a fair amount of commercial work. I recently did commercials for Sprite, Mercury Villager Van, Sprint, and Hewlett Packard. Martial arts spoofs, mainly.

As if you don't have enough to do already, I hear you are also working on another book.

Actually, two books.

My first book was *The Art of Stretching and Kicking*. That was pretty much an experiment for Unique Publications, which was a new company at that time. Curtis Wong wanted to get into book publishing aside from just publishing *Inside Kung-Fu,* so my book was the trial. Twenty years later, it is still selling well. When Unique decided to get into the instructional video business, I was one of their first Guinea pigs also. I did two stretching videos which kind of updates what I have learned about the topic since my book came out.

The first new book I am working on is on fight coordinating for film and television. It will be a "how-to" book from how to break down the script, how to look at it, how to put together all of the moves, how to figure out the best camera angles, how to work with the actors that will be in the fight scenes, and so on. Then I will tie all of these things together into how you create a realistic-looking fight scene out of the individual parts. It will be a real overview of the trade.

The other book will be the ultimate book on kicking. It will be my answer to the coffee table book on kicking. Every kick imaginable in the world of kicking will be in this book. Basically, one stop shopping for the kicker.

It seems as though you have fought everybody who's anybody in the martial arts and film industry. Can you name them all?

Actually, I think it is easier to name those who I haven't fought. I will write a list of names of who I fought for you. When I think about it, I have to break it down into separate lists of who I fought, who I coordinated, who I trained, and not to mention all of the martial artists I shot self-defense sequence photos with during the early days of *Inside Kung-Fu*. The lists are quite long. I'm like Timex: I take a lickin' and keep on tickin'.

So with all that you have done in the martial arts and action film industry, where do you see yourself headed?

My approach at this point is to have more control over my life and career. Like I said, I am looking to get into directing and also to do more acting than I have in the past. I am also working on some projects of my own that I am in the process of writing and would like to produce and direct.

Do you have any words of advice for martial artists who are looking to get into the film industry?

Well, they must first do their homework. You must know the business you want to get into. It is all about longevity in this business. If you do your homework and have talent and can get into the business, that's great. However, you may only get one shot. So, the key is in the preparation. Just like in martial arts training, you must always prepare yourself since you may need to use your skills at any moment. And when that moment comes, you only get one chance and you better not blow it. So, if this is the career path you would like to pursue, put one hundred and ten percent into it and nothing less.

PART FIVE

MARTIAL ARTS RESEARCH AND PUBLISHING

HUNTER B. ARMSTRONG
Hoplology and Combative Culture

Hunter Armstrong and his family lived in Japan for about ten years, spread out over a twenty-year period. Starting in karate in the early sixties, he has been training consistently for the past thirty-five years. Now primarily concentrating on the classical Japanese martial arts, he has also trained in a number of Chinese systems.

Professionally, as director of the International Hoplology Society, founded by the late Donn F. Draeger, Armstrong is engaged in the research and development of hoplology—"the study of human combative behavior and performance". In his efforts to gain a broader perspective on hoplology, he has spent considerable time on field research in Japan, Taiwan, Hong Kong, Malaysia, Indonesia, Thailand, Sri Lanka, and India, researching the fighting arts of those areas.

Hoplology is a rather strange term and one that certainly is not in wide use today. Yet, it is an important science when studying the combative arts. What exactly is hoplology?

We have both a formal definition, which we hardly ever use and a more realistic one—"The study of the evolution and development of human combative behavior and performance." In short, hoplology is the study of "how people fight, why they fight, and how different cultures manifest those behaviors." Essentially, what we are doing, and have been doing, is looking at human fighting and trying to really delineate the natural aspects of it, as well as the dysfunctional and unnatural aspects.

Hoplology sounds like a truly encompassing study of the universal art of combat. A name that comes up frequently when researching the roots of hoplology is Sir Richard F. Burton. Is he the founder of this research method?

Sir Richard Francis Burton was definitely one of the forerunners of hoplology. Actually, though, we have found references to the word prior to Burton's use of it. In Greek, the root word *hopl* refers to "armed" or "armored." As well, when Burton was doing that kind of work, from the 1850s through to the 1880s, there was another fellow B. Henry Lane Fox Pitt-Rivers, who was also doing hoplological work if you will. However, I would have to say that it was Burton who was the real father of hoplology.

Hoplology appears to be a lot like anthropology, although anthropologists tend to focus their studies on the culture of an event and not on the practice of it as much.

Hoplology was developed in a period when anthropology itself was really starting to grow. At that time, I think the people who were doing what we now call anthropology were, for the most part, amateurs. At the same time, in almost a parallel development, there was hoplology. I think at that time these two fields really weren't separated, and probably they shouldn't be separated now. But somewhere probably after the wars in Europe in the late 1800s and of course World War I, warfare, fighting, and that study of that kind of thing took on a very bad taste. As a result, researchers began looking at human cultures almost without regard to their fighting behaviors of those cultures.

Now Burton, on the other hand, was very interested in people's fighting behavior. He was a widely published author of a number of travel books and book on the cultures he had visited, as well as on weapons and fighting manuals. His most famous book on this topic is *The Book of the Sword*. He did a number of military training manuals, and was himself considered a master swordsman inEurope.

Was Burton from England?

He was from England and he spoke several languages fluently. He trained in schools of Italian fencing, French fencing, etc., and he was a British military officer who saw limited action in India. He was also in combat in Africa. He received a face wound from a spear through the cheek while in Africa. So he was a man who had both experienced battle, and who had a deep, abiding interest in it. Again, his great curiosity about human behavior in general carried over into human fighting behavior.

What is not so well known is that at the other end of the continuum of human behavior, Burton had one of the better erotic art collections in Europe at the time. He was one of the first people to translate the *Hindu Book of Love*.

The *Kama Sutra.*

Yes, the *Kama Sutra*. He actually did one of the better translations of the *Arabian Nights* series. Of course, a lot of the versions that we see of that now are kind of the expurgated versions. The material he kept in there would be shocking to many. He would footnote with pieces like the Arab methods of doing this or that particular combative movement. This was in the footnotes. He was a very interesting character.

Burton was interested in both the weapons and the use of the weapons—the whole context of that behavior. What happened after his period was that the study of weapons kind of took on an artefactual perspective. There are plenty of great weapons museums in Europe and Asia, but generally speaking there is very little interest in how the weapons are used. The weapons are generally looked at and studied for their size, their shape, their morphology; where they were found, what groups used them, and so on.

They are basically collectors and curators rather than practitioners.

Right. And in this context they are essentially museum shelf implements. That has been the predominant study of weapons since Burton's time, and even now.

We, members of the International Hoplology Society, were in India in 1986 for a month-long field survey. We were trying to see what areas would be worthwhile for doing a longer-term study. We went through a lot of great Indian museums, just fantastic pieces. But people from the museums just had no idea how the weapons were used. On the other hand, if you go out on the street, there were still people around still who knew how to use them.

The late Donn F. Draeger was one of the first Westerners to seriously research, practice, and write about Asian combative systems. He was also the first torch holder, so to speak, of hoplology since Burton. How did Draeger get involved in hoplology?

What happened, as far as the study of hoplology is concerned, was that Donn Draeger came on the scene in the early Fifties, shortly after World War II. Draeger, of course, had been a career Marine officer who saw action throughout the Pacific and in Korea, had done intelligence work in South America after the war, and had been studying Japanese martial arts of one type or another since the age of seven. He had started in one of the old jujutsu classes, I think in Chicago. So he had quite an extensive combative background. After WWII, while he was stationed in Japan, he became associated with the Kobudo Shinko Kai, the Classical Martial Arts Preservation Society of Japan, a research society, which he was allowed to join. By that time he had already begun training in Japanese classical martial arts. In that organization, he formed the international branch. Of course the Japanese being as inward-looking as they are, pretty much ignored what he was doing, so he broke it off and formed what became the International Hoplological Research Center.

Where did Draeger come across the field of hoplology?

Draeger was an incredibly gifted athlete. He was probably a world-class athlete as far as genetic capabilities. He was also a very intelligent fellow, very well read. He was near genius if not genius—in fact, in combination of capabilities, I would have to say he was genius. Draeger was incredibly well read across a broad area, from engineering to cultural studies. Essentially, his interest was in weapons and warfare. Having been a combat Marine, he had seen more weapons and warfare than most people of our generation.

Draeger came upon the word hoplology in his readings of the early European hoplologists themselves; essentially Burton. Many of us who later knew Draeger and worked under him, often joked of him being the reincarnation of Burton. Unfortunately, Draeger didn't have quite the language capabilities of Burton; he had the language capabilities of a Marine. Actually, he was a very erudite fellow. But he often came across as a jock. And I think this is part of the reluctance of serious academics to take him seriously, as they would look at this fellow and see someone who was obviously a jock. Unless he was in his professorial mode, they would consider him to be a meatball. I have been in on a few of the academic challenges he had received, and he was formidable.

Wasn't Draeger doing something through the University of Hawaii, or connected to it in some way?

Actually, not the University of Hawaii but the East West Center, a graduate institution at the University of Hawaii. I think he received two grants there. Essentially, they were cross-cultural studies grants. At the same time, he was also doing a project for the Bishop Museum in Honolulu in going through their collection of Polynesian weapons. He did a pretty extensive morphology survey of the weapons they had on hand. It is a pretty dry piece, basically being a physical description of all of the weapons. And while he really couldn't get into the use actions of the weapons, he did offer some hypotheses of how these weapons might be used, based on biomechanics and the known combative aspects of Hawaiian or Polynesian cultures. Surprisingly, he was probably the foremost expert on Hawaiian weapons until his death, although he was relatively unpublished in this area.

I, for one, never knew this, and I have all of his books. Why didn't he publish more on this topic?

We actually do have some of his writings on it, but they are more in the form of notes and things on those lines. Part of the reason is that Hawaiians are as secretive as anyone else, and he was asked not to release anything until he had gotten permission from the Kahunas he was working with. He died before that happened. But his research work on those weapons is the foremost work on Polynesian weapons ever done.

Draeger lived in Japan for most of his adult life?

He was based in Japan. At the end of World War II he also spent some time in China.

Really? Since he wrote so little on Chinese systems, I don't think most people are aware of his research in China. Do you know in what part of China he stayed?

I know he was in Shanghai for a short time, but I couldn't tell you for how long. He was later based in Tokyo. I believe he was what they call "riffed out"—part of the reduction in forces that was going on after the war—and he actually did not serve a full-career term in the Marines as a result. He was riffed, as they put it, I believe, in 1956. He took his discharge in Japan.

At that time he stayed in Japan, although he had first done some work for the Marine Corps and the Department of Defense in South America on some kind of special duty. But after that, what he basically concentrated on was his martial arts training and writings. During that period, the early sixties, he was doing some of his earliest writings, articles for *Strength and Health* and *Muscular Development* magazines, published by the old Bob Hoffman empire. He did some articles on Shindo Muso-ryu jo, as well as some stuff on Oyama karate. It was really the first introduction of non-pop martial arts to the Western world.

When did Draeger begin his extensive travels and doing his extensive research throughout Southeast Asia, India, and other places?

I guess his seminal studies in that regard were while he was still in the Marine Corps. When he was doing work with the military, wherever he went he was either challenging or checking people out—a very competitive guy. I think his early researches, as it were,

were more in the form of "Let's see what you've got and I'll show you what I got." As he went on and got more serious about actually finding out about these systems, his approach was smoothed out, and he became much more sophisticated as a researcher. But I know by the mid- and late-Fifties he had a much more sophisticated approach to what he was looking at and seeing. It was also somewhere during that period that he started getting more interested in the weapon arts, as versus the purely empty-hands stuff.

I think most people are familiar with Draeger's background in judo. What other martial arts did he study while in Japan?

Draeger was a grappler, first and foremost. The guy was roughly 6'2" and ranged in weight from his peak as a judo man of two hundred and fifteen pounds to around 195 later when he specialized in weapons training. He was a real solid guy. When I first met him, he was fifty-five years old and could still squat five hundred pounds. That's pretty impressive for anybody, much less a fifty-five year old guy.

As you are probably aware, he was associated with Mas Oyama in the early days. He was not a member of the Kyokushinkai, but he helped Oyama out in his books and with some of his PR work. Draeger was also associated and co-authored some books with Nakayama of the Japan Karate Association. Again, he wasn't really a karate man at all, and never really formally entered any of the dojo or training schools of that time, but he often did train with those people. So he had a pretty good grasp of what they were doing, and being a formidable athlete, and a combative athlete at that, he could pretty much hold his own in anything he went into new.

Again, looking at his background as a combat Marine, somewhere along the line I think the same realization came to him that has come to a lot of us who have gone on that track: reality says that the last thing I want to do in a real fight is do it with my hands empty. So, he was introduced through, I believe, one of his judo teachers to Shindo Muso-ryu under Shimizu Takaji Sensei, who was head of that ryu at the time. From there, he was introduced to the Katori Shinto-ryu. This was the basis of his weapons training.

Draeger has done a wealth of research that has yet to be published. I am curious that although he had been to China, Taiwan, and Hong Kong, the three books he published on Chinese martial arts featured two masters and systems from Malaysia and one from Indonesia. Why did he choose to write books on three Chinese systems in Southeast Asia?

Well, of course, at the time Draeger was writing his Chinese martial arts books you couldn't get into China. Also, the Chinese martial arts that you can see in Hong Kong, basically, he was not real impressed with. He had seen much better stuff when he was in Shanghai. He had seen much better stuff when he was in Malaysia. As far as the Taiwan stuff goes, I suspect that because he was such close friends with Robert W. Smith, he stayed clear of it; Taiwan was Smith's territory, so to speak. When they collaborated on the book, *Asian Fighting Arts,* essentially Smith took the Chinese and Southeast Asian realm and Draeger did Japan and India. I think part of it was just out of friendship with Smith and part of it was the political situation in China. He had though, and we have of his, a tremendous amount of material on Chinese culture, history, and fighting systems.

Will the International Hoplology Society be publishing any of this material in future issues of its Hoplos and Hop-Lite newsletters?

I'll tell you the problem with that. The material is in notes, we would have to do the background checks to make sure everything is proper with it. It is not how-to stuff. It is basically historical and cultural information. That information, it's not that it's hard to back up, it's just that I don't have the time or the people who can do that kind of work. It is some really fascinating information, and I think frankly it is a political thing as well. I don't mind getting into people's faces when I can thoroughly back up what I have got to say.

Draeger went to a lot of effort to maintain historical and factual accuracy. And frankly a lot of the stuff that has come out in the last twenty-five years in martial arts doesn't care about history or other facts.

Sure, practitioners are still stuck on the old myths and legends of masters.

Right. Again, if I am going to go out there and challenge a lot of the myth and legend aspects of the Chinese arts, I want to have real solid information, other than just saying, "Well, I've got Draeger's notes." At this point I am not really interested in popping any balloons in that field; we are popping enough balloons in other areas as it is.

Draeger also went to India a few times and did extensive research there. Again, he wasn't able to publish his research on that region before his death.

No. Again, when he went to India it was in the earlier days. And, we have some of his notes. At that time he was primarily interested in the grapplers, so most of his information on the Indian arts was in the grappling. He did gather some information on the weapons and armor, but it was in a more primitive form than he would have done later on. So actually when we did our India trip, it was really part of a program that Draeger had originally outlined. When I first joined up working under him in 1977 or 1978, one of the long term plans was to do a long-term field study in India, particularly Northern India. We kept putting it off for this reason or that reason. We did do a trip to Sri Lanka, which ironically turned up absolutely nothing. Then a couple of years later they had a major civil war. The only thing we could find was modern wrestling. But we couldn't find anything regarding classical or traditional wrestling systems. It could be that we just didn't look in the right places at the right time. But later on, of course, we found out that they are very combatively capable people.

It is widely known that Draeger spent a good deal of time in Malaysia and Indonesia, and he wrote three books on silat. Did his research ever take him into the Philippines?

Draeger did go into the Philippines. Again, I think his original trip into Southeast Asia was from Japan through the Philippines, then down into the Indonesian and Malaysian areas. I really couldn't tell you why, but he found the Indonesian and Malaysia fighting arts to be of greater interest than those of the Philippines. I don't know enough about the Philippines arts to say whether it was because they had already predominantly moved from classical into modern systems, or what. Indonesia and Malaysia, when I was there in the late seventies, were still fairly pristine. You could still see fighting arts that were for fighting. Since then, of course, we now have silat oloraga for sport tournament fighting, a complete distortion of what the classical systems were.

What are some of the tools or what is the primary methodology a hoplologist takes into the field with him when documenting a fighting art?

The biggest point is perspective. This was something that Draeger really drummed into all of us who worked with him. There are terms he used and borrowed from aspects of behavioral studies: emic and etic. The emic observer is the observer who is part of the culture being observed. Etic means you are an outsider looking in. The problem with observing any outside culture is your view is distorted by your own culture.

Sure. Ethnocentrism.

Right. So it was very important to Draeger that if you were going to go study fighting systems in any culture, you better have a good grasp on fighting. If you are going to go to a new culture, there is not much you can do about being a member of that culture's fighting arts, but if you have an understanding of the basic biomechanics and behaviors of fighting that are normal in human beings, you'll have a better understanding of what you are seeing. Of course, the whole study has been aimed at finding out what those behaviors are. And we have found these behaviors to be universal. So, the primary tools are having as emic a perspective as possible. So, if you are going to go look at a weapons fighting art, being a karate man doesn't do you much good; you have to have a weapons background. In particular, Draeger was also concerned that the observer was trained in a fighting system that was aimed at combat as versus sport. So, perspective was one big one.

The challenge there is that when you go in is being objective. If you are Joe Black Belt and you are a big tough guy from the States, and have been training in Japan for a few years, and you go to Malaysia, for example, where the average guy is half your size and half your weight, then your first impression is likely to be, "Well, I can take that guy." That was certainly natural for me, and was something that Draeger kind of slapped out of us all of the time. He was adamant that we look at these things as objectively as possible. He was constantly pushing on us that we were not seeing everything; we were only seeing (1) what they wanted to show us, and (2) we don't really fully understand in what context that this system is being used. At that time, I was primarily a karate man and into Japanese weapons arts. A karate guy, especially a modern karate guy, is used to training on a nice, smooth, hardwood floor. But look at what these guys are training on: mud or loose dirt. Draeger would tell us that a hardwood floor karate guy would have no idea what it's like to train on that kind of ground. It is something that is easy to miss. And frankly, it took me a while to catch on to these little things and try to figure out how the material differences worked. We had to learn to really look, to see all the actual physical differences in the training context. And these are relatively easy to see compared to the cultural differences.

Exactly. Context is the most important thing to consider when viewing a fighting art. You wrote an article about this idea where you mentioned how you viewed an apparent empty-hand silat system in Malaysia that looked impractical. Yet, it was designed to be used with a *kerambit* held in the hands, which, of course had you known this, the movements would have made better sense.

Right. The Western mind and especially British sense of fair play is to stand up and say, "Okay, you and me, let's stand up and go toe to toe." Whereas in Asia, a real fight means that probably real weapons are going to be used. This means that you don't want to stand there and exchange blows with your opponent; you want to kill him before he can hurt you. This is a totally different mindset in dealing with an enemy from what the American or Brit has as an idea of as a fair fight. When I was a kid, before the karate movies came out, when we got into schoolyard fights, you never kicked. It was considered cheating or dirty fighting to kick, and only girls kicked. Of course now it has completely changed, as the martial arts movies constantly remind you. Everybody kicks now.

And that's a cultural thing, an evolution of the fighting culture. That was something you have to learn: to stand back and remove the blinders from your own culture and objectively look at other cultures. These things are hard for a normal human being.

It was impressive to watch Draeger because he was so capable. Most of us were in total awe of him physically. It was amazing how he could go in there and charm these people into showing him their stuff. When we went in as mid-twenties to thirty-year-old guys, there was still a fair amount of testosterone coming out of us, and they would tend to look at us as young guys as challenging them. Draeger could go in there and in just a very smooth manner convince them that he thought their system was the best in the world, and they would show him things that otherwise we would never be able to see.

At the time you were going into the field with Draeger, you were going into basically uncharted territory as far as the martial arts are concerned. Assuming, then, that you have an open mind and are entering the field with a proper perspective, you still had to locate the fighting arts. How was that end approached in an area like rural Indonesia or Malaysia?

Aside from perspective, the standard tool for going into a culture where there had been little research was to show them what we did. You couldn't go into a village and say, "Hey, we want to see your fighting system." The first thing they are going to do is, "Yeah, we'll show you our fighting system," and go at you for real. So, what we did in a lot of cases—as silly as it may sound—we would go to a local coffee shop, which often was kind of an outdoor shack, and drink coffee. And maybe if we were in that village for a day or two we'd actually go out and do some training. But what almost inevitably would happen was that we would show them something. And often when they saw what we were doing, they'd want show us what they did. The exchange basis seemed to work pretty well. A number of times we would be in places where absolutely nothing seemed to be going on, and we'd do some kind of training. Somebody at a table would say, "Hey, my uncle does something like that." And that would be a kind of key into getting into seeing somebody's system.

Quite often, in the more industrialized areas of Malaysia and Indonesia, we'd talk to members of that culture who would absolutely swear that nothing like that was being done any more. Or there is only kung-fu, and that is only done in movies. Or, no fighting silat, only sport. Yet, we could go out into the *kampung* somewhere and find people who were still doing old-style training.

Part of the hoplological study of fighting arts is their classification. Was Draeger able to design a practical fighting arts classification system that was easily put to use when doing such research?

We have a macro analysis system for weapons and systems. Draeger had started one for unarmed fighting systems, and we had been working on it for years. In the late Seventies, when we started *Hoplos*, the first newsletter for the International Hoplological Research Center, there were about four or five of us in Japan (Meik Skoss, Larry Bieri, Phil Relnick, and myself) who were at one point going through monthly courses with him. We would go out to Draeger's village at Narita, and spend all day Sunday in his apartment being instructed on the how-tos of hoplology—everything from weapons morphology to systems analysis. As we got more skilled in that, we actually became involved in developing the systems analysis method. Even now, that is ongoing.

Don't you find such classifications of fighting arts to be rather limiting in their stereotypical classifications of systems? After all, just because a system chooses to employ a sword with a curved edge doesn't necessarily mean that the system couldn't be applied to a straight-edged sword.

The system analysis was purely meant as a field tool to provide a shorthand idea of how a system or weapon was being used. It was to be a backup for photos and video. For example, we would look at a weapon, its striking edge or point, the target it was being aimed at, and how it moved to the target. So, for example, you say a curved sword. Well, it is a cutting-edge weapon, and its aimed effect on the target is to achieve some type of trenchant action, a cut; generally speaking, the blade moves through an arc. If we look at a spear, you are not looking for a trenchant action so much as a perforation or penetration effect on the target and the spear point is going to move to the target in a line. All right, so these were the basics of it, and you can pretty much define any weapon in that manner. Now, perhaps you can also take that curved weapon, and use it similar to the spear, but it wouldn't function in as effective a manner as would the spear. And I think you would be hard put to find a system that strictly used a curved cutting-edge weapon, such as a saber, in a manner like a spear, and vice versa. So, that is basically what the system and weapons macro-analysis was used for; it was not supposed to be clearly defined, black-and-white descriptions of weapons use or the weapons themselves.

This is something we've run into throughout hoplological descriptions and also in any field of human studies or human behavior. There is the tendency to look at these things when they are written down in black and white as saying it is black or it is white and there is nothing in between. Our feeling is that everything is in shades of gray.

In hoplology, then, we are real fond of the word "continuum" in regard to fighting systems, particularly with the evolution of systems still going on. So you can still find fighting systems that are being strictly used for combat in the jungles of Malaysia, but very few of them. Most of the silat now is undergoing an evolution into sport. This is true in Japan, China, India, anywhere you go—there are transitions going on.

When we say a system is primarily combat oriented, meaning not sport oriented, it is toward the combat end of a continuum that runs from pure mortal combat at one end to solo nonconflict at the other. That doesn't mean that that combat system has no use in sport. *Vice versa,* you can look at a combative sport like boxing, for example, that has strictly been evolving for sport for over a hundred years now; it doesn't mean that boxing can't be used in a fight. It just means that boxing is most effective for what it has been evolving for. So, these are the problems with describing weapons and systems.

Now, the nice thing about weapons is that since they are hard material objects, they are a little easier to describe in the sense that we can ascribe them to specific uses. If you look at the Indian *talwar,* you are probably not going to jump to the conclusion that it should be used in sport fighting. On the other hand, take a look at the Japanese bamboo *shinai* used in kendo. The man doing kendo is likely to say that the shinai is a bamboo sword. It is not a bamboo sword; it doesn't even come close to looking like a sword, although the Japanese people who do kendo still like to call it a bamboo sword. However, it has no use or application in its movement or in its shape and structure any similarity to the real weapon. As a material object, the weapon is a lot easier to look at in that regard. And that really puts the lie to a number of systems that claim to be strictly a combative system…the weapon says not.

This is one of the problems serious martial art researchers, who actually know the difference between actual combative systems and purported combative systems, come across on their research. And the practitioners of those purported arts tend to get overly defensive when you try to tell them why what they are engaged in is not truly a combative system.

It comes down to these people's belief systems. In a system that, for example, strictly trains in a solo manner, there is no training for distance, no training for timing, no training for targeting—how can it be combative? Of course, we constantly get arguments on this point from taiji people and iaido people. That's the nature of it: there is absolutely no way to train for combat with other people without training for distancing and timing and targeting. And those systems don't do that. The same holds for weapons. If you are only training with an implement that not even superficially simulates the real weapon, chances are that system is going to be so distorted that it is no longer nearly as functional as a truly combative system. Unfortunately, people take that as a qualitative statement, and it shouldn't be. Boxing, I think, is a great sport. But to say that boxing is the best means of engaging in combat on the street is silly. That doesn't mean it can't be used on the street; as a good boxer can certainly handle himself in a one-on-one fight. But if you think you are going to win all street fights because you can box, you are going to run into a problem. Even more so if the boxer goes into a more combative or battlefield combat realm, he's going to be in real trouble.

I agree. As you said, it comes down to belief systems and also, I believe, exposure to many different fighting arts to come to this realization. Let's talk about your background in the arts a little.

I started with Ed Parker's kenpo karate in Pasadena, California in about 1962. At that time I didn't stick with it for more than a few months. I started again in about 1965, then I tore some cartilage in my knee and due to attitudinal problems at that particular dojo at the time, I decided that I'd like to try a Japanese style. I ran into a dojo that opened up in Alhambra, California by a man named Ben Otake, a Japanese-American of great character who, at that time, and I believe still is, was under the newly arrived Kubota Takayuki, or Tak Kubota of *kubotan* fame. I guess it was about 1966 that I started training under the International Karate Association, and trained with Ben Otake and Tony Tulleners and those guys.

I heard that Tony Tulleners used to beat Chuck Norris quite often on the tournament circuit.

I've seen a number of "names" get their clocks cleaned in the Hollywood *dojo* of Kubota's a few times. I saw a number of people famous from the tournament world come in there and never show up again.

But at that time, at that *dojo*, it was all Los Angeles-area cops. They were all mean and nasty, and ninety-five percent of all the scar tissue I have now is from that period of time that I trained there. It was incredibly rough. I remember at the age of sixteen riding my motorcycle on Sunday afternoons to the advanced training class, with such a total feeling of fear in my gut. And to this day I have no idea why I continued doing it. I never came away from training without damage of some kind. I remember coming home one time and knocking on the door because my hands were bashed so badly I couldn't open the door. At one point my eyelid was hanging over my eye. It was very tough, hard-core training. The good side was that after that, I never ran into a *dojo* that I was afraid to enter, including in Japan.

When I graduated from high school, I went to the University of Hawaii, where I trained with the Japan Karate Association for a while. After a year or so, I started training for a while with Chuzo Kotaka of the International Karate Federation.

Why was I under the impression that you were a Goju-ryu man?

Well, I went to Hawaii in 1968 and in 1970 I went to Japan for six months of training. I was introduced to several instructors there by Kotaka. I ran into some interesting styles there, but Japan was pretty much sport-oriented by that time. I did run into one old Okinawan system called Mihara-ryu, which was interesting. It was just slowly being introduced to the sport stuff, and was kind of in a state of transition. Because I was a sport karate guy from Hawaii, they had me teach them sport sparring. And I was actually teaching them some of the Shito-ryu *kata* that I had learned under Kotaka. Until that time, all the kata they did was two-man *kata*.

Like most of the Chinese and Southeast Asian empty-hand systems.

Right, and again, referring back to what I was saying about solo practice, all their training was two-man. Almost all of the older guys in this *dojo* didn't have any front teeth.

I went back to Hawaii in 1971 pretty disenchanted with what was going on in Japan and what was going on in Hawaii because of the sport aspect, and essentially trained a little bit more with Kotaka. I then went pretty much on my own for the next couple of years.

Not happy with self-training, in 1973, I started training in Hawaii with a man named Nozaki, who originally was a friend of Kotaka. Nozaki Sensei's style was a cross between Goju and Shotokan, although he was the head of the JKA in Honolulu at that time. From 1974 to about 1976, I became more and more determined to get back to Japan and train with the JKA.

Do you believe that the modern martial arts systems are, as Draeger once wrote in reference to Japanese karate-do, "an ass in a tiger's skin?"

Again, this gets back to what we discussed before regarding belief systems. Karate that has evolved in Japan since it was taken out of Okinawa, never evolved for combat nor was designed for combat nor had anything to do with combat. Modern Japanese karate evolved toward a totally different end. Now, there are plenty of good, functional karate guys who can go out and do fine in a fight, but it's probably more to do with their own personal abilities than the type of karate they train in.

The problem is that we lump all karate together, where you should have the old classical Okinawan karate-jutsu as versus the modern Japanese karate-do. Again, the modern karate-do is not designed for real fighting, it's not evolved for fighting, and it isn't very good for fighting. Again, that doesn't mean that somebody couldn't use it in a fight.

What is your opinion on these ultimate no-holds-barred competitions?

Those guys are tough. There is no system there. We are seeing some great grapplers beat the crud out of some not-so-great punchers/strikers. I've seen some really top-quality grapplers get in there, but I haven't seen many top quality boxers, for example. So, what are we saying with the UFC: that grappling is the best fighting art? For what context? For the UFC context it is the best. However, it is a sport and if you put that type of fighting out on the combat field, it won't do you nearly as much good. If you take a guy to the ground on the battlefield, he may have a weapon on him or his buddies will shoot you.

The real key is looking at the functional end of a system, its application. Almost any system that has been going for decades is going to be reasonably efficient for its application. The problem occurs in the difference between what the people are doing and what they say they are doing; what they claim their system is for and what the system has actually evolved for. For the most part, what they claim the application is and what it is really are generally two very different things. Let's go back to kendo again. If I have been training with the bamboo *shinai*, and then I tell you that this is training in swordsmanship, are you going to believe me? I hope not! You've got to look at the realities behind the systems.

Again, though, for karate's functional application it is great. I am speaking of modern karate-do in a modern karate-do *dojo* context. But what is that functional application? It's not for going out onto the battlefield or entering the UFC. It's for *dojo, shiai* (contest), sparring.

When did you meet Draeger? I assume it was at the University of Hawaii.

I met Draeger in about 1975 or 1976, when he was on one of

his research programs with the East West Center. I started working with him, helping him on a Hawaiian project. I worked at night, and so was available to drive him around during the day. That's when I first ran into a classical Japanese system, Shindo Muso-ryu. Draeger had a small group training in Honolulu (Pat Lineberger was one of them, and is still training there), and I came out and watched several times, and eventually asked if I could join. I was very politely told no.

Why wouldn't Draeger allow you to join his class? I mean, after all, you were helping him out quite a bit.

He told me that in classical training, in training for real fighting, a teacher could only handle no more than four or five students at a time. I thought that was kind of interesting. In karate we were training fifteen or twenty guys in the *dojo* with no problem.

However, because I was working with him so much, he encouraged me a lot. In late 1976 I had arranged for my visa back to Japan through karate. Once there, Draeger had arranged for me to go see a number of classical systems scattered around Japan. These were *ryu* I had seen in films that he had shown. He then wrote letters of introduction for each of those I indicated I would like to visit. My wife (at that time my lady friend) and I went to Japan and spent two or three months traveling around Japan and visiting these classical traditions.

Did you abandon your karate training at this time, with the hopes of being accepted into a classical system?

No, I was still heavily biased toward karate. One of the things Draeger had told me was that if I was still interested in karate, as far as he was concerned the best karate man he had ever met was Higaonna Morio, an Okinawan Goju-ryu man teaching in Tokyo. So after visiting these different classical *dojo* in Japan I really couldn't settle down on one, so we came back to Tokyo and decided that since Draeger does Shindo Muso-ryu, I might as well join that. So I started training at the Shindo Muso-ryu *dojo* in Tokyo.

How is it that, especially as a foreigner, you were able to gain accep-

tance into a classical ryu in Japan, but while in Hawaii you were not?

Draeger was teaching his students in the classical, old-style method. However, the Renbukan Dojo, the main one in Tokyo for the art, was basically open to anybody. It was also a system that was in transition from the old classical method of instruction to a more modern method, and since then has gone almost completely in that direction.

At the same time, I decided that as far as karate goes I should go to the JKA. So I went to the Hombu Dojo of the JKA, and was again immediately disenchanted with the ultramodern approach to karate instruction. It was good karate, mind you, some terrific instructors were there, like Kanazawa and Asai, but it was not classical fighting.

Why didn't you seek out Higaonna, as Draeger advised?

Well, I originally had kind of a bad impression about Goju because of all the Yamaguchi Goju Kai stuff published by *Black Belt* magazine.

You mean like photos of Yamaguchi in his "Cat" posture and practicing karate under a waterfall?

Yes, all the silly stuff that was put out. That was my impression of Goju, so I was a little surprised when Draeger told me that Higaonna was the best karate man he'd ever seen. At that time, I was still a little more oriented toward systems rather than people. So, in my mind, the style of Goju was more important that the man teaching it.

When I became totally disenchanted with the JKA, I did go over to the Yoyogi *dojo* where Higaonna Sensei was teaching, and introduced myself. He was a very fine and cordial gentleman. And the rest is history, as they say, because I switched over to Goju very quickly. As it turned out, Higaonna Sensei and I had many things in common as far as our beliefs about fighting arts. And Higaonna Sensei is one of the finest gentlemen I have ever run into, probably the finest karate men I have ever run into. He had and has an interesting ability to maintain the dichotomy between classical Okinawan fighting karate-jutsu and modern karate-do. Most arts that are going through that transition from the old into the new, are not able to maintain many aspects of the old system in the new. Higaonna Sensei was able to maintain the traditional combative aspects. His real interest was in the old style, but at the same time he truly believes that modern karate as done in Okinawan Goju-ryu is a boon to mankind. And so he is quite capable of teaching modern Okinawan karate-do, while at the same time, for himself and a few others, he still teaches and trains the classical karate-jutsu.

So that was my karate background. At the same time I started Shindo Muso-ryu, and that was around 1977.

You are also an exponent of a classical spear system. How did you get involved with that art?

Draeger was determined that all the members of the Japan core group of the IHRC would be trained in Japanese battlefield weapons systems. Of course, we were all determined to be in Katori Shinto-ryu, just like the master, but he was determined to keep us out of that ryu.

Why? One would think that Draeger would want to increase the membership of the classical *ryu* to which he belonged in an effort to promote and perpetuate it.

It was his belief that the classical traditions were going to fall by the wayside as modern culture set in. And he was determined that his people were going to help preserve the classical traditions. He didn't want a bunch of foreigners in Katori Shinto-ryu because he felt we could be better used in other traditions to help preserve them. And also because he knew too many foreigners would corrupt the system. I am sorry to say that this appears to be happening.

So Draeger introduced me to the tradition of Tatsumi-ryu. I trained at the Tatsumi-ryu *dojo* in Chiba prefecture from 1979 until I left Japan in 1981. I did go back for a couple of summer trainings.

Then in 1985 my wife was hired by Brother Industries to help set up a chain of fitness centers in Japan. So we were based in Nagoya for that year. I asked some friends if they new of any classical systems to go visit while in Nagoya. I was only going to be there for a year, so I didn't really think it would be responsible of me to try and go train in a new classical tradition for only a year. One friend, Larry Bieri, suggested I go check out Owari Kan-ryu So-jutsu, a classical spear tradition headed a man named Kato Isao Sensei.

I did go to that *dojo*, and it turned out they did both Shin Kage-ryu *heiho* and Owari Kan-ryu. I watched and was impressed to the point that I actually asked to join on the spot. I told Kato Sensei that I was very impressed and realized that it was rather rude of me to suggest that I would like to train since I was only going to be there for one year, but if I could train with them I would be very honored. He agreed that a year was too short, but was still kind enough to invite me in. I am still with that classical system today.

That is probably the most important training I have ever done and am doing now. It is a complete battlefield tradition, as they've maintained all of the weapons, tactical instruction, the whole thing. It has been quite an eye opener for me.

At the end of that year, I moved back to the States for about a year-and-a-half. My wife was then asked to take over the operations of the Brother fitness center chain (another book in itself). So, we moved back to Japan in 1988, and stayed in Kyoto through 1990. I went back to training in Nagoya, and was actually taking the train out from Kyoto to Nagoya two-to-three times a week. That was an expensive little commute.

Wasn't it also around this time that you established the International Hoplological Research Center in Hawaii?

Yes, that's right. We moved back to Hawaii in 1990, where we stayed for four years and got the ball rolling a little more seriously in the IHRC. Then in 1994, we moved out to Sedona, Arizona, where we live today.

What are the types of things that the International Hoplology Society is doing today. How are you applying the knowledge of human combative systems and behaviors to the modern world?

In a nutshell, we've done quite a bit of work in the behavioral area. Combative behavior and biomechanics are the two legs of combative performance. Essentially, in hoplology, we have been descriptive over the past thirty-some-odd years, in our studies in Asia as well as in Europe and South America, Africa, and so on. Now we have been able to get enough information to look at that descriptive material and say, here are the commonalties in mechanics and here are the commonalties in behavior. And the behavioral aspect is the real key point. So, just since we relocated to Arizona, we are for the first time becoming prescriptive.

I am not sure what you mean by prescriptive? Can you give an example of what you mean by prescriptive?

Sure. We have been taking this information on classical fighting systems from all parts of the world, but more importantly those that are still using what you might call natural weapons—swords, spears, sticks, clubs, etc. By looking at all the systems that are still being used for real fighting, as opposed to sport, we can look, for example, at a modern law enforcement defensive tactics instruction course or at shooting instruction course or at a military bayonet program, and we can see that while some of what they are doing is viable, much of it is not. Based on what classical systems are doing—that is, systems developed in real fighting for real fighting—some things are very wrong with what these courses are doing.

Of all the areas that could be better developed in these courses, what is one that stands out the most?

Probably combat handgun use is the best example. In the predominant shooting school of thought, you are taught to focus on the front sight of the handgun, not on the person you are shooting. This is, basically, unquestioned by most. The only real controversy in shooting is what size cartridge, or whether to use a revolver or a semi-auto. But these are secondary things, as, according to the classical combative systems, the primary factor is training the individual.

As another example, a lot of defensive tactics is based on modern aiki. However, modern aiki was neither evolved for nor designed for law enforcement uses or real combat.

What the modern systems tend to lack is an understanding of behavior. The stress of somebody actually coming back at you in real life is very different than the stress of even a competition type of martial sport where someone is trying to smack you. Shooting again offers probably the most glaring illustration of this, as the great majority of modern police or military handgun training is based on shooting at static, nonreturn firing targets. One can become quite accurate and very effective with virtually any shooting system you want to make up using that method. But, when the bullets start coming back at you, and if you have not trained any behavior behind it, your shooting system will fall apart pretty quickly.

So this is what we mean when we say as hoplologists we are becoming prescriptive. We are not teaching shooting or defensive tactics per se, but we are teaching an integrated combative behavioral system. We now have a training organization within the IHS, that deals specifically with developing training programs for the military, law enforcement, and similar fields of professional combative application. The ICS (Integrated Combative Systems) has already done work with the Marine Corps on bayonet training as well as law enforcement groups in combative behavioral training. A huge benefit for us from this work is that we find that we are getting tremendous information back from the professionals we've been working with. But there is also a lot of resistance from the current instructors of these courses. Again, it comes down to belief systems and the fact that no one likes change.

The idea that the principles found in classical martial arts can be effectively applied in our modern world, even with guns, is very interesting. Do you have any final statements regarding the research, theoretical, or practical application of hoplology you would care to share?

Yes. I have been involved in hoplology now for twenty-five years, and I think what we are really doing here is looking at human combative behavior as being a normal human trait. It should be viewed as neither good nor bad, as it has been an adaptive trait that has helped us adapt to and survive all sorts of contexts and environments on this planet and in all kinds of conflicts.

The problem is, that technology has perhaps surpassed our abilities to deal with combat through our natural combative behaviors. In this day of guns and bombs, our own behavioral responses are too slow to deal with the speed of the bullet. However, the solution is not to get rid of the guns, or to change the behavior, but to better understand our combative behavior and be able to apply it to these days and situations.

CURTIS F. WONG
Martial Arts Book and Magazine Publishing

Curtis Wong has been involved in various aspects of the martial arts for over thirty-five years. Starting out as a student of kung-fu and taekwondo, Wong landed a role as an actor in 1972 on the "Kung Fu" television series. Riding the success of the show, he soon opened a kung-fu school and began to design and manufacture his own kung-fu uniforms. Finding that he needed a place to advertise his school and uniforms, but not wanting to pay the ad prices charged by the martial arts magazines of the time, Wong started publishing Inside Kung-Fu *magazine in 1975. Since then, he has published over two hundred different magazine titles, the most popular being* Inside Kung-Fu, Inside Karate, Martial Arts Legends, Martial Arts Illustrated, Bruce Lee, *and* Action Pursuit Games. *In addition to his magazine business, Wong also founded Unique Publications, a martial art book and video publisher, and has published over one hundred martial art book titles and over two hundred martial art video titles.*

Curtis, the story of how you got into the martial arts publishing business, and built your company into one of the leading martial arts publishers in the world, is quite interesting and inspirational.

Well thank you, Mark. Actually, I didn't start out in the martial arts publishing business, but in the entertainment industry. First I studied kung-fu under Ark Wong and taekwondo under a Mr. Cho, who died while a member of the Green Berets. I started my career, though, as an actor and stuntman on the "Kung Fu" television series, in August of 1972. I was hired by David Chow, the show's technical advisor, and was in twenty-one episodes of the series.

How did David Chow, as the technical advisor to the show, come to hire you?

David was the technical advisor, a position almost as strong as producer for this show. In fact, I think he invented the term "technical advisor." On the show, he would tell the producer things like what religion a Shaolin monk was, how he meditated, what he wore, the history of the temple, what type of philosophy to put in the dialogue, and so on.

So I got into the show almost by chance. Our insurance agent and friend of the family, who also happens to be a friend of David Chow, informed my brother Douglas of the *Kung Fu* movie pilot. David put Douglas in the pilot. I was invited to the pilot wrap party, which is where I was introduced to David Chow. David hired me to work on several episodes on the series and I got my friend James Lew involved also. On the first episode we met Harry Wong. Harry and James ended up being my two best friends throughout the years.

Didn't you also open a martial arts school at this time?

Yes. Actually, I was going to college at night for a degree in art. But after four years of study, I had only completed about twenty-two credit units. So I decided to open the Sil Lum Kung-Fu School in December of 1972.

Were you no longer with the "Kung Fu" series at this time?

I was still with the series, but at that time I had most of my days free. You see, as an actor/stuntman on a television series there is not much to do most of the time. Since my part only required a day or two a week of shooting I had a lot of extra time on my hands. So I worked as a delivery man for a pharmacy and worked the graveyard shift as a grocery store clerk to earn extra money.

Since I always wanted to open a kung-fu school, I thought now was a good time to do so since I could capitalize on the timing of the show. So I just went out and looked for a location. I opened the school, but my brother Douglas actually ended up doing most of the teaching.

Didn't you also start your kung-fu uniform company called Mantis Supply during this time?

Yes, that's right. As I stated, while on the series I had a lot of free time during the day. I really wanted to go to college during the day, rather than at night, so what I did was I started to think that I could make uniforms for the students. All throughout my college years, I went to school from 6:00 to 10:00 pm. During the day I worked from 7:30 to 5:30 at a pharmacy. Since classes at my kung-fu school were held at night I couldn't go to night school anymore, so I decided to quit and I would later attend day classes. Well, as things happen, I never went back to school. My kung-fu school was successful. After the first three months of opening the school I had amassed two hundred students. I wanted to earn more money so I started Mantis Supply.

Wasn't the Mantis Supply company actually the impetus for beginning your publication of *Inside Kung-Fu* magazine?

Right. The way the whole thing started was that I decided that I could make kung-fu uniforms for my students. So I started to design them and I had my mother sew them up, and we sold two-hundred uniforms. Since that was a pretty good profit I thought I would take an ad out for the company in *Black Belt* magazine. I called them up and their ad rate at that time for one page was six-hundred dollars. I couldn't afford it. So what I did was to just sketch a cover for a kung-fu magazine, using a picture that appeared on the cover of *Black Belt*. There were five people from the "Kung Fu" show that appeared on the cover photo of *Black Belt*, and I was one of them. So I took the photo and just put the word kung-fu on top of it. It looked pretty good so I decided to start my own magazine.

At the time, I didn't know anything about how much it was going to cost to publish a magazine or how to distribute it. So I went to the bank with four-thousand dollars and borrowed ten thousand against it. I used that money to put together a brochure for the magazine and mailed it to six thousand martial arts schools. I said that if the schools would subscribe to fifteen copies of the magazine or more, they would get their address listed in the directory in the back for free, and they would make fifty-percent profit on all the magazines they could sell to their students. Right off the bat we sold twenty-five thousand copies of *Inside Kung-Fu*.

In May of 1973, I opened our editorial and production office in Hollywood. By August we had the first issue of *Inside Kung-Fu* out. It was out in August but the cover date was December 1973. It was fifty or sixty cents a copy.

Why did you eventually close down the Mantis Supply company?

What happened was that we continued Mantis Supply until we ran out of money. We ran out of money for it because our main concern was to keep the magazine going. Later on we cut out Mantis Supply altogether because the advertisers were complaining that we were competing with them.

I know that it is terribly difficult to get nationwide distribution for a new magazine. How did you eventually get such good distribution for *Inside Kung-Fu*?

First of all, we couldn't get our magazine distributed nationwide right away because our distributor handled *Black Belt* magazine. *Black Belt* had the exclusive at that time. But, if we were to come out with a second, non-martial arts magazine, the distributor would also have to take our martial arts title. So, in 1977, we came out with a new magazine called *Racquetball Illustrated*. It did fantastic, and that helped launch *Inside Kung-Fu* nationally.

What made you decide to publish additional martial arts titles. Wasn't it tough enough and costly enough just doing one, or did you see an untapped market potential?

At that time, there was only a handful of martial arts magazines. The largest was *Black Belt,* which also had a few sister magazines. So I thought that if I came out with a few more titles, we would actually have our own little martial arts section on the newsstand. We felt that would be better than having only two or three martial arts titles on the newsstand mixed in with hundreds of other titles. With all of the mixed titles no one would even know our titles were there. So, although we competed with *Black Belt* and competed with ourselves, we could have more newsstand space available for our own products. So, in 1978, I started publishing other titles like *Kick Illustrated,* which later became *Inside Karate.*

When did you start publishing books under the Unique Publications imprint?

In 1975 we started publishing books. Basically, we just followed *Black Belt's* format, which incorporated Rainbow Publications books. They were so successful that we just wanted to follow in their footsteps. At the time, they were mainly doing the Japanese arts and so we were doing mostly the Chinese arts.

I think the first couple of book titles we published were *Sil Lum Kung-Fu* by my brother Doug Wong, *Dynamic Tension* by Harry Wong, and *The Art of Stretching and Kicking* by James Lew. We just used guys we hung around with. We were all friends so there was no hassle. It was a fun learning experience.

How did you go about getting national distribution for the books?

Basically we just did that ourselves via direct mail through placing ads in our own magazines. Once we started we became pretty successful in our first couple years of publishing. And quite a few people from Rainbow Publications came over to join our company. For whatever reason they just wanted to work for me. For instance, Bob Matheny, the former publisher of *Black Belt* came over to us, their head book salesperson, Margorie Tijiri, came over, and then some editors came over, Ed Ikuta, their photographer came over,

Mark Komuro their art director came over, and Nancy Lem the assistant art director came over.

You got the whole crew. You must have done something right for everyone to jump ship.

Yes, we got quite a few people from their company. And after twenty-five years, most of them are still with us today.

More than anything, Curtis, it says a lot about you as an individual.

Oh, well, thank you.

When and how did you start to get your books into the chain book stores?

As soon as Marjorie came over, I think it was in something like 1977 or 1978. Since she had been dealing with the book buyers in the past, especially with B. Dalton, we got in there right away. That made a big difference for us in terms of sales and establishing our name and titles.

I recall seeing ads in your magazines a few years ago for Unique front list titles with a line saying they were available through B. Dalton Booksellers. You must have had a strong relationship with them.

In fact, at one time we had orders where we would ship out to them thirty thousand books at a time. This was just to B. Dalton. We were lucky because we caught the tail end of the whole Bruce Lee phenomenon. Rainbow was there and did really well, and we came on the scene in 1973, the year Bruce Lee passed away.

At one point you moved your offices from Hollywood, where Rainbow was located, to Burbank. Was this for political reasons or financial ones?

Well, at that time we really needed a larger office space, and Hollywood was becoming trashy. So we moved to Burbank because it was a lot safer and I was able to buy a large warehouse space for the editorial, marketing, and shipping offices.

It certainly marked a turning point in your business as you were able to

expand. In fact, after the move you were able to produce a least a dozen monthly magazines.

Yes, that's right. We have probably started about two hundred and fifty titles. I think in 1991 we actually had fifteen different magazine titles on the newsstands at one time, including *Inside Kung-Fu, Inside Karate, Inside Martial Arts, Masters and Styles, Martial Arts Masters,* and *Martial Arts Legends.* We also had four comic books; one was called *Robo Warriors.* We also had a skateboarding magazine called *Power Edge,* and *Racquetball Illustrated, Outdoor Gear, Golf Lifestyle, Action Pursuit Games, Paintball,* and others.

So why do you now have only about half of those titles still in print? Was the interest no longer there, or were other mitigating factors involved?

Well, the comic book sales were always up and down, so when they came down again we decided to kill the titles. The golf market was a tough one to crack since we were up against the big boys. *Outdoor Gear* was a good magazine, but the sales just weren't there. The advertising was there, but not the sales.

Do you attribute lack of sales to limited distribution?

It is always hard to launch a new title, and back then it was especially difficult. If you don't have money to advertise a new title and nobody knows it's there, sales are left to impulse buyers who chance by it in stores. Like now, if you want to come out with a new magazine title, the company must advertise it well in advance of actual publication so that people will know to look for it.

Another problem was that paper prices went up drastically in 1990. That one event really hurt the entire publishing industry. Even Bob Guccione had to sell off a few of his titles. A lot of magazines dropped twenty to thirty percent in sales, and at the same time, for some reason, the price of producing them almost doubled.

Why do you think the price of paper went up so high while sales dropped?

I think in part it was because of the Internet. The biggest reason, I think, is because there are now four thousand magazine titles out there on the newsstands, and there is only so much space to sell them. The average newsstand only carries about three hundred or four hundred titles. And now they are categorized into A titles and B titles. A lot of the grocery store chains require a sixty-five percent sell-through for a title or they won't carry it. No martial arts magazine comes close to that percentage of sales.

Also, the whole distribution business has changed. Over the last two years a lot of the small local wholesalers, secondary distributors have been bought out by larger distributors. Before, they had like four hundred local wholesalers, while there is only approximately one hundred and fifty around today. Because of that, fewer distributors have more control. The secondary wholesalers control which magazines will go out and which will stay in the warehouse. And they want to do what is most cost-effective for them. So, push the big A titles like *Time* and *People*, and forget about the B titles like *Inside Kung-Fu.* In fact, now you even have to get authorization from the individual grocery store chains. And if they already have one martial arts magazine, they don't see a need to carry another one—they simply don't have the shelf space.

I also think another factor that slowed down the sales is that the cover prices are now so high. Before, the average buyer would go out and buy four or five martial arts magazines in a weekend. Now they only buy one, maybe two. So that hurts, too.

You were also one of the pioneers of producing martial arts videos. I think today you have over two hundred titles. How and why did you get into that end of the business?

We always wanted to produce martial arts videos, even ten years ago. But at that time we didn't think there were that many people who were into buying videos or even learning from them. We found out differently after watching Panther Productions and others coming out with strong-selling titles. So we decided to start our own production company. We did, and produced two hundred video titles in the first two years alone. We were able to keep production costs down by owning three cameras, an editing bay, and using our own studio space.

Well it seems, in this regard, that Rainbow followed Unique.

Yes, I would say so. They actually had a couple of videos out first, but they weren't produced by Rainbow Publication. Instead, Rainbow licensed out the *Black Belt* name to the producers. But now Rainbow Publications is producing their own videos full force.

What do you see as some of the major trends over the past twenty-five years in the martial arts?

I think in the mid-eighties the ninja era was a huge business all around for the martial arts. They brought out the mystique in the art that people like. Everyone likes mystique, and any kind of mystique sells. Of course Bruce Lee started the whole martial arts business thing. Even today he is really big. And the new guys like Jackie Chan, Chuck Norris, Steven Seagal, and Jean Claude Van Damme have also done their part in popularizing the arts.

The problem today is that there is no more mystique in the martial arts. I think if twenty years ago you said you were a black belt and could break fourteen boards, people were impressed by the mystique of it all. Today, they don't care because they know it is not a big deal. Everyone knows the tricks involved in doing these stunts, like breaking ice and bricks and lying on nails.

You know what really killed martial arts, I think, was events like full-contact karate and the Ultimate Fighting Championship. People realized, after watching these events, that you couldn't kill somebody with just one punch. You don't see those mystical techniques, only street fighting or boxing or wrestling. So what happened to the promise of the death touch and chi power and invincibility? They went out the window.

Within the past two years you have launched a new publishing company called Multi-Media Communications Network, which has diversified your place in the publishing world. Can you tell us a little something about the new company?

Yes, Multi-Media was launched with the publication of *Bruce Lee* magazine. *Bruce Lee* magazine is actually the official publication and voice of the Jun Fan Jeet Kune Do Nucleus. We also have *Martial Arts Illustrated,* and we are in the process of coming out with an alternative health title called *Rejuvenate,* and a celebrity fitness title called *Fit and Famous.* We are also publishing an entire new line of martial arts, alternative health, and fitness books and videos to complement the magazines.

Ten years ago you could have been a single publisher, but today you have to be a publisher of multiple titles. In the past few years a lot of the big publishing companies have been acquiring the smaller ones, making themselves stronger in the process.

So the key is to diversify and stay in the game as long as possible.

Exactly. Communications will always be big. If you look at these big chain stores like Barnes and Noble, books are here to stay. Regardless of the Internet, people will always buy books. You can't take your computer with you, or be near your computer every time you want to look up something or learn a new technique.

You have also recently diversified even more with the production of fitness supplements. How did you get into that business?

Joe Weider has always been a sort of mentor for me over the past twenty years. His company has done fantastic. The thing is the martial art and fitness fields are similar, and our companies too—although Weider is a hundred times bigger. There has never really been a supplement drink or nutrition bar for martial artists. Now there is, but no one really focused in on it until last year. We realized that people want to maximize all the energy that they will need for the martial arts, just as all the bodybuilders and other athletes do in their sports. So we designed a supplement just for martial artists so they can say "Hey, this is ours." Our formula was so good that we decided to go to the "extreme sports" market, not just to martial artists. So we came out with Nitrokick powder supplement and nutrition bars.

It's really just something to give you energy. You know, before a workout you really can't eat a full meal, or if you're on the road. So someone can eat a bar or drink a shake on the go and they are satisfied, but not so full that they can't work out—but they have that extra needed energy.

Throughout your years in the martial arts business you have seen and

done a great many things. Are there moments that stand out in your mind as extraordinary?

Yes, a few. In 1974, a guy named Dennis Ritz came to my office looking for information on the martial arts. He represented Howard Hughes Corporation in Las Vegas, who were putting together a variety show called "Orient '75." I said, hey I got the guys right here for your show—me, James Lew, Harry Wong, Tadashi Yamashita, and a guy named Todd Taguchi.

Anyway, we agreed and went to Arizona to do the first show at a small fair. Then we went to the Landmark Hotel and did a show there for eight weeks. So every night they would announce "Lloyd and Keigo and Curtis Wong proudly presents the Orient '75 Show." It was a variety show where Pat Suzuki sang the original flower drum strong. There was also a magic show, topless girls—it was pretty cool.

While I was doing that, I still had the school and I was doing a lot of TV shows at that time, like "Different Strokes," "The Hardy Boys," "Police Story," "Night Rider," "Quincy," and many others. I worked as both an actor and stuntman.

Speaking of "Quincy," weren't you slated to be the star of the movie Men of the Dragon, of which the lead eventually went to "Quincy" co-star Robert Ito?

Yes, that's right. I was supposed to be the lead in that film. But I was advised to stay at home to run my magazine, rather than go to Hong Kong for six weeks of filming, as the magazine was just getting started. So I passed on the part.

I was also supposed to have been the martial arts choreographer on the "Kung Fu" TV series, but Kam Yuen ended up with the job because he was good friends with David Carradine.

Throughout your travels and appearances, who were some of the stranger martial artists you crossed paths with?

Well, the strangest thing that ever happened to me was when this one time we kept getting letters from this guy named Rodney Sacharnoski. The letters said that he could take a baseball bat shot to his throat and nothing would happen. I thought this guy was totally nuts and I didn't want to put him in the magazines. I ignored him, but he just kept writing.

Then one day I was at work cleaning the office on a Saturday and three guys in suits walked in. One of the men introduced himself as Dr. Rod Sacharnoski. Even though they all looked like decent people I thought there was going to be trouble. They asked if they could do a demonstration for me right then and there. I told them to hold on; I was thinking lawsuit. I mean, if someone were to get hurt and I am the only one from the office present, it would have been their word against mine as to whose fault it was. So I told them that I would set it up for them to come back the following day to demonstrate, when I would have a proper audience of top instructors from the area present and we would have our cameras and recorders ready to go. They agreed.

I called Ed Parker, Tadashi Yamashita, Tino Tuliosega of the lima-lama system, Kim Kahana, James Lew, and Harry Wong. So the next day we all got together, and Rod Sacharnoski and his guys did some stuff that was so scary, I'm telling you, that my arms literally got cold.

Our guys hit their guys in the eyes and balls and head with bats and punches and kicks, and it didn't phase them. This was some real stuff because it wasn't like they were hitting each other; we were doing it to them. Scary. I'm telling you, man, if you had seen this you would have fainted. Even Ed Parker said he couldn't believe his eyes and that he had never seen anything like this in his life. In fact, Ed left early because the whole thing just scared him. And Tino had this big Samoan black belt hit this guy right in the temple, and nothing happened. Then Tino got scared. We had one guy stand in a horse stance and one of our guys kicked him square in the balls with front kick. The kick was so hard it lifted the man off the ground—but no damage. So then I asked them, what if you placed your head against the wall and someone side kicked it? Now, you know, there is no room "to give" in a situation like that, so we figured they would back out. Well, they didn't. I'm telling you, this guy placed his head against the wall and one of our guys did a side kick smack into his temple. We all started to panic when we heard this loud crack sound on impact. But the guy just stood up as if nothing had happened. We all got the chills.

The next day Ed Parker called me and said, "Curtis, we got to get to know these guys, they are amazing." And it wasn't just one guy; all of his students could take the shots without showing any signs of damage. Ed became good friends with Rod; they even appeared in a movie together.

That event was probably one of the highlights of the martial arts for me. They actually performed the same demonstration on a televised episode of "Wide World of Sports," but it bombed because everyone thought it was fake. But they were unbelievable, and the nicest guys. I have since lost contact with Dr. Sacharnoski, but I know he is still around. I don't know how he does it, but he is one of those martial artists who is truly for real.

Out of all the martial artists that have come by the office or you have met on the tournament or seminar circuits, who had the strongest and hardest punch?

Without a doubt, Joe Lewis definitely hit the hardest. In the early days of the magazine when everyone started coming out of the woodwork, we used to have all the martial artists come in and James Lew would hold the heavy bag or focus mitts for them—just to see who was real and who wasn't. Of all the people, when Joe Lewis hit the bag or mitts you could really feel it and also hear it. The impact from his punches was awesome. He is a really tough guy.

You have not only rubbed elbows with not only the greatest martial artists in the world, but also with the world's greatest celebrities. Who was the most memorable celebrity you have met?

The biggest thing for me ever was meeting Elvis Presley and being invited to his house. I am a huge Elvis fan. In 1974, I had a party in my office to celebrate the second year of my publishing company. I invited Ed Parker along with Elvis Presley, who couldn't make it. But Elvis told Ed to invite me along to RCA to watch him rehearse for an upcoming gig in Las Vegas the following day. So I went to RCA and stood behind the booth and watched Elvis; I was the only guy there. Ed Parker was in the other room with Elvis and the other boys. He finished rehearsals around twelve o'clock midnight and we met each other. As we were walking down to his car, Elvis told Ed to come to him and whispered something in his ear. Ed then came over to me and said Elvis wanted me to come with them to his house with them right then.

So Ed gave me the address and said they would meet me there. He also said I had to park two blocks away to avoid the press, who would be all around the front gate. This is when Elvis lived in Beverley Hills. So I parked my car two blocks away from the house, and Red West, Elvis' right-hand man, came to pick me up in Elvis Presley's little red Mercedes and we went to the house. Meanwhile, Ed Parker had gone home to go pick up his wife.

When I walked in the room there were some people there like Micki Garcia, the head of Playboy Talent, and George Waite, Elvis' stepbrother. Then twenty minutes later Elvis came down. We sat down and actually talked for like four hours. Then he gave me a tour around the house. And I didn't leave the house until about seven o'clock the next morning, and I was so tired. Ed Parker had come back around three or four o'clock in the morning, and they gave Red West a third degree black belt in kenpo. They had a whole ceremony and everything.

The experience was cool since I have always been a huge Elvis fan. And Elvis told me that while his first love was music, his second was the martial arts.

With your vast experience in martial arts acting, equipment sales, magazine, book, and video publishing, and now supplements, where do you see the arts headed in the future?

I think that what is going to happen is that you are going to see a lot of martial arts publishing companies fall off to the side, including some of our titles that aren't doing so well. I think we will end up with magazines and books on the stands and in stores that focus on quality and have a lasting value to martial artists as a whole. Another two or three years down the line will see only three or four martial arts magazines still on the newsstands. Aside from problems with distribution and authorization, the production costs are simply becoming too high.

There is a lot of magazine competition out there right now, so we were forced to add more color, more pages, and better paper quality to our titles just to keep up. This, however, raises our costs almost to a point of exhaustion. Martial artists are also getting more and more sophisticated, and you can't give them just any kind of information anymore; they know what is real and what is bogus. However, since we are firmly established, I know we will be here for the long run.

Books, on the other hand, will always be there and strong since they don't contain dated material, like magazines do. Again, I think quality and packaging will prove to be of utmost importance, whereas in years past it wasn't. And there are a lot of people who, even though they are not practicing martial arts, want to know about it.

PART SIX

MARTIAL ARTS
AND LIFE

CHRISTOPHER D. HESS, SMAC
Toward a Total Quality Martial Art

Chris Hess is a twenty-year veteran of the martial arts, having practiced such styles as Shotokan karate, taekwondo, aikido, tai chi, and jeet kune do. In 1996, Hess became the first certified "specialist in martial arts conditioning" through the International Sport Sciences Association. Hess' articles on the martial arts and fitness have appeared in such international magazines as Martial Arts Illustrated, Black Belt, Karate International, MA Training, Inside Karate, Karate/KungFu Illustrated, *and* Wushu KungFu.

In recent years, Hess has become known in the martial arts field as an inspirational and lifeplanning leader. He has taken a base of ideas from time management, psychology, sport science, Eastern and Western philosophy and spirituality and condensed them into the development of an approach to using the martial arts as a vehicle for not only personal growth, but a means of integrating the physical, mental, business, and interpersonal aspects of life. He calls this approach Total Quality Martial Arts.

Chris, you have hit on an interesting approach for martial artists, which you have labeled Total Quality Martial Arts, wherein you relate physical practice with interpersonal, business, and spiritual matters in life. What are the roots of your approach?

In one sense, the true root to this approach is simple curiosity. I have always been curious and have read so much that I think I literally fulfill the warning of Solomon who, in the *Bible,* cautioned that "much study wearies the body."

On a serious note, my intellectual life has gone through many phases. As an adolescent I was compelled to read Freud and similar behavioral theorists. In college, I most enjoyed the study of existentialism (which is about the irrational nature of man). Throughout my twenties, I focused on Christian ethics. Each of these studies "prepared the ground," so to speak, for my introduction to a business approach called Total Quality Management—which occurred in my early thirties. All of my previous studies and attempts to understand life and improve myself brought certain satisfactions and certain disappointments. However, they made my introduction to Total Quality unusually relevant.

After my first exposure to Total Quality, I took everything that was important or an issue in my life at that time, and subjected it to the Total Quality process. And I mean everything. There are a variety of quantitative and qualitative tools available to analyze any process in Total Quality, and I used each of them to assess myself physically, spiritually, vocationally, and in every other manner I could conceive. The spiritual analysis was particularly humbling, both because the process showed me where I was stuck and because it's easy to not fully appreciate spiritual concerns when fully committed to physical training, as in the martial arts.

This rigorous approach, sort of laying myself open to the knife, helped me learn the Total Quality process in a very intimate way and suggested to me that it could be especially useful in the martial arts (which often seem to resist analysis). So, after mastering the fundamentals of Total Quality over a couple years time, I created the Total Quality Martial Arts approach. I have recently presented this approach in a new book by the same name.

You are saying, then, that martial artists need to carefully consider the spiritual concerns in our lives. That while many of us diligently train our arts we, in effect, neglect the nonphysical aspects of our lives. How, specifically, does TQMA address this?

Total Quality Martial Arts invites martial athletes to look at their lives in the most comprehensive manner possible. Since I sense that anyone who picks up a copy of my book will do so primarily because of martial arts interest, I address sport science first in the approach. My intention is to help satisfy that curiosity, then invite readers to the fuller dimensions of the Total Quality approach.

What I do next is remind readers that even those athletes who have become successful in their arts show the effects of not fully addressing the spiritual aspects of life. What I mean by this is that there are those who are title holders, movie stars, and so forth, but whose names are also associated with, perhaps, drug abuse, interpersonal problems, and similar types of disorders. So, my exhortation to martial artists is to not assume that if victory occurs all will be well. Many times, success brings a whole new host of problems that need be addressed. That's why we need an unqualified emphasis on spiritual matters as martial artists. If someone can defend themselves in a street fight but is unable to successfully negotiate a matter with their employer, spouse, or child, that person is not very high up the ladder of human achievement.

The Total Quality approach says, in effect, that we must all plan and address our spiritual life as we do our physical one. We read books, study videos, and attend seminars to improve ourselves as martial artists. We need to exercise the same diligence in the spiritual realm as well.

Another fundamental area addressed in your approach is sport science. For thousands of years martial artists have neglected the scientific study of movement and principles of physics. Why do you now place such an emphasis on sport science in you TQMA approach?

I was one of the millions of people who thought that the key to athletic success was to find out how the top performer in any given sport trained, to then copy that program, and "voila!" success would be mine. It doesn't take too many injuries or long walks home after a bitter loss to realize that the "copy the star" approach is severely lacking.

There are literally millions of nuances to sport science regarding physiology, nutrition, and so forth, but I've found that if people are equipped with even the most basic fundamentals of sport science they can begin to interpret training recommendations and elite programs on their own. By "basic fundamentals," I'm referring to the human body's primary muscle fiber types and three primary energy systems. We can talk about these in greater detail if you want in a few moments. But I don't want to lose the initial point about sport science yet.

If athletes only use the recommendations or programs of elite athletes without understanding the underlying sport science of those endeavors, most will overtrain themselves. As a practical example, someone might read that a track athlete runs one-mile repeats at a 4:45 pace and think, "I'll need to do those as well to be a good miler." Well, I can tell you right now that someone able to run 4:45 miles in training has a high proportion of slow-twitch muscle fibers. If a prospective athlete has a high proportion of fast-twitch fibers (which would enable someone to run short distances very quickly), no amount of training will turn that person into a 4:45 miler. Conversely, that 4:45 miler will not be turning in any sub-eleven second, one hundred meter dashes. If either one tries to copy the training program of the other, without realizing their inherent muscle fiber types, overtraining will occur.

To help martial athletes address sport science, I've included no-cost "field tests" in my book, *Total Quality Martial Arts,* that can be used to determine approximate muscle fiber types, the degree of aerobic conditioning, and whether their mental temperament is similar to those who dominate the combative arts. This is an individualized use of sport science that can help anyone design and use a training program that reflects their inherent abilities and their martial arts goals.

TQMA warns that martial artists should avoid the training myth that if a program worked for one person it will work for all. Why wouldn't the

program of a national champion necessarily be beneficial for an aspiring champion?

This is a very difficult concept to articulate. I'll try to explain it in two ways. On the one hand, elite athletes are successful because they are genetically predisposed to success. This is not to say they don't train hard; they do. But certain types of success are only available to those who have the inherent, genetic talent. This is most apparent, perhaps, in endurance athletics.

World-class endurance athletes have, for instance, a "VO2 Max" with values in the eighties while otherwise healthy adults have values in the forties. (VO2 Max is a measurement of how well oxygen is utilized). Aspiring endurance athletes aren't generally aware of the VO2 Max and, furthermore, aren't aware that it's only trainable to perhaps fifteen percent. In other words, if a person is born with a VO2 Max of forty, it might only be raised to perhaps a value of forty-six, even with rigorous training. Conversely, a person with a genetic inheritance of seventy could raise theirs to eighty. As you can see, the difference between someone with a forty-six and another with eighty translates to a great amount of distance between competitors when the two line up against one another on bicycles, in the pool, or whatever. If the person with a forty-six tries to emulate the training program used by the person with an eighty, that person will undoubtedly overtrain and experience a tremendous amount of disappointment that he or she can't achieve the same results.

How are these differences seen in the martial arts?

Differences in the martial arts are the second way I want to answer your question. However, to first clarify myself, one reason a champion's program can't just be blindly adopted is that genetics may be an inhibitor to emulation. The other reason is that many athletes, and martial artists in particular, are successful despite themselves. And that is an equally difficult concept to articulate and accept.

Earlier I hinted at the difference in muscle fiber types. Many people are aware that there are "slow twitch" and "fast twitch" fibers. The former are good for endurance activities and the latter are good for short periods of high intensity. Now, if readers open any martial arts magazine, they will find some competitor who currently holds a title of some sort or another talking about their training program. Frequently, these training programs contain aspects that these successful competitors don't realize are actually blunting their full potential.

For example, a successful kickboxer might say he or she does an hour of stairmaster work each day and they will attribute a portion of their success to that endurance work. But, an hour of stairmaster work recruits and trains slow-twitch muscle fibers and enzymes. And martial athletes don't generally use slow-twitch fibers in training or competition. In effect, the training stimulus, which in this case is the stairmaster, is actually training the wrong energy systems and muscle fibers for a kickboxer's competition demands. But, because the kickboxer is successful despite these incorrect training methods, the reality of properly trained fibers and systems is obscured by that success. "If they do it and they're a success, it must be right," the reasoning goes.

The difficulty in communicating this concept is further compounded by the fact that the negative results of improper training don't always show up at the present time, which enables elite athletes to consider their programs as "proof positive."

So, trainers like myself are frequently confronted with these difficult situations of trying to explain to aspiring athletes that the programs of their heroes aren't necessarily suitable for their own dreams, regardless of the degree of success. They might be, after careful analysis, but they shouldn't be accepted at face value. Admittedly, this is a tough sell, and it takes a long time to persuade and convince athletes not to blindly accept elite athletes' training programs.

So there is some truth to the notion that champions are born and not made. Can you further explain how human energy systems and muscle types differ in each of us, and how this effects our progress?

Sure. We've touched on energy systems and fiber types in several instances so this is probably an appropriate point to clearly state the fundamental aspects of martial arts sport science. There are three energy systems that exist in the human body, although they are frequently summarized as five due to some functional overlap. Generally speaking, the three core systems are the phosphagen, glycolytic, and oxidative energy systems.

The phosphagen energy system is the one that supplies short-term, high intensity effort such as a front snap kick. Physical efforts that use this energy last from zero to six seconds in length. In contrast to the other energy systems that I'll describe, phosphagen describes stored energy within the muscles and cells. Stored energy means that your exertion is not dependent on either oxygen or calories deriving from carbohydrates or fats. Martial athletes are primarily anaerobic and therefore primarily use this phosphagen system.

The glycolytic energy system is not as distinct as the other two systems. According to the level of intensity, the glycolytic system is either its own independent energy system or it interacts with the phosphagen or oxidative system to supply energy. This energy system is apparent in efforts that range from thirty seconds to approximately two minutes in duration. Whereas the phosphagen system uses stored energy, the glycolytic system is an energy-producing system deriving from carbohydrate sources in the body. The process of glycolysis is frequently referred to as the "lactic acid" system.

The oxidative, or aerobic system, describes those activities that are longer than three minutes in duration. The fuel for this energy system is stored fat in the body.

Now, with regard to muscle fiber types, the type and size of muscle fibers determines the speed and force of an action, such as kicking and punching.

This seems like a lot to digest for martial artists who aren't biologically inclined. Can you summarize for us the various muscle-fiber classifications in easy-to-follow terms?

Sure. To a large extent, these muscle fibers are genetically determined. There are four classifications of muscle fiber types.

Type I: These fibers are predominant in a long distance runner. They are fatigue resistant but have limited potential for rapid force development and low anaerobic power—which means they won't help create fast, powerful kicks. As I've alluded to, martial art training should not overemphasize the recruitment or development of slow-twitch fibers and enzyme systems.

Type II: While these fibers fatigue more easily, they generate much greater speed and power than aerobic type muscles, although for shorter periods of time. Type II muscles are understood as two subtypes.

The first is Type IIA. This type of fiber, because it is a derivative of Type II, creates fast and powerful movements but is not the maximum power fiber. These muscular contractions contain an oxidative component and therefore developing them involves the fast oxidative glycolytic (FOG) enzyme system. Whereas a Type I fiber person will be seen in endurance type events such as distance running or swimming, a Type IIA fiber person will be seen in road cycling, or in running events such as the 880.

The second is Type IIB. These fibers are the least fatigue-resistant of all muscle fiber types because they are designed for short-term, maximal efforts. The enzyme system is Fast Glycolytic (FG) because there is no oxidative property to the contraction. A person with these fibers will be seen in events such as the hundred-meter dash, shotputting, or other power events. It's what martial artists use in events less than six seconds in duration.

With all that said, the second part of your question becomes quite apparent. Our progress is, in many respects, correlated to the specific training of these energy systems and muscle fibers. If we say we want to be a champion karate point fighter, but then spend two hours a day on a bicycle, progress will be slow and hindered. Instead, if a point fighter evaluates his or her competition needs and realizes "I need a well-developed phosphagen energy system and Type IIB muscle fibers" and trains them accordingly, great progress will result.

Where do periodization and training cycles fit into this approach?

Periodization is an applied sport science term that essentially means adding variety to a training program. By definition, it means periods of overload followed by periods of recovery. Let's assume that someone is currently training ten hours per week. To periodize their training, they would overload for a three week period, say eleven, twelve, and then thirteen hours on the third week, followed by a one week recovery period of perhaps only seven or eight hours of training. This type of periodization enables athletes to progressively overload their current capacity and systematically recover before it's necessary to do so.

"Before it's necessary" is an important precept of periodization. Numerous athletes won't take a break from their training until injuries force them to slow down. And, of course, some of these injuries occur precisely because training has been occurring too long without an adequate opportunity for recovery. Just as the old maxim says "drink before you're thirsty," periodization says "recover before you need to." In other words, whether someone personally feels like it or not, in a periodization approach every fourth week is an "unloading" week of reduced training volume and intensity. This allows for physical and psychological recovery from intense training.

Training cycles are the natural fruition of periodization. Let's use resistance training as an example. In a general sense, to periodize means to follow that three-week overload and one-week recovery approach I just outlined. In a more specific sense, training plans can be further broken down into alternating cycles. For example, in resistance training, each new three week overload cycle can feature a different type of training stimulus. The first might be hypertrophy where an athlete lifts a certain weight with repetitions in the eight-to-twelve range to cause muscle fiber enlargement. The second cycle might be for strength, where someone lifts a heavier load with repetitions in the four-to-six range to increase contractile strength. A third cycle might mean lifting a lower weight with a fifteen repetition range at an accelerated lifting speed to enhance power and speed.

Periodization and training cycles are directly related to the energy systems and muscle fiber types we just discussed. Through sport science, we know how much stimulus and how much recovery is needed to properly train high and low intensity energy systems and fast or slow twitch muscle fibers. Each has it's own unique periodization and recovery needs that any qualified conditioning coach or trainer can help athletes in training realize.

In reviewing your book, I noticed you don't recommend just any weight training or physical fitness program, but advocate only certain activities for martial athletes. How did this come about and why did you see a need to be training specific?

Specifically tailored programs, including weight training, are the results of several significant factors. The first is that resistance training is absolutely a non-negotiable item for any serious martial athlete. I'm well aware of those who shun it and tell others to avoid it. In my opinion, avoiding resistance training sacrifices at least ten percent of someone's potential and invites all sorts of strength imbalances that arise from rigorous martial arts training, not to mention serious injuries.

However, I personally don't like resistance training. I'd rather spar, hit the bag, or do cardiovascular work. I like continuous exercise. But because resistance training is so important—not only to martial art training but to our long-term health as well—I perform it and tell anyone who will listen to do the same.

I think that most martial artists find it hard enough to make it to the training hall three time a week, let alone throwing weight training into the mix. Is there a way of better maximizing time in the gym?

When I first began resistance training, I spent from five to seven hours a week in the weight room because I was guilty of trying to use the "stars" programs. I used Arnold's recommendations in the *Encyclopedia of Modern Bodybuilding.* Since then, I've researched what muscle groups are most important in martial arts training and which ones can become neglected through the same. Through that research, I've pared resistance training down to the essentials, which has focused my training and greatly reduced the amount of time I now need in the weight room to be successful.

Can you offer a concrete example?

Sure. As a practical example, I no longer feel a need to do squats or other types of resistance training that emphasize the quadriceps because I train them plenty through bicycling and with Shotokan and taekwondo training. But the hamstrings are another matter altogether. These muscles aren't targeted through my normal training and, if not strengthened, will actually cause an imbalance that can adversely affect either bicycling or my kicking ability. As a result, I now regularly include stiff-leg dead lifts that train the hamstrings (as well as the lower back) and let the quadriceps resistance training go.

By paring these resistance training exercises down to the essentials, I now only spend two to three hours per week in the weight room, sometimes only thirty minutes at a time. Psychologically, I find that acceptable and I'm physically strong in the areas I need to be. It also leaves me with more energy for the activities I inherently enjoy.

In my book I address the core resistance training exercises needed by martial athletes based on my research and personal experience. Readers can use that information to develop their own tailored programs. This will, again, focus their efforts, reduce their time in the gym, and enhance their success while promote lifelong wellness.

You hold some interesting perspectives on the martial arts, can you tell us a little about your background?

I'm celebrating my twentieth year in the martial arts during 1998. I began training in judo and Shotokan karate during my freshman year of college in 1978. Throughout these twenty years, I've also practiced taekwondo, tai chi, and jeet kune do. Martial arts are one of three activities that I regularly practice. I also strength train and I raced bicycles competitively for ten years.

Although I'm not a professional athlete, I actually consider fitness to be my vocation in life—what I'm called to do. That sounds a little strange, I realize, because my actual salaried career is not fitness, but it's in fitness—whether martial arts, strength training, or cycling—that I feel I "meet myself" and God. That's why I consider fitness my vocation. In other words, performing exercise, researching it, writing about it, or training others is where I am most "present." In any fitness endeavor, I most encounter who I am as well what I'm not. And because of the many nuances to sport science, like human energy systems, fiber types, and mental temperament, I'm frequently confronted with the reality of God's creative design. I find that particularly exhilarating.

So, I've been an athlete my entire life. In the beginning it was team sports, but I was soon bored by those activities because of the amount of "dead time" involved—I didn't like depending on others in order to have a successful training experience. In high school, I began more individual pursuits such as boxing and distance running. Then, in college, I evolved into the three activities that are my "main menu" to this day.

As far as my knowledge or expertise is concerned, I've used that curiosity I mentioned earlier to nurture a solid foundation of applied sport science. I was introduced to periodization and other types of sport science in 1992 and from there studied the programs offered by the National Strength and Conditioning Association (NSCA) and the International Sport Sciences Association (ISSA). As a matter of fact, I became the first certified specialist in martial arts conditioning through an innovative program offered by the ISSA in 1996.

My knowledge has been greatly increased by writing as well. In my very first published article, I simply wrote about periodization because that is what I knew best at that time. But as my writing career flourished and editors actually began asking me to cover certain topics, I was stretched to learn many new things I otherwise might not have investigated. This has broadened my understanding considerably.

Another one of your learning approaches in TQMA is that everyone should create and use a "thought notebook." I get the sense that your idea of a notebook is more active and broad than a person just jotting down some temporary ideas.

Yes, exactly. I take measured steps to ensure I'm aware of, and can recall, the most relevant sport science considerations. For years I've used a "thought notebook" that is especially effective. When I read a book I highlight (with a marker) particularly important portions. When I finish the book, I type those highlighted portions into notes and place that summary into a larger collection of authors notes in my "thought notebook." On a periodic basis, I review those notes so that I maintain some top-of-mind awareness of the things I found interesting during my readings. I can also use these during preparation of my articles. A practice like the "thought notebook" makes what I read meaningful for a long time. Otherwise, like a movie, the image quickly fades from consciousness. This is an inherent part of my Total Quality approach.

You mentioned "presence" as a major element of your fitness endeavors. Can you explain what you meant by that?

Martial arts inherently possess the characteristics to help us become more "present" in our lives, and that learning is what makes the arts priceless. I've been influenced tremendously by the writings of people like Wendy Palmer, Kathy Park, and Richard Heckler. While they can certainly explain this much better than myself, I'll describe what presence means to me.

Presence is a characteristic of spiritual maturity that transforms our lives and make us people of more depth, wisdom, and human capacity. To be present means to experience a transformation that enables us to participate in our life right this second. As Americans, in particular, we're not too adept at being present.

I really learned the hard lessons of presence in various jobs I've held throughout the past twenty years. We all encounter those aspects of our jobs that we don't want to do, that we consider unsavory. When we do, we usually want to mentally imagine ourselves someplace else. While a certain amount of that tendency is inherent in any job, martial arts and fitness are another matter altogether, and hence more illustrative of my definition of "presence."

What I mean is that sure, there are certain aspects to a job I won't want to do and, even if I increase my "spirituality," might only do under a sense of obligation. But when the tendency to mentally "spin off" occurs in fitness endeavors, you learn something about yourself. Unless you're a professional athlete, no one is forcing you to do exercise. That's a free, volitional choice. So, I've chosen to exercise but during the course of it I find myself "spinning off" or daydreaming. What this literally means is that, while lifting a weight or hitting the bag, or only being forty miles into an eighty mile ride, I might find myself wanting to be somewhere else. Maybe drinking a coke or reading with my legs propped up. When that phenomena occurs, I'm no longer "present" but split— my body is doing one thing but my mind is doing quite another.

I think human beings in general have a tendency to look elsewhere most of the time. The old saying, "the grass is greener," illustrates this point. In the martial arts, I can't count the number of times I've seen students and instructors alike looking bored or distracted.

Right. Our collective tendency in adversity is to try and protect ourselves from suffering by mentally stepping outside of the present. In martial arts, if the *kata* practice seems long and tedious, we may look at the clock and begin thinking of the relief we'll experience when class is over. If we're defeated in sparring or competition we may begin to dream of a "comeback" training program where we avenge our loss. In other words, at those moments when our full concentration is not invested in the moment, but we're daydreaming about another time, we're not present. We've literally stepped away in order to blunt the full impact of the moment.

When the pressure mounts, we don't want to pay attention, or be fully present, because those situations are not always pleasant—they don't suit us. Instead, we "spin off" from the rigors of the moment—diverting our attention away from arduous training, work, or relationship needs to daydream or create an imaginary life where everything is pleasant. When we do this, we can't see "now," the present moment, because we're filtering it through the prism of our daydream.

This is the inherent value available through the mindful practice of the martial arts. By fully experiencing the emotions initiated in the martial arts—from fear to the desire to conquer—we have a reference point for our spiritual growth. Some of the Eastern teachers call this "grounding practice." By this, they mean that we should carefully observe ourselves in those situations where we tend to go off-balance, or lose our center. Too often, we take off on our reactions—launching ourselves mentally into another plane. That's the untrained reaction to life, thinking about something else when the pressure mounts. But our martial art practice invites us to pay attention instead.

Learning to come to the present involves a sense of gathering ourselves together. This means ensuring our minds are in the same place as our bodies. If my body is doing kata but my mind is on the clock, I'm not unified or present. The martial arts specifically, and fitness in general, invites us to unify ourselves, to literally have both our mind and body in the same place at the same time. That type of presence is the priceless value I'm referring to.

All of these components, from sport science to spirituality, seems like a great deal to come to understand and work within—not to mention taking a great deal of time. But in TQMA you mention concepts like "life-planning" and "training in the margins" as ways of working around tight schedules and addressing life holistically. Can you explain these concepts for us?

The concept of "training in the margins" can transform anyone's life. During a typical workweek, I estimate that on *paper* I have probably four hours available for training (Monday through Friday). But I routinely train for up to eight hours during those five days. I do this by "training in the margins."

If we look at our martial training in a "box" then we'll assume that any training means very distinct activities such as driving to the *dojo*, changing clothes, working out, driving home, etc. (about a two-hour ordeal for a one hour workout). But if we view training as a free flow experience, there are numerous opportunities to train in the margins.

When I used to take my daughter to piano lessons (which lasted a half hour each) I didn't just sit in the car and wait. I stretched, or ran, did push-ups, or any number of things, depending on my training cycle and what we were doing after we left the piano lessons (I wouldn't do something sweaty if the next activity would make that inappropriate). That's what I call "training in the margins." It's the time that's available if you maximize it. If you look at your life, you'll find there are numerous opportunities for "margins" training.

Everyone has margins if they look closely. How about five minutes of stretching during a break at work or between school day classes? How about ten more minutes when you find yourself waiting for a late appointment? Or another fifteen while watching the opening of Monday Night Football? There are a wide range of possibilities if we don't "box" or compartmentalize our view of training. Some people will look at the training components inherent to martial arts—such as technical practice, strength training, etc.—and think that they must all be performed in the same training session, one after the other. Actually, each component can be addressed individually which enhances our "lifeplanning."

My recommendation for martial artists in our fast-paced age of numerous responsibilities is to split training into manageable pieces and maximize the margins. I personally average one-and-a-half to two hours of training per day, but almost never at one time.

There seems to be a lot of controversy in the athletic fields about the place and true benefits of nutritional supplements. What is your opinion on the real effects of supplementation?

I have to tell you that I can answer this question from a wealth of personal experience and research. If it's legal, I don't think there's a single supplement that I haven't ingested during the past ten years. No steroids or anything else illegal, mind you, but I have fully explored every legal and ethical performance enhancer known in the nineties.

To specifically answer your question, it depends on a particular athlete's needs or aspirations. If someone wants to be a successful martial artist and is not particularly concerned with muscle mass, there are only two things I think are truly necessary: creatine and a daily multi-vitamin. Creatine is absolutely and unequivocally capable of enhancing performance in martial artists. And if an athlete is ingesting a well-rounded diet, special high doses of various vitamins aren't necessary, but a daily multi-vitamin is a little "insurance" I feel safe to recommend.

On the other hand, if someone want's huge muscle mass, supplements are a nonnegotiable requirement. Supplements like glutamine, ion-exchanged whey protein, and the like are scientifically designed to be absorbed faster and more efficiently than similar types of nutrients available through ingestion of whole foods. Bodybuilders aren't getting big on what's available in the supermarket (unless it contains a supplement section!).

In general, I'd say people desirous of muscle mass need supplementation. Those who only want increased strength don't necessarily need supplementation and neither do martial artists—with the exception of creatine. Anyone can get stronger through resistance training without supplements. Most people are aware that Mark

McGwire, who now holds the single-season home run record, used a testosterone precursor as a supplement. I can unequivocally state that his seventy home runs were not the result of that supplement, although it does partially account for his tremendous muscle mass.

Aside from the use of a "thought notebook," your approach also advises the use of a Total Quality Performance Log. Exactly what is it and how is it used?

Earlier I mentioned the "thought notebook" where I record the notes from various authors I've read as well as my own observations about life. The Total Quality Performance Log is similar to that practice, but only in the physical realm. It's a means of recording important training routines and their results. For example, I keep a daily log of my training time, sleep, pulse rate, and other factors that I can use as comparative performance indicators. If I attend a seminar by Bill Wallace and decide to use his recommendations for training, I enter that information in my Total Quality Performance Log then assess the results by using comparative performance indicators.

You have written in your articles that you believe the martial arts to be the best exercise. With all of the sports and recreations out there, why do you make such an assertion?

Partially because of the inherent emphasis on "presence" within the martial arts approach that I outlined earlier. Other sports have a form of that emphasis, but not the "full meal deal." For example, in bodybuilding you'll hear the term "be here now," which means to be fully engaged in a particular lift. You'll also hear things like the "muscle–mind" connection—things that hint at presence. In football, baseball, and so forth, you'll hear the word "focus" a lot which also hints at presence. But in those activities, the end result is either mere improvement of oneself or winning a game. In the martial arts, the application of presence is much broader.

In a tradition like aikido, for example, the emphasis is on harmony and connection with the universe. Love and compassion are also inherent emphases. You simply don't, and won't, hear that type of emphasis in other sports. Those qualities are seen as antithetical to the ultimate goal of winning.

Additionally, I believe the martial arts are simply more practical. There are no rain-outs, expensive equipment, or waiting on someone or something that can't be controlled (like the weather or a teammate) to have a satisfying experience. While bike racing for ten years, I was constantly frustrated by trying to fit rides into the weather or length of daylight despite how much I enjoyed riding itself. These frustrations are never an obstacle in martial arts practice.

I also find that martial arts welcome anyone willing to be an athlete. Earlier I talked about how certain athletes in endurance activities are genetically predisposed to success. That's not nearly the case in martial arts, although it has some degree of influence, albeit smaller. Since martial arts are primarily a technical activity, anyone who is willing to invest the time can become proficient. This isn't necessarily true in other sports. You could be a person of great commitment and determination but, if you only weigh one hundred and forty pounds, you're not likely to appear in the NFL no matter how hard you train. That feature makes the martial arts very unique.

Martial arts are also the most portable of any exercise, which I particularly like. As a martial artist, I don't have to worry about carrying a bike on a plane, whether I'll find a gym for weight training in a city I visit, or any other unusual equipment or location problems. Give me a space equal to the outstretched dimensions of my body and I can stretch, kick, shadow box, or do any number of things. I like the idea that a martial artist's "equipment" is primarily his or her own self.

Clearly, the American public has a fascination with the martial arts as fitness. This can be seen in the plethora of cardio-kickboxing and karate programs that have emerged in recent history. What is your opinion of these programs?

I welcome any activity that introduces more people to the martial arts. Some people object to an activity like cardio-karate because they believe it waters down the true arts. But that is only true if you see something static—that those who begin with cardio-karate will only stay in cardio-karate. Instead, a new activity like cardio-karate may be a segue—an introduction to something that a person might not otherwise consider.

Show a teen-age female a portrait of a grimacing martial artist with clenched teeth and spittle flying out and that person will not likely be compelled to start the arts. But allow that same person to start in cardio-karate and her interest may be aroused to start looking at other expressions of the martial arts. In a few years, she might cross-over to a more traditional art and get all the benefits that go along with that endeavor.

The martial arts are very decentralized, which is how they should be. Decentralization means that there will always be hundreds of physical expressions to it. Unless a particular expression is intended to emotionally, socially, or physically injure or suppress another person, I don't believe we should criticize new innovations. I'm reminded of that verse in the *Bible* where a speaker says, "If the movement be of men, it will fail. If it is of God, it will prevail despite our efforts." I feel that way about martial arts innovations. If it's without true usefulness or value, it will wither on it's own without harsh criticism. If it's valuable to some people, it will continue regardless of our opinion so why act arrogantly against it?

With all of the changes in sport and fitness martial arts, where do you see the martial arts headed?

I see some very positive signs and some areas that need more emphasis in the martial arts community. In one important perspective, my research indicates that the population of practicing martial artists in the U.S. has doubled since 1990, which is obviously very encouraging. In the wake of this growth, there are some strong and influential personalities that are nurturing further growth and professionalism in our community. For instance, Michael DePasquale, Jr. has accepted the invitation to merge traditional arts with technology via the introduction of his extremely comprehensive Internet website. Watching developments like that are very critical to long-term growth.

Similarly, John Graden's creation of the National Professional Martial Arts Association is providing a degree of professionalism, marketing and sound business practices that, in my opinion, are very needed. So, technology and professionalism, along with the interest in new outlets such as cardio-karate are very encouraging signs.

On the other hand, the same research that indicates the practicing U.S. population has doubled since 1990 also indicates that there is a tremendous turnover rate among people who begin the martial arts. This is a problem that has not yet been adequately addressed by our marketing and business practices.

AFTERWORD

Martial arts represent a never-ending, yet ever changing and evolving continuum. That is, there is no clear-cut Darwinian progression to their evolution, as evidenced in Patrick McCarthy's discussion on the history of Okinawan karatedo—a discipline that has evolved over time and across space into many forms. However, as Hunter B. Armstrong so noted in his discussion on combative behavior and performance, the continuum of these disciplines stretches far and wide, with many stops along the way. And what is found in one combative culture is generally also found in another, and still another. Moreover, what was found to be useful on the battlefields of yesterday still holds true on the battlefields of today: the violent cities and streets we call our home.

Martial arts, then, are not mere rigorous physical disciplines or cultural artefacts. They are "ways of life." As such, one can enjoy the very real combative aspects of the arts, the serene philosophical precepts, the intellectual study of history, the scientific breakdown of technique, or the athletic appeal of physical fitness or sport. What is of value and interest to one, may seem quite ridiculous to another. Yet, the martial arts and their many incarnations are here to stay, and they will continue to evolve, change, and come full circle many times.

With this in mind, we must not judge another's choice of involvement in the arts as better or worse than our own. Indeed, in the martial arts, as in the vast cultures around the world, there is neither better nor worse, only different. And it is in fact these very differences that make the arts so appealing to a vast audience. It is the perceived value and intended use of these arts by the people who embrace them that distinguishes one art from the next. And yet, almost every culture has practitioners involved in various aspects of the arts for any number of reasons.

As my dear friend Oscar Ratti has impressed upon me many times, the various systems of martial arts are not important, and one should strive to not become "stuck" on them. When we become blinded by the dogma of style and master, we are eventually no longer able to see "the forest through the trees." The arts are, then, ethnographs of what Oscar calls the universal art of combat—"an expression of the ways diversified human beings confront and solve problems that arise from violent confrontations—as well as the evolving ways of transcending them through the culture of movement."

I have tried to keep Oscar's advice in mind while constructing and writing this book. I have also attempted to stay clear of dogma and the deification of a single master or "martial arts personality." Indeed, when I direct reference in the conversations to the lives and careers of the interviewees, it is done to establish background and perspective in an effort to better orient the reader as to how these individuals arrived at their conclusions.

It is hoped that this collection of conversations has shed some light on the historical development, cross-fertilization, philosophy, worldview, and career opportunities that the martial arts represent and have to offer. At the very least, if not educated or inspired, I hope that you have been well entertained.

ABOUT THE AUTHOR

Mark V. Wiley is an internationally renowned martial artist and scholar whose involvement in the arts spans more than twenty years. He holds advanced rank in the Filipino arts of Cabales serrada escrima, Biñas dynamic arnis, kalis Ilustrisimo, arnis Escorpizo, and modern arnis; the Chinese arts of ngo cho kun and wing chun kuen; the French art of boxe Francaise savate; the Japanese art of Shiho Karano-ryu ju-jutsu; the Korean art of taekwondo; and the American arts of kenpo karate and jeet kune do concepts.

In addition to training for several years in Western-style boxing and wrestling, Mark has also received instruction, without formal rank, in Filipino pekiti tirsia arnis and kabaroan, Malaysian bersilat, Indonesian pencak silat, Indian silambam, lathi, and hatha yoga, Japanese kenjutsu, Chinese Yang and Wu style tai chi chuan, hsing-i, Chuka Shaolin, and qing long san dian xue mi gong fa qigong, and Theravada Buddhism's vipassana meditation.

After many years of intense study and scrutiny, Mark integrated the essence of these various methods into the formation of talahib, a cross-cultural martial arts training methodology.

Mark has written several other books, including *Qigong for Health and Well-Being* (with FaXiang Hou), *Filipino Martial Culture*, and *Filipino Martial Arts: Cabales Serrada Escrima.* He has written martial arts entries for the *Encyclopedia of World Sport, Encyclopedia of Body–Mind Disciplines,* and *A Martial Arts Encyclopedia,* and is the author of over one hundred articles which have appeared in the leading international martial arts magazines and journals, including *Journal of Asian Martial Arts, Hoplos, Hop-Lite, Martial Arts Illustrated, Martial Arts Legends, Inside Kung-Fu, Black Belt, Karate/Kung-Fu Illustrated, Martial Arts Training, Wu Shu Kung-Fu, Qigong Kung-Fu, Karate International, Tambuli,* and

Phoenix. Mark has traveled internationally throughout Europe, Southeast Asia, and the Far East—spending most of his time in the Philippines, Malaysia, and Japan—to train and conduct field research on various martial arts and healing traditions. He has been nominated to four martial arts halls of fame, but declined induction feeling that such things are too often motivated by political and monetary gain, which is also why he resigned after only one year as chairman of the North American Fellowship of Soke/International Headmasters Society.

Mark has served as executive martial arts editor for the Charles E. Tuttle Publishing Company, in their Tokyo and Boston offices, as associate publisher of *Martial Arts Illustrated*, editor of *Martial Arts Legends*, and associate editor to the *Journal of Asian Martial Arts*. He is currently the publishing manager for Multi-Media Books and Unique Publications, and resides part of the year in suburban Philadelphia and part of the year in Quezon City, Philippines, with his wife, Janet, and son, Alexander.